ESQUIRE'S 1945

JAZZ BOOK

.

A Da Capo Press Reprint Series

THE ROOTS OF JAZZ

ESQUIRE'S 1945

JAZZ BOOK

Edited by

PAUL EDUARD MILLER

Introduction by

ARNOLD GINGRICH

DA CAPO PRESS • NEW YORK • 1979

This Da Capo Press edition of *Esquire's Jazz Book 1945*
is an unabridged republication of the first edition
published in New York in 1945 by A. S. Barnes & Company.

Published by Da Capo Press, Inc.
A Subsidiary of Plenum Publishing Corporation
227 West 17th Street, New York, N.Y. 10011

ESQUIRE'S 1945 JAZZ BOOK

ESQUIRE'S 1945

JAZZ BOOK

Edited by

PAUL EDUARD MILLER

Introduction by

ARNOLD GINGRICH

A. S. BARNES & COMPANY

NEW YORK

Introduction

Esquire's 1944 Jazz Book, originally issued only as a dollar pamphlet, was reissued this past September by Smith & Durrell, Inc. as a two-dollar book, in a reduced format suited to the proportions of the normal bookshelf and bound in cloth covers for permanent preservation. Having accomplished its mission of extending the frontiers of jazz appreciation, which it did through a vastly larger sale than had ever before been achieved by any single volume concerned with hot jazz, not to say larger than the combined sales of all of them, the original newsstand edition of the 1944 Jazz Book promptly went out of print. Nothing could be done about that because, as the Pennsylvania Dutch would put it, "the paper was all." But the oblivion that threatened it was averted by the action of Smith & Durrell, who, as the publishers of *The Jazz Record Book* by Charles Edward Smith and *The Record Book* by David Hall, not to mention Panassié's *The Real Jazz*, were the logical ones to keep Esquire's 1944 Jazz Book in print, as a needed reference source in the fast-growing body of literature on this subject. The logic of this choice has been extended, through its obvious corollary, by awarding to Smith & Durrell (and their parent company, A. S. Barnes & Co.) the publication of both the paper and clothbound editions of this second Jazz Book for 1945.

This year's Jazz Book is much improved, chiefly because last year's attracted the interest of people who were able to help make this one better. For example, Richard M. Jones of Chicago, who might be called the John the Baptist of righteous jazz recording, has been of almost immeasurable help with this book. It was he who, as head of the race division of the old Okeh recording studios in Chicago, brought before the mike the one and only Louis Armstrong, to record the Hot Fives and Hot Sevens that were and remain the highwater mark of the flood-tide of recorded jazz. The greatness of the recordings he made of performances of others has served to overshadow the excellence of his own re-

v

cordings, which is unfortunate. You can scan both *Hot Discography* and the *Jazz Record Book* in vain for any mention of his record of *29th and Dearborn* (OK 8260) with Albert Nicholas on clarinet, himself at the piano, and what sounds like a very "sincere" banjo (to strain at a pun), yet to these impressionable ears it should merit a place on anybody's list of the fifty greatest jazz records. But Richard M. Jones must long since have become accustomed, if not reconciled, to being the forgotten man of jazz, for more than once others have taken credit for things he has done. (Just one instance was the transmutation of his *Jazzin' Babies Blues* into the infinitely better-known *Tin Roof Blues* by the New Orleans Rhythm Kings.) But that's only all the more incentive for us to make sure that his special help on the New Orleans portion of this book, and on the map of Storyville that forms its end papers, should not go unacknowledged.

Both William Russell of Pittsburgh and the Standard Oil Company of California were extremely helpful in the garnering of material for the picture sections, particularly those devoted to New Orleans jazzmen. Bill Russell also lent his invaluable assistance on the New Orleans biographies.

Since the varying viewpoints of the different members of the Board of Experts are vigorously presented at first hand in Chapter V, it is probably not necessary to comment on them here, except to say that whatever the several camps of experts may think of each other it should be obvious to anyone with more than the most rudimentary knowledge of jazz criticism that they do, among them, constitute the most competent as well as comprehensive coverage of the field. That the differences between the fundamentalists, or purists, on the far right and the modernists, or progressives, on the extreme left, should have become so much more embattled during this past year is perhaps just a reflex reaction to the vastly greater progress jazz has made in winning general recognition during this period.

Because of our interest, here at *Esquire*, in trying to accelerate the advancement of hot jazz to the status of a big-league factor in what our Gilbert Seldes first charted as the realm of the Lively Arts, we have tried to straddle, if not to reconcile, the two extremes of jazz ideology, and have been roundly cursed by both camps for the effort. So far, that has only added zest to our program of jazz-advancement, but it is probably only realistic to recognize the possibility that if anything can wreck that program, further aggravation of the dissension between the two schools of jazz critics would be the one thing that could do it. Meanwhile, however, it is perhaps more fitting to save such dark forebodings for some gloomy Sunday afternoon when it's raining, and confine our comment here to the cheerful truth that the Board of Experts served well this year, if somewhat reluctantly in some instances.

The gold and silver Esky statuettes, which were awarded last January on the stage of the Metropolitan in New York, are being awarded this January in three corners of the country, New York, New Orleans and Hollywood. To a degree this symbolizes and reflects the increase of jazz-consciousness that has come within this twelve months. Jazz concerts, as opposed to dance dates and movie stage-shows, had been a relatively isolated phenomenon before 1944. The same was true of real jazz broadcasts. But this past year has seen both become comparatively common occurrences. The change has been signalized by the success of the Eddie Condon concerts on Saturday afternoons at Town Hall and the Mildred Bailey radio program on Friday nights. And where the appearance of the Ellington band in a concert at Carnegie Hall was a seven-day wonder not so long ago, this year's All-American Award Tour will have brought that great aggregation to the concert halls of a dozen cities from coast to coast by the time you read this. It's a far cry, messieurs, from the honky-tonks of Basin Street.

But even more startling is the realization that jazz is at long last coming back to Basin Street, whence it first wandered all over the world, for New Orleans itself, which once disowned jazz as its wayward child of which it was anything but proud, has finally awakened to the cultural significance of its historic role as the birthplace of this newest and most vigorous of the lively arts. Credit for this must go to that indefatigable jazz-missionary, Robert Goffin, who aroused the interest of some of the Crescent City's leading citizens in his pet project, the founding of a National

Jazz Museum. A New Orleans newspaperman, Scoop Kennedy, caught some of Goffin's highly contagious enthusiasm during a visit the latter made to New Orleans early last spring in the course of research for his recently completed book on Louis Armstrong. The result was the formation of the National Jazz Foundation, Inc., with offices in the Cotton Exchange Building in New Orleans and an impressive roster of directors, which has as its goal the acquisition of a suitable site (such as the fabulous Mahogany Hall) for the National Jazz Museum, and already has accomplished some noteworthy achievements. For one thing, it has had Basin Street's name restored. (It had somehow been changed to Saratoga Street, as if the town deliberately wanted to forget everything about its function as the cradle of jazz). For another, it has staged two hugely successful jazz concerts, this past October, in the beautiful, big Municipal Auditorium which fronts on storied Congo Square, having with John Hammond's help imported the Benny Goodman Quartet, (with Teddy Wilson, Sid Weiss and Morey Feld) for the occasion. And this January it is holding another jazz concert, timed to coincide with other presentations of *Esquire's* All-American Awards in Hollywood and New York.

When you stop to consider that until this Fall there had never before been a jazz concert in New Orleans, the birthplace of jazz, this intensive activity on the part of this non-profit civic organization augurs well for the rapid realization of its immediate goal, announced as the establishing of a National Jazz Museum in which will be preserved the most comprehensive collection of jazz records in the world, historical relics of jazz instruments, books, papers, and made available to the vast, international jazz public.

Membership in the National Jazz Foundation is by no means limited to residents of New Orleans, and while its first activities, up to the time of the establishment of the museum, are bound to be localized, if jazz enthusiasts from the rest of the country join in sufficient numbers, it will soon be able to extend its activities and its influence to a national scale. Active membership is ten dollars, but associate memberships are three dollars and the latter are especially suited to nonresidents, at the present stage of the organization's development. Since this modest amount represents the approximate premium that we would have had to pay, up to a couple of months ago, to obtain a single Muggsy Spanier or Goodman Quartet Bluebird, it's obvious that any record collector can now afford to send this much to the National Jazz Foundation, Inc., 407 Cotton Exchange Bldg., New Orleans 18, Louisiana.

For that matter, there are several other things that the individual jazz fan can do to make his presence felt in the now burgeoning jazz scene. One is to write both Victor and Columbia, in appreciation of their alleviating the "record famine" by the recent reinstatement of 118 Victor and Bluebird titles and the restoration to active standing of the majority of the Columbia Hot Jazz Classics, at the same time making your suggestions as to which titles you would like to see reissued next. And don't forget Decca, for its splendid Brunswick albums. Another is to write to the Networks and the local radio stations every time you hear any real jazz on the air. The only way to get more, in both instances, is to register our appreciation for what we get, as we get it. And a good rule to remember is that one letter written to one of these outside agencies, which are in a position to bring more jazz to the general public, outweighs ninety-nine letters written back and forth among the brethren in the endless bickering that goes on between "the boys in the back room" over the hairsplitting questions constantly raised by the little magazines specializing in jazz exegesis. For instance, it is more to the point to write the editors of *The New Yorker* or *The Saturday Evening Post*, in appreciation of an Ellington article, or the editors of *Life* for a spread of jazzmen's pictures, or the officials of Victor for including Jelly Roll's *Pearls* and *Beale Street Blues* in their list of restored reissues, than it is to go on wrangling interminably with other readers of *The Record Changer* over whether Johnny Dodds did or didn't play the clarinet on this or that disputed date with Jimmy Bertrand's Washboard Wizards or Lovie Austin's Blues Serenaders. Such questions will keep—in fact they have kept, for a long time. But silence in the former instances will only confirm those worthies in their belief that jazz is just a concomitant of jitterbugging, something that jumps with James and swoons with Sinatra.

On the discography front, the year's biggest news is the commencement of publication of Orin Blackstone's monumental *Index to Jazz*, which at last tackles the job of filling in the gaps left by *Hot Discography* in the tabulation of all records of jazz significance. Blackstone, a New Orleans newspaperman, is a member of the board of directors of the National Jazz Foundation, of whose record library he has made his own huge collection, numbering over 12,000 sides, an integral part. Thus, on two counts, he merits the thanks of every record collector in the country. His *Index to Jazz* is being published serially by *The Record Changer* (which has been flourishing during this past year like the proverbial green bay tree), where it is subject to collectors' verifications and emendations before being committed to book publication.

Other welcome new activities of the past year have been the launching of two new collectors' periodicals, *The Needle* and *Recordiana,* and the resumption of Bob Thiele's *Jazz* Magazine upon his discharge from the Coast Guard this Fall.

To get back to the book you hold in your hands, it speaks so well for itself that we have felt no compunction about wandering away from it to talk of other items of interest to the jazz minded. In it, you will find everything that has happened in this past jazz year, covered like a tent, and a wealth of original research covering the continuing history of jazz over the fifty years since Buddy Bolden began to blow the horn ultimately heard round the world. To us, reading it all over just before publication, it seems a rare enough wine to need no bush. And certainly if you don't find it a treasure chest of jazz information, nothing we can say about it here will turn it into one.

There remains, then, only the very pleasant duty of mentioning the fact that the compilation of this year's JAZZ BOOK attracted the attention, interest and help, not only of critics but also of musicians, with the result that for this year's pictures we find ourselves deeply indebted to the Messrs. George Filhe, Edmond Hall, Baby Dodds, Bill Johnson, George Hoefer, William Russell, Dave Dexter, Jr., and Sidney Bechet, as well as to the Standard Oil Company, the helpful staff of *Down Beat* and the secretary of the National Jazz Foundation, Miss Pat Spiess.

So from here, to corn a phrase, is where we "get off."

ARNOLD GINGRICH

Chicago: December, 1944.

CONTENTS

ESQUIRE'S 1945 JAZZ BOOK

Chapter I

Fifty Years of New Orleans Jazz

by PAUL EDUARD MILLER

NEW ORLEANS: seaport shipping center to and from which boats and peoples from waters far distant and near swish and mix, in and out, interminably; city inhabited by peoples of semitropical climes, peoples accustomed to abandon and freedom in the living of their personal lives; peoples from Spain, France, from Africa. New Orleans: city of countless fraternal societies and lodges; city of carnivals, parades, picnics, excursions, outings, lawn parties, street dances, festivals; city that had open and legal relationships between politics and activities usually *sub rosa*. New Orleans: a city in which the economic position, not only of the Negro, but also of the "poor white trash" engendered an attitude and an atmosphere conducive to the pursuit of an easy way to make money —of which music was one. New Orleans: city that gave the world its Louis Armstrong, its Sidney Bechet, its Freddie Keppard, its Edmond Hall, Jelly Roll Morton, King Oliver, Johnny Dodds, Barney Bigard, Bunk Johnson, Richard M. Jones, George Lewis, Kid Ory, Mutt Carey; city of *High Society, Oh Didn't He Ramble, Riverside Blues,* stomps, rags, cannonballs, more blues, the Blues in B Flat. Especially the city of the blues and the men who knew how to play them, to lift them to high emotional levels.

It no longer is necessary to insist that New Orleans nurtured jazz and brought it to its first flower just before the turn of the century. So much is patent. But *why* and *how* jazz found such fertile soil in the Crescent City rather than in some other part of the country yet remains in considerable obscurity. The tendency to romanticize and color has been apparent in all that has been published about New Orleans in relation to jazz. We have been regaled with tales of gaudiness and bawdiness, with stories of the musical "characters" who lent their talents and their frenzy to jazz and to the atmosphere of New Orleans itself. But the long-view approach has been neglected. What I hope to accomplish in this capsule impression of fifty years of jazz based on its New Orleans origins is to emphasize and portray the panoramic sweep of the sum total of events in the developments of jazz and the jazz spirit.

The map of Storyville (inside front and back covers), depicting the actual block-by-block location of buildings in the heart of New Orleans' tenderloin district, may well serve as an introduction to a panoramic view. Careful inspection of the map will reveal that side by side with the honky-tonks, saloons, cribs, cabarets, theatres and houses of assignation were cemeteries, churches, hospitals, business establishments, pawn shops, restaurants, tailoring and pressing shops, drug stores, grocery stores, private homes, barber shops and music publishing houses. Perhaps it was more than coincidence that the Court House and Parish Prison are found—conveniently, no doubt—in the very midst of this sea of sin and that the fire department is located on Basin Street between the super-notorious Emma Johnson Studio and the Mae Tuckerman mansion. In any event, it is not difficult to grasp the significance of this admixture of diverse activities. Only a city imbedded in Old World traditions could have produced it: the psychoreligious philosophy that Man, creature of Sin, needs and must have intermittent outbursts of indulgence—when steam can be blown off at a time and in a place proscribed by the authorities. Storyville was such a place and the Mardi Gras was such a time. Such a time also was the occasion of parades, festivals, picnics and

The Onward Brass Band of New Orleans, 1913. Another great parade band, another star-studded personnel. Left to right: cornetists Manuel Perez, Andrew Kimball, Peter Bocage (Bocage doubled on violin in many bands); clarinetist Lorenzo Tio, Jr; Adolph Alexander, alto horn; drummers Baby Matthews and Dandy Lewis; Paul Barbarin, Sr., alto horn; trombonists Buddy Johnson and Vic Gaspar; Eddie Atkins, baritone horn, double trombone; and Eddie Jackson, sousaphone. These men formed the backbone of many another band. George Hoefer photo.

The Tuxedo Band: 1916. The name of Oscar (Papa) Celestin most frequently is associated with the Tuxedo. Although he did not lead the band during its earliest days, from about 1916 on he took over the reins and produced some of the best jazz heard in New Orleans. Even as late as 1934, when he broadcast over radio station WWL, his group played great jazz. Front row, left to right: Ernest Tripania, Armand J. Piron, Tom Benton, Johnny St. Cyr; rear: Jimmie Noone, Bill (Baby) Ridgley, Celestin himself, John Lindsey. George Hoefer photo.

The Manuel Perez Band at the Arsonia Cafe in Chicago, 1915. Although Chicago had heard New Orleans jazz prior to this date, the Perez group was the first Crescent City jazz outfit to play at a location spot for dancing, contemporaneous with an outfit headed by George Filhe. Perez played for Mike Fritzel (at Madison & Paulina) while across the street at Tommy Thomas' Filhe held forth. Left to right: trombonist Eddie Atkins, drummer Louis Cottrell, Perez, pianist Frankie Haynie and clarinetist Lorenzo Tio, Jr. Paul Eduard Miller photo.

| *Mutt Carey*
(trumpet) | *Kid Shots Madison*
(trumpet) | *Bud Scott*
(guitar) | *Jelly Roll Morton*
(piano) |

Distinguished New Orleans musicians. Carey and Scott photos by Standard Oil Company: Madison by Wm. Russell; Morton by RCA Victor

| *Bill Johnson*
(bass) | *Baby Dodds*
(drums) | *Louis Armstrong*
(trumpet) | *Kid Ory*
(trombone) |

Distinguished New Orleans musicians: Dodds, Armstrong and Ory often played together. Ory photo by Standard Oil; others by Jim Ferstel.

| *Wingy Manone*
(trumpet) | *Big Eye Louie Nelson*
(clarinet) | *Charlie Elgar*
(leader) | *Sidney Desvigne*
(trumpet) |

Distinguished New Orleans musicians: all have fronted their own bands. Nelson photo by Leonard Bechet and the National Jazz Foundation.

funeral processions for which the many fraternal societies provided.

Thrown against such a background was the economic position of large sections of the Crescent City's population. Storyville and its environs gave work not only to musicians, but to waiters, cab drivers, gamblers, bartenders and a host of other occupations always an adjunct to sinful pursuits. With men and women such as these, it was not a "choice" but a necessity. Their jobs forced them into an attitude toward life which does not have the approval of solid citizens; nevertheless, for them it was life and the solid citizen was their best customer.

With only a limited number of respectable jobs open to them, young Negroes, to idle away the time and with no thought of the money which might be earned that way, took to playing different instruments. One of the salient characteristics of the poor New Orleans Negro family was the interest taken in music. Many of the jazz greats who later made a name for themselves were reared in families possessing not only musical instruments, but a musical tradition in the person of some member or members of the family. In addition, every young boy in New Orleans heard so much music that he developed genuine interest; the parades inspired the kids; they heard music all around them, all the time. They constructed their own homemade instruments or they worked until they had enough money to explore the musical possibilities of pawn shops and junk shops. They learned from their friends: literally it was person-to-person individualized education and invariably it began as a pastime. The demand for musicians was heavy and it is for that reason that so many New Orleans jazzmen began playing while they were still mere boys. The older, initiated musicians seemed to take pride in "discovering" some youngster who showed promise; they gave their protégé patient tutoring and almost always this resulted in his performing with some brass band on parade or at a picnic or for an excursion or tour of nearby towns. The youngsters were caught up in a wave of enthusiasm; fired high, their spirit of adventure carried them through the hardships—the actual physical hardships—of a long parade march or tours requiring them to sit up all night in some railroad station because they could not find accommodations.

The Mardi Gras was held during the eight days and nights preceding Lent, with festivities ending at midnight Tuesday, official beginning of Ash Wednesday. On St. Joseph's Day, in mid-Lent, the lid was off for that one night only, when masked balls were the ruling favorites. During Mardi Gras musicians often worked two or three jobs in one day: a parade in the morning, another in late afternoon or early evening and a dance at night. Each carnival day a different fraternal society or lodge or merchant or group of merchants would finance the floats (costing a thousand dollars and up); between floats, a brass band comprised of from ten to thirty musicians ranging in age from twelve to fifty. The "kings" of the Madri Gras—Rex, Momus, Comus, Proteus—originated their march at the foot of Canal Street (at the river), proceeding up Canal to Claiborne to Jackson and St. Charles and back again. The King of the Zulus entered at the head of The Basin (see Storyville map, Rampart and Howard) and marched with his parade, floats and brass bands, downtown toward Canal and then followed the same route. All the kings, usually some rich, popular and/or political figure, arrived at their points of origination by boat, then were joined by their retinue.

The carnival season was only the climax of year-round festivities. During the entire year dances, parties and celebrations of all kinds, and held for innumerable never-ending reasons, required music in a ceaseless stream. A long season of picnics and outings began on Easter Sunday; invariably these called for music. Both boat and railroad excursions were common: these demanded music. There were even night and day flatboat excursions on the river. The boat was drawn by mules (ropes attached to boat) twenty miles down the river and back. The band was placed in the center of the boat and played for dancing and entertainment. A bar was set up near the musicians—but for the indulgence of the patrons. The resort spots on Lake Ponchartrain, at Milenburg, West End, Algiers—all these attracted the festive crowds, mainly those of the lodges and societies and the clubs, such as the Tramp and Pickwick Clubs.

In short, New Orleans was a city in which the demand for musicians was excessively great as compared to other urban centers. Youngsters became interested in brass bands because they saw so many parades and other festivities in which bands took a prominent part. Having themselves grown up in the same parade-brass band atmosphere, the fathers and mothers, too, were favorably inclined toward music; they lent encouragement to the children who showed an interest in music, for music had a specific functional value in the life of New Orleans.

It is little wonder, then, that from such surroundings should emanate great jazz musicians. The music itself, of course, was an expression—natural and without regard for academic niceties—of the Negro's response to his environment. The men who played jazz gave it that expression because they found more than ordinary opportunities for projecting it into society. The music was accepted; socially and economically, it fulfilled a function. When it took a definite trend toward what we now call hot jazz, it still was accepted and fulfilled a function, although the people who responded most fully to it usually were those on the lower economic levels. Thus, the better class of houses did not allow their pianist to play the blues; this emotional music was reserved for the cheaper houses, the honky-tonks and saloons and the cabarets. A band like John Robichaux's, on the sweet side, garnered some of the best paying jobs in town, although he led a small contingent of hot men too, at times. Nevertheless, with so much music being played, genuine hot jazz inevitably crept into the ears of people on all economic levels; and with so many musicians playing and being influenced by one another, the percentage of great and near-great jazz virtuosi was bound to be high. It *was* high.

As early as the 1880's a musical group in Donaldsonville, some ninety miles from New Orleans, was setting the pace. It often made appearances in the Crescent City, winning the band contest at Lincoln Park year after year and playing as well at all the Fairs throughout the entire state. It was the *St. Joseph Brass Band*, led by cornetist Claiborn Williams, who also fronted a band under his own name which played for dances. The collective personnel: Claiborn Williams, William Daley, Sullivan Spraul, Edward Duffel, Israel Palmer, Lawrence Hall, cornets; Harrison Homer, George Williams, Ernest Hime, trombones; Freddy Landry, trombone and piano; Jill Williams, string bass; Marble Gibson, Bean Bauddurs, clarinet; Joe Walker, Buddy Kyeri, Bow Legs, drums. Williams himself was a great all-around cornetist, but more of a straight man than hot; but he knew his music, knew how to pick his men and gained a wide reputation as a teacher, since he could play most of the other instruments of the band too. Some of the other men in the band, however, were playing plenty of jazz: cornetists Daley and Spraul; pianist Landry; drummers Walker and Kyeri; clarinetist Gibson; trombonists Harrison and George Williams, brother of Claiborn. According to Richard M. Jones, whose information about New Orleans has proved to be extremely reliable, the Claiborn Williams bands are the oldest (leaning toward the hot) in the state of Louisiana.

The Excelsior Band, too, dates back to the eighties. About 1885, its personnel consisted of T. V. Baquet, leader-clarinetist; Lorenzo Tio, Sr. and Louis Tio, clarinets; Fice Quiyrit, cornet; Anthony Page, valve trombone; Hackett Brothers, alto horn;

Boisseau, baritone horn; Lee, drums. The Tios were the renowned teachers, while the senior Lorenzo was the father of Lorenzo, Jr., who became one of the great New Orleans clarinetists. By 1900, The Excelsior Band boasted a group of really hot men: cornetist Edward Clem, clarinetist Alphonse Picou; trombonist Buddy Johnson; cornetist Manuel Perez; and bass drummer John Robichaux.

The Adam Oliver Band and Duce Manetta's Band in Bay St. Louis, Mississippi, were two other early bands, but of no great consequence to hot jazz history. The stage was now ready for the appearance of Buddy Bolden, whose band solidified the trends toward the hot style which had been hinted at by the Claiborn Williams groups. During the 1890's Bolden became the acknowledged "king" of the trumpet. In 1895 his outfit was comprised of Bolden himself on cornet; Willie Warner on clarinet; Willie Cornish on valve trombone; Jimmie Johnson on string bass; and Brock Mumford on guitar. His band endured as an actual unit for about twelve years—perhaps a little longer, but not much. During that time his collective personnel included some of the greatest hot men of the time: Trombonists Frankie Duson, Vic Gaspar, Willie Cornish; clarinetists Frank Lewis, Big Eye Louie Nelson, William Warner; drummers Cornelius Tilman, John McMurray, Henry Zeno; guitarists Lorenzo Stall, Jeff Mumford, Brock Umphrey; string bassists Bob Lyons and Jimmie Johnson; and the hot piccolo player, Bab Frank, who worked with practically all the famous New Orleans hot groups at one time or another.

Born approximately in Civil War days (between 1860-65), Bolden undoubtedly was one of those rare natural, instinctive musicians who had a flair for the right *jazz phrasing* and intonation. However, judging from the overwhelming consensus of reports from old-time New Orleans musicians, he was a reasonably good musician too and not all his playing was sheer spontaneity or so-called improvisation. His technique too, was good and was acquired by a natural bent for the medium rather than protracted study, although there is little question that he was given considerable instruction on the cornet before he approached the zenith of his career as a jazz virtuoso. Contrary to expectations, Bolden rarely, if ever, played in the Storyville district. He had come and gone from the jazz scene before Storyville nightspots hired bands either for entertainmnt or dancing—that is, anything but string bands, which were found in profusion prior to 1909. Bolden was primarily a parade and dance man. Not only would he book his own band for parades and the dances which followed, but often he would work in some other musician's band, bringing his own coterie of sidemen over to his competitor—but for that day only. Monetary offers were not the deciding factor; rather, with whom and for whom he would play on any given day was a matter of his own mood and which fraternal lodge boasted the most members whom he regarded as his friends. On most such occasions he played for the Crescent Lodge, whose membership consisted of a fast, sporting crowd. On a carnival day in 1902, according to the remembrances of old-time New Orleans musicians and natives, the crowd at a dance in Longshoreman's Hall (Jackson and Franklin streets, where Bolden often played) was so great and so emotional that a brawl turned into a riot in which several persons were killed and during which many patrons of the dance jumped from the windows of the building and were injured. There can be no doubt that Bolden's personality was vigorous and colorful, that his influence on hot jazz was great. He was a pioneer. During a parade in 1908 or 1909, he was stricken with a severe illness, which eventually sent him to an asylum, where he died in 1931 or '32.

Contemporary with Bolden, many other bands, both brass-parade and dance, sprung up to make New Orleans fairly vibrate with the vitality and exuberance of a new American music. John

Robichaux's first band, a small hot group (1895-1905) consisted of Dee Dee Chandler, drums; George Baquet and later Lorenzo Tio, Jr., clarinet; Ed Cornish and later Battice Dellile, trombone; James Williams, cornet; Henry Kimball, string bass; Arthur Budd Scott, guitar. Later Robichaux formed big bands, played at class spots such as the Lyric Theatre, the Gruenwald Hotel, the Yacht Club and the Antoine and Louisiana restaurants. From 1920-23, at the Lyric, where vaudeville was three-a-day (four on Sunday) his personnel included: Charlie McCurtis, clarinet; Andrew Campbell, cornet; John Lindsey, trombone; Walter Brundy, later Louis Cottrell and Zutty Singleton, drums; Henry Campbell, string bass. At these and other times the Robichaux outfit boasted these hot hornmen: Vic Gaspar, Lindsey, Delille, trombones; Baquet, Tio, McCurtis, clarinets; George Kimball, James Williams, George McCullogh, Andrew Campbell, cornets.

Because complete personnel information has never been available to jazz fans, I believe it is a worth-while use of space to devote most of the balance of this chapter to such information. Therefore, without comment, here are the line-ups of most of the famous New Orleans bands contemporary with Bolden and during the ten-year period following his retirement, when Storyville played such an important role in the development and acceptance of jazz.

The Olympia Band. (1900-09): Joseph Petit, valve trombone, later replaced by Zue Robertson, Eddie Atkins; Freddie Keppard, cornet; Alphonse Picou, clarinet, later replaced by Big Eye Louie Nelson; John Vigne, drums, later replaced by Louis Cottrell, Ernest Tripania. 1912: Freddie Keppard, cornet; Eddie Vincon, trombone; Lorenzo Tio, Jr., clarinet, later replaced by Sidney Bechet; Louis Keppard, guitar, later replaced by Steve Lewis, piano; John Lindsey, bass, later replaced by Billy Marrero; Ernest Tripania, drums; Willie Santiago, guitar; Armand J. Piron, violin. 1914-15: King Oliver, cornet; Zue Robertson, trombone; Sidney Bechet, clarinet; Henry Zeno, drums; Louis Keppard, guitar; Billy Marrero, bass.

The Peerless Band (1906-13): Bab Frank, piccolo; Andrew Kimball, cornet; George Filhe, trombone, also probably Hamp Benson; Charlie McCurtis, clarinet; Coochie Martin, guitar; Walter Brundy, drums, later replaced by Baby Matthews.

The Superior Band (1905-12): Bunk Johnson, cornet; Buddy Johnson, trombone; Big Eye Louie Nelson, clarinet; Walter Brundy, drums; Billy Marrero, string bass; Richard Payne, guitar; Peter Bocage, violin.

The Imperial Band (1909-12): Manuel Perez, cornet; George Filhe, trombone, later replaced by Eddie Atkins; George Baquet, clarinet; Rene Battice, guitar; Walter Brundy, drums, later replaced by John Vigne; Jimmy Brown, string bass, later replaced by John Lindsey.

The Original Creole Band (1912-17, in California and vaudeville tour across country): Freddie Keppard, cornet; Eddie Vincon, trombone; George Baquet, clarinet, later replaced by Big Eye Louie Nelson, Jimmie Noone; Bill Johnson, string bass; Dink Johnson, drums; Leon Williams, guitar; Jimmy Palao, violin.

The Tuxedo Band (1910-13, opened and closed the Tuxedo Café, staying together three years and closing the Tuxedo on Easter Sunday, 1913): Oscar Celestin, cornet; George Filhe, trombone; Bab Frank, piccolo; Lorenzo Tio, Jr., clarinet; Manuel Manetta, piano; Louis Cottrell, drums; Peter Bocage, violin. 1913-16: Oscar Celestin, cornet; Baby Ridgley, trombone; Sam Dutrey, clarinet; Johnny St. Cyr, guitar; Ernest Tripania, drums; Johnny Lindsey, string bass. 1917, at Suburban Gardens, first roadhouse cabaret in the New Orleans area: Oscar Celestin, cornet; Baby Ridgley, trombone; Lorenzo Tio, Jr., clarinet, later replaced by Johnny Dodds; Richard M. Jones, piano; Ernest Tripania, drums, later replaced by Vic Gaspar; Willie Bonti, guitar. Others who worked with the Tuxedo at other times: Jimmie Noone, clarinet; Armand J. Piron, violin; Eddie Atkins, Sam Henry, trombone.

The Eagle Band (1913): Bunk Johnson, cornet; Frankie Duson, trombone; Sidney Bechet, clarinet; Brock Umphrey, guitar; Henry Zeno, drums; Dandy Lewis, string bass. Collective personnel, 1907-15; Freddie Keppard, Bunk Johnson, Frankie Keeley, Mutt Carey, cornets; Jack Carey, Frankie Duson, trombones; Lorenzo Tio, Jr., Big Eye Louie Nelson, Sidney Bechet, Zep, clarinets; Bob Lyons, Dandy Lewis, string bass; Henry Zeno, drums; Brock Umphrey, guitar.

The Onward Brass Band. This was another early band of the eighties, but which had only mild tendencies toward the hot spirit, although drummer Chandler, cornetist Perez and trombonist Filhe might well be classed as hot. 1892-1912: Bellevue Lanair, Sylvester Cousto, Manuel Perez, cornets; George Filhe, trombone; Steve Johnson, tenor horn; Paul Barbarin, Sr., Joseph Bruno, alto horns; Albert Tucker, string bass; Mike Gillin, bass drums; Dee Dee Chandler, snare drums. 1913-17, an entirely new personnel, now definitely hot: Manuel Perez, Andrew Kimball, Peter Bocage, cornets; Lorenzo Tio, Jr., clarinet; Baby Matthews, snare drums; Dandy Lewis, bass drums; Paul Barbarin, Sr., alto horn; Buddy Johnson, Vic Gaspar, trombones; Eddie Atkins, baritone horn; Eddie Jackson, sousaphone.

Armand J. Piron Orchestra (1917) at Transchino's: Piron, violin; Peter Bocage, trumpet, violin, guitar, banjo; Arthur Campbell, piano, later replaced by Steve Lewis; John Lindsey, string bass. 1923-24, the group which recorded in New York: Piron, violin; Peter Bocage, trumpet; John Lindsey, trombone; Lorenzo Tio, Jr., clarinet and tenor; unknown alto; Steve Lewis, piano; Robert Ysagguirre, string bass; Louis Cottrell, drums. Collective personnel of other musicians who played with Piron at one time or another: George Baquet, Louis Warner, clarinets; Andrew Kimball, cornet; Bab Frank, piccolo; Vic Gaspar, trombone; Bob Lyons, Henry Kimball, string bass; John Vigne, Willie Wannich, drums; Arthur Budd Scott, Johnny St. Cyr, guitar; Hall Brothers, drums and guitar.

Bob Lyons Orchestra (1919): Lyons, string bass; Kid Rena, trumpet; George Boyd, clarinet; Lorenzo Stall, guitar; Joe Lindsey, drums.

Allen's Brass Band (partial collective): Jack Carey, Yank Johnson, Buddy Johnson, trombones; Peter Bocage, Joe Howard, Oscar Celestin, Henry Allen, Jr., cornets and trumpets; Collings, baritone horn; Lawrence Dewey, clarinet; Baby Matthews, drums.

Magnolia Sweets (1910): Tig Chambers, cornet; Ernest Kelly, trombone; Zep, clarinet; Yank Johnson, trombone; Minique, drums.

Hill City Band (1906): John Hime, trombone, later replaced by Hamp Benson; Andrew Kimball, cornet; Charlie McCurtis, clarinet; Charles Pearson, guitar; Cato, drums.

Primrose Orchestra (1912): Joe Johnston, cornet; Hamp Benson, trombone; Herb Lindsey, violin; Cato, drums; George Williams, guitar.

Richard M. Jones, at George Fewclothes cabaret in the Storyville district, (1912-13): Jones, piano; Freddie Keppard, cornet; Roy Palmer, trombone; Lawrence Dewey, clarinet, later replaced by Sidney Bechet, Jimmie Noone; John Vigne, drums.

Noone-Petit Orchestra, at Frank Early's cabaret, (1915-16): Buddy Petit, cornet; Jimmie Noone, clarinet; Honore Dutrey, trombone; Kirk Tripania, piano; Arthur Depese, drums.

Jack Carey's Band (1913): Jack Carey, trombone; Mutt Carey, cornet; L'il Mack, drums; Sidney Bechet, clarinet; Tom Benton, guitar; unknown bass.

Kid Ory's Band (1915): Ory, trombone; King Oliver, cornet; Sidney Bechet, clarinet, later replaced by Johnny Dodds; Henry Morton, drums; Louis Keppard, guitar.

At the "25" (1916): King Oliver, cornet; Sidney Bechet, clarinet; Annison, piano; Peter Bocage, violin; John Vigne, drums; Arthur Campbell, piano and entertainer.

At Pete Lala's Cafe (1915): Freddie Keppard, cornet, later replaced by King Oliver; Sidney Bechet, clarinet; Frankie Haynie, piano, later replaced by Louis Wade; Joe Pierre, drums; Herb Lindsey, violin.

At the Claiborn Theatre (1917): Sidney Bechet, clarinet; Buddy Christian, piano; L'il Mack, drums.

In Storyville (1914): Willie Hightower, cornet; Roy Palmer, trombone; Black Pete, piano; Armand J. Piron, violin.

At the 101 Ranch (1910): Big Eye Louie Nelson, clarinet; Arnold Mywtiet, cornet; Black Pete, piano; John McMurray, drums.

Original Dixieland Band (1913), at Peg Etstet's: Nick La-Rocca, cornet; Georg Brunis, trombone; Yellow Nunez, clarinet; Anton Lada, drums. 1915-18, in Chicago and New York: Nick LaRocca, cornet; Eddie Edwards, trombone; Larry Shields, clarinet; Harry Ragas, piano; Johnny Stein, drums, later replaced by Tony Sbarbaro.

The Louisiana Five (1915-20): Anton Lada, drums; Yellow Nunez, clarinet; Charlie Pannelli, trombone; Joe Calway, piano; Karl Karlberger, banjo.

What happened in New Orleans during the first two decades of our century has continued to happen, though at a slower pace and on a smaller scale. The Crescent City still has its parades and festivals (curtailed by the war), still sends forth its musicians to join the ranks of the jazz greats (Irving Fazola, Eddie Miller and Edmond Hall, for example). If this quick panoramic sketch has highlighted anything, it is that early New Orleans jazz was played by many different musicians in many different bands; that there was little organization, commercialization; no recordings or radio and therefore practically no evidence, except hearsay, of who was great—but that evidence is conclusive enough. Recent recordings of some of the old-timers has verified it.

The Storyville spots indicated by a check mark (see map, inside covers) identifies many of the honky-tonks, theatres and cabarets in which the old-timers played. An inspection of the map will reveal that numerous establishments and many streets have been celebrated in titles of jazz tunes. In addition to the checked spots, all the *maisons* and most of the saloons featured music at the hands of a pianist, usually blues but often operatic and popular songs too.

Chapter II

A Survey of Jazz Today

by LEONARD FEATHER

THE past year of 1944 was an extraordinarily good one for jazz. In spite of draft depletions, which in any case eased off considerably later in the year, the general quality and quantity of good jazz to be heard throughout the country, through the media of records and radio and in the flesh, was higher than ever before.

Before going into details concerning this exceptional output of good jazz, it might be best to start with a brief discussion of what the word "jazz" is assumed to mean.

Among the critics, there is considerable dissension regarding the meaning not only of this word, but also of "swing." Some writers consider this merely another term for the same thing, while others differentiate sharply between the two, claiming that jazz is the genuine article and swing a despicably modern synthetic product.

Among the musicians themselves, who should know best, there is a little, but considerably less, dissension on the meaning of these two words. Many musicians scorn "jazz" as an old-fashioned word; Red Norvo says, "Jazz, to me, means something very obnoxious." On the other hand, Zutty Singleton points out that "Swing is just a modern term to denote jazz." Cootie Williams states emphatically that "There is no difference between jazz and swing," and the majority of the other top jazzmen (swingmen) concur in this view.

Whether it be called jazz or swing, whether it be improvised or arranged, played by a honky-tonk pianist or a six-piece Dixieland band or an eighteen-piece orchestra, the musicians themselves are agreed that all this music has the same basic technical characteristics, such as the uses of syncopation and the blues scale. In view of this, any critical analysis of swing music should pay equal attention to all its various forms instead of insisting that one is the real thing, one phony.

During the past year or two a sharp schism has developed between the proponents of the old-time jazz and the critics whose views are more modern. The former group generally believes in the music of New Orleans musicians and of the kind of Dixieland music dispensed on Eddie Condon's broadcasts, but seldom listens, or gives serious consideration, to music of the same genre when it is played by a large band, or by any group that has had a resounding commercial success.

The musicians themselves are the first to point out the fallacy of this reasoning. Men like Barney Bigard and Edmond Hall, despite their own New Orleans background, have reiterated forcefully that the old New Orleans style, as exemplified by Bunk Johnson and by such tunes as *High Society*, is musically obsolescent and that the fans who take nothing but this kind of music seriously are betraying their complete ignorance of music. Hall, for instance, described the music recorded by a veteran New Orleans clarinetist as "horrible," and is at a loss to understand how anyone with a pair of ears can fail to appreciate the genius of Benny Goodman. Hall also points out that it is not simply for his technique that he idolizes Goodman, but for his ability to play brilliantly and with unflagging inspiration in any style and mood.

Similarly, Mary Lou Williams, Duke Ellington, Earl Hines, Teddy Wilson, James P. Johnson and every other top pianist idolizes Art Tatum, not just as the most accomplished technician, but as the most inspired of all jazz pianists. Their views are more likely to be sound than those of the men who belittle these musicians. A musician can explain his views in factual terms, whereas the jazz fans in question are musically illiterate and are unable to explain their dislikes in musical terms or in anything but rhetoric and vague invective.

Assuming, then, that you are willing to accept the views of the musicians elected by *Esquire's* board of experts as the world's greatest, I shall broaden the scope of this survey to include all the "musicians' musicians," the artists and orchestras that have come in for most of the comment among fellow musicians during the past year.

BIG BANDS

In the big band field, the outstanding event of the year has been the complete public acceptance of Lionel Hampton's great orchestra. Sparked by the great personality of its leader and by his work as vibraharpist, occasional drummer and pianist, this band has become the greatest draw at colored theatres and dances and a potent attraction among white audiences. It is a loud, boisterous band that can cope just as effectively with a subtle, melodic arrangement as with a screaming flag-waver.

Benny Carter, after a long struggle, seemed at last to be making an impression with his fine band. He spent some time on a combined theatre tour with the King Cole Trio, and the success of his own records as well as Cole's made this a happy union. Curiously enough, the Capitol records that have helped Carter to establish himself with colored audiences are, musically, among the least interesting he has ever made, being devoted mostly to mediocre vocals. In person, however, Benny still plays plenty of wonderful music.

Cootie Williams benefited greatly from a theatre tour with Ella Fitzgerald and the incredibly popular Ink Spots. His Hit records, including the Echoes of Harlem album, did surprisingly well, and

Eddie Vinson's blues singing proved to be the band's most valuable selling point. Cootie, Vinson, pianist Earl Powell and the other fine soloists in the band deserve every break they can get.

Louis Armstrong broke up his band, led by Joe Garland, and a new one of similarly erratic quality was formed for him by Ted McRae. Louis made a number of Spotlight Band broadcasts and was set for his first New York location in several years at the Zanzibar toward the end of the year.

Benny Goodman also disbanded, spent most of the summer in idleness, then returned slowly, mostly in isolated radio appearances, with a quartet including Teddy Wilson, Sid Weiss and Morey Feld, to which Red Norvo was later added. Charlie Barnet had three different bands during 1944, the last of which was below his usually high standard; however, he has some interesting Decca records due out at this writing.

Among the outright commercial bands, Tommy and Jimmy Dorsey and Harry James and the rest of them, there were the customary fabulous grosses and the customary assortment of good jazz, bad jazz and music and that does not pretend to be jazz by my standards or anyone else's. Tommy's band, as well as James' and others that added a plethora of strings, offered relatively little music of importance to the jazz lover; but, as Muggsy Spanier, Max Kaminsky and other contemporaries have pointed out, James still is a great trumpeter who does occasionally still play good jazz.

Among the new bands of the year the biggest surprise came from Woody Herman. I call this a new band because it bears so little relation in style and personnel to the old Herman group, though actually he has worked continuously as a band-leader for the past eight years. Herman no longer has Billie Rogers, the girl trumpeter who formed a competent band of her own, heard fre-

Sidney (Big Sid) Catlett continues to beat out his jazz rhythms in his characteristically powerful manner for numerous studio recording sessions as well as for his own small group which Los Angeles night-lifers have had the opportunity of hearing during his long stay there. A veteran of no less than seven top name bands, Big Sid was chosen by Esquire's experts over little Davey Tough, who ran Catlett a close second (24 points to 19). It is significant that both these drummers' reputations rest on their well-controlled drive and their steady beat.

The fierce "growl" style of Cootie Williams, once a distinguishing trade-mark of the Ellington band, is now heavily featured in his own full-size orchestra. No other jazz trumpeter has handled that style quite so artistically and powerfully as has Cootie: the records on which it may be heard number in hundreds, but among the best, surely, are Concerto for Cootie, East St. Louis Toodle-O (on the Master label) and Echoes of Harlem. His open bell playing, however, is no less arresting: remember Black Beauty, West End Blues? Down Beat photo by Arsene.

The swift rise to prominence of young Oscar Pettiford was probably due in no small part to his winning position in the 1944 Esquire All-American. His decisive victory in the current poll indicates that his talent was not overestimated. Kriegsmann photo.

- The altoing of Johnny Hodges still imprints its personal stamp on
the Ellington orchestra, where his style has developed from its
clipped, accented rhythmic phrasing of 1929 to its present-day
super-romanticism. He won over Carter 42 to 33.   Apeda photo.

quently over the air later in the year; but he has a remarkable new discovery in Marjorie Hyams, a vibraharpist who has learned plenty from Norvo. The Herman band, during its last New York stand in September, provided some excitement unequalled by any white band in recent years. Ralph Burns' arrangements and piano solos, Flip Phillips' tenor, Neal Hefti's trumpet, Bill Harris' trombone, Woody's own clarinet, alto and vocals, Billy Bauer's guitar, Dave Tough's drumming and Chubby Jackson's bass work were all individual kicks. Our board of experts testified to the importance of this band by selecting four members as winners in this year's voting.

Lee Castle (Castaldo) and his excellent Armstrong-inspired trumpet headed a promising new band which impressed me in a number of airings. The band plays plenty of jazz arrangements featuring the leader and other good soloists. Billy Eckstine, the "sepia Sinatra," went on the road with a big band formed with the aid of the unique trumpeter and arranger, Dizzy Gillespie. This group is shaping up wonderfully and boasts of a great girl vocalist, Sara Vaughn, as well as several outstanding soloists, among them tenormen Dexter Gordon and Gene Ammons (son of Albert Ammons), trumpeters Shorty McConnell and Dizzy.

Boyd Raeburn, a fugitive from Mickey Mouse music in Chicago, impressed New York and other cities with a fine modern band in which the superb Hodges-like alto of Johnny Bothwell, the bass of *Esquire's* All-American man, Oscar Pettiford, and the arrangements of George Handy stand out. Georgie Auld, a great man on alto, tenor and soprano, has a most impressive young band which is more than a mere secondhand Basie bunch. At this writing it includes two fine colored musicians, Shadow Wilson and Howard McGhee. Herbie Fields, another versatile reedman who has had a tough time getting started, should go places with his latest band.

Gene Krupa plunged into the much be-stringed morass of commercial music that has enveloped Dorsey and James. His new band has some good talent, but the proportion of jazz played is dismayingly low. Gene's ex-trumpet star, Roy Eldridge, has been scuffling with a big band of his own that deserved to do better; discouraged, he joined Artie Shaw as a sideman.

There were a number of other big bands that boasted enough superior soloists and arrangements to be of some musical interest from time to time during 1944.

Cab Calloway, whose place as a hot jazz singer is acknowledged by only a handful of critics, the majority considering him more of a showman and entertainer, must nevertheless be reckoned with as the leader of a consistently fine orchestra combining swing, precision and finesse in its ensemble work with a high standard of inspiration. The arrangements are mostly by Buster Harding. Soloists with Calloway, as heard over the air during the year, included many men who are at least on a level with the more highly publicized men who play the jam sessions or the Village and 52nd Street clubs. They include Jonah Jones, Paul Webster and Shad Collins, each a talented solo trumpeter; Tyree Glenn, Keg Johnson and Fred Robinson, all of whom take solo trombone parts; Al Gibson, clarinet; Ike Quebec, a fine tenorman; Dave Rivera, pianist, who, along with Danny Barker, guitar, Milton Hinton, bass, and J. C. Heard, drums, forms part of a virtually perfect rhythm section. Although Calloway's band plays a relatively small number of unadulterated jazz pieces, there is usually a large enough proportion of jazz in his performances (except stage shows, when, like so many bands, he almost entirely sacrifices musicianship for showmanship and a plethora of vocals).

Earl Hines, during 1944, gave up his contingent of girl musicians—string quartet, harpist, vocal quartet—and settled down to a band with normal instrumentation, the only girl retained being the able bassist, Lucille Dixon. Earl is still a superior jazz pianist, with a band of variable quality in which the clarinet work of Scoops Carey is a major attraction. Hines suffered the loss of vocalists Billy Eckstine and Sara Vaughn, but he found an excellent replacement in Betty Roché, the former Ellington star. Though unable to get much radio time because Jim Crow still keeps Negro bands out of many of the best wired locations, Earl has remained, musically and commercially, an important figure.

Andy Kirk and Lucky Millinder, two of the perennials in the colored band field, still have better-than-average organizations. Lucky made a brief and unhappy attempt to launch an augmented band with woodwinds, but soon reverted to normal instrumentation. His new blues singer, Wynonie Harris, is a Joe Turner-styled shouter of considerable promise.

Stan Kenton, a pianist whose style is strongly akin to Hines' and whose orchestrations have highly individual characteristics, was one of the few admirable leaders of big bands who preferred losing commercial opportunities to sacrificing good jazz. He appeared for some time on the Bob Hope air show and refused to be made into a comic bandleader-character in the script; he resisted the advice of bookers and stuck to an advanced jazz style for his band. He has several powerful assets, among them our winning New Star vocalist, Anita O'Day, and the versatile and inspired ex-Hampton man, Karl George, playing both first and solo trumpet.

Freddy Slack had an up-and-down career, breaking up his band several times but impressing with his piano work on record releases. Jack Teagarden similarly was on shifting sands, with too many complete turnovers of personnel to allow for any accurate appraisal. Sonny Dunham, whose band was obviously modeled on Lunceford lines in its early days, is the leader of a typical surprising commercial swing band, by which I mean that one minute he may be playing a hammy trumpet or trombone solo, or leading the band through a dull arrangement of a dog tune for one of his singers, but three minutes later he may be riding through an excellent instrumental number which could easily be confused with a performance by one of the best colored jazz orchestras.

Bobby Sherwood, a cornetist who ranks with Max Kaminsky, Muggsy Spanier or Bobby Hackett, playing in a style similar to Hackett's has been leading a big band which supplies a good framework for his versatile and musicianly personality. Sherwood doubles on guitar, sings pleasantly in a Teagarden style, plays occasional trombone and piano and is altogether a talented musician worthy of more recognition.

Les Brown, another leader who seemed to be on a Lunceford kick awhile back, still has one of the better commercial bands, though perhaps in need of some stronger jazz soloists and more of a beat in its rhythm section. Like so many unfortunates tied to Victor and Columbia, he has had no chance since July 1942 to preserve any of his band's music on records.

Jerry Wald, whose own clarinet style, like the style of his band as a whole, is blatantly modeled after Shaw's, plays good jazz occasionally and has a good guitarist in the former Joe Venuti partner, Hayden Causey. Dean Hudson and George Paxton were other bandleaders whose work was of occasional interest.

The conversion of Mickey Mouse bands to a more modern style continued apace in 1944. In addition to Shep Fields and Horace Heidt, such bands as Jan Garber's and Tommy Tucker's have come up to date, with Tucker even getting arrangements made by Claude Hopkins and Fred Norman. The kind of music that Benny Goodman's band helped to propagate less than a decade ago has spread so far and improved the general standards of big band jazz so immeasurably, that many orchestras which a jazzman or jazz fan would have found thoroughly painful to listen to a couple of years ago are now acceptable and listenable much of the time.

The outstanding event in the field of small jazz orchestras during 1944 was the renaissance in the record industry.

After Decca signed the first armistice with Petrillo in the Fall of 1943, several of the independent record companies decided that they might as well make a deal on the same terms. Even paying royalties to the Union would not prevent them from making money with jazz discs. Before long such companies as Commodore, Keynote, Blue Note and Signature were waxing furiously. Musicians, relieved to get back on wax again at any price after a lull of a year and a half, often did sessions for flat scale.

Although the hot jazz market was and is limited to a five or six figure audience of fans, the fact that they could record most of these musicians cheaply and that the discs could be sold for 75c or a dollar, instead of the usual 35c or 50c, brought a swarm of new companies into the recording field. Most of them wanted to cut jazz dates featuring small bands, trios, quartets and sextets specially assembled for the occasion, with never a color line. A glance at our Discography of the Year (Chapter VI), or at the list of currently active record companies, will give you a small idea of the deluge that followed.

As the competition got keener, musicians started to ask higher prices and they managed to get them. Most of the recording men knew that owing to restrictions of production processes and manpower they would not be able to release the majority of these recordings until after the war. Meanwhile, though, they considered it a good investment to build up a catalogue while they could still build it reasonably cheaply.

Coleman Hawkins, who led a small band of his own most of the year along 52nd Street, was probably the most prolific of all recording artists in this hot jazz field. He made sessions with various combinations for Apollo, Beacon, Commodore, Delta, Keynote, Savoy and Signature. Also prominent both in the recording studios and along 52nd Street were such men as Hot Lips Page, Pete Brown, Cozy Cole, Johnny Guarnieri, Stuff Smith, Red Norvo and Emmett Berry.

Among the permanently organized small groups that stood out in 1944 were King Cole and Louis Jordan. It would have been hard to foresee, four years ago, that these groups, a trio and a quintet, both then barely making an adequate living, would today be among the nation's top juke box favorites (Capitol and Decca respectively) and still featuring the same blend of first-class music and fine entertainment. Jordan, a capital entertainer and showman, must not on this account be underestimated as a tenor and alto saxman and vocalist. The same applies to the singing and piano of King Cole and the guitar of Oscar Moore.

Eddie Heywood's little band sprang up fast after a good start via Café Society and records on Commodore. He features intricate and highly original arrangements with a sextet of such superlative men as Vic Dickenson (trombone) and Lem Davis (alto).

Café Society produced two other six-piecers, both led by Teddy Wilson alumni, Edmond Hall and Benny Morton. The former did a great deal of recording during the year, though never, curiously enough, with his own band, which included such excellent men as Mouse Randolph (trumpet) and Ellis Larkins (piano). Members of Benny Morton's new band included a talented young pianist, Sammy Benskin, also trumpeter Bobby Stark and clarinetist Prince Robinson.

Two veterans of the 1920's, Miff Mole and Red Nichols, got into the jazz groove again leading sextets in Hollywood and New York respectively. Nichols' "Five Pennies" started out with men like Milt Raskin (piano) and Don Lodice (tenor) both well-known for their work with Tommy Dorsey. Mole had an all-star Dixieland bunch at Nick's with Muggsy Spanier, Pee Wee Russell and a rhythm section. Max Kaminsky, out of the Navy, spent half the year leading his own group at the Pied Piper in the Village, his sidemen including Willie (the Lion) Smith (piano), Wilbur de Paris (trombone) and a very good new bass-man, Jack Lesberg.

The Red Allen-Higginbotham sextet played another entire year through at the Garrick in Chicago and did not record as a unit. Red Norvo had a great little band along 52nd Street which brought out two of our New Stars, Aaron Sachs and Remo Palmieri. Before Norvo joined Benny Goodman in the fall, his own band was preserved on wax, with a couple of personnel changes, in a Keynote session.

Eddie South, with the up-and-coming Billy Taylor on piano, has been on the Coast, as has Joe Venuti, who gave up his own band in favor of studio work. With the disbanding of Art Tatum's trio when Tatum departed for the Coast, both Slam Stewart and Tiny Grimes went out on their own and figured prominently in the 52nd Street and recording studio scenes.

Among the solo artists who came into the limelight in 1944 were Maurice Rocco and Dorothy Donegan, both fairly good pianist and better showmen; Herman Chittison, who landed a network sustainer series, and Nat Jaffe, featured in the Fats Waller Memorial Album on Signature.

RADIO

The business of hearing good jazz through the medium of radio still remains largely a catch-as-catch-can affair. If a good jazz orchestra happens to be working at a spot where there is a network, you're in luck. None of the networks goes out of its way to present the best in swing music in the best possible setting.

One of the heartening signs during the year, however, was the Mildred Bailey show on CBS. The overambitiousness of Paul Baron's house orchestra which accompanied Mildred on this series was partly compensated by the relaxed atmosphere of the sextet within the band which had one featured item on each show. In this group were Red Norvo, Charlie Shavers or Roy Eldridge, Teddy Wilson, Remo Palmieri, Specs Powell, and Al Hall or Billy Taylor, Sr. The program also introduced some guest stars playing good jazz.

Eddie Condon's Blue Network jam sessions every Saturday afternoon were the first series of this kind to go from coast to coast. This series has presented a great deal of good jazz and has done much good for jazz as a whole. It could have done a great deal more had Condon not been tied rigidly to the Dixieland instrumentation—trumpet, trombone, clarinet—and insisted on a policy of playing Dixieland tunes, often against the wishes of the musicians themselves. Thus no alto or tenor saxmen, no guitarists and relatively few colored musicians, have benefited from the substantial network time allotted to these shows.

Many of the musicians themselves feel that opportunities are being wasted at these Condon affairs, which in addition to the broadcasts from Town Hall and the Ritz Theatre, included four unbroadcast concerts held at Carnegie Hall. After the first of the Carnegie affairs I talked to a number of the musicians. The general opinion was that the affair had been a disorganized clambake. Edmond Hall confessed that he never feels relaxed, can never play his best, at such sessions; Joe Marsala admitted he hadn't wanted to do *Wolverine Blues*, but they had insisted he do this Dixieland tune. Hot Lips Page, Sammy Price, Muggsy Spanier, Benny Morton, Sid Weiss and several others told me they had been uneasy and unable to play their best under the circumstances. What this all boils down to is that there are a few musicians who are born Dixielanders, but many more have Dixieland thrust upon them. Such men as Spanier and Wettling have often stated that they dislike being classed as Dixieland musicians. But the individual ability of some of these men sometimes saves the concerts and broadcasts from being a collective mess.

Another important radio event was the cornering of two months on the Old Gold show by the great Woody Herman band, which unhappily had to turn it back to Frankie Carle when the latter returned to New York. Count Basie made regular appearances for a while (without his band) on the Kate Smith program, a notable item in the crashing of the color line on commercial airings. Lionel Hampton, earlier in the year, had a Sunday morning series for the War Manpower Commission, and plenty of good orchestras, white and colored, were heard on the Spotlight Bands show over the Blue Network.

As for movies, this remains the worst medium for hearing jazz. Plenty of good bands made movies during the year, but in most cases they were so much embroiled with corny settings, cutaways to dialogue and other distractions, that it didn't amount to much. For all the good Hollywood has ever done jazz, the jazzmen might as well have stood in bed.

To sum up, 1944 was an extraordinary year for swing music. By the time the musicians in uniform come marching home, the music business will be ready, both artistically and commercially, to hit a new all-time high in jazz history.

Chapter III

The Main Currents of Jazz

by PAUL EDUARD MILLER *and* JAMES CRENSHAW

JAZZ has taken its assured place among the arts. After years of sniping, the intelligentsia have beat a hasty retreat, a little awed by the appearance of *Jazz Books, Record Books, Yearbooks,* and considerably disconcerted by the Carnegie Hall (New York), Symphony Hall (Boston), Ravinia (Chicago), Philharmonic Auditorium (Los Angeles) and Metropolitan Opera House (New York) concerts by jazz orchestras. Critics supposedly in the know suddenly realized that for years they had been championing jazzmen and jazz music of an inferior art-quality—the orchestras of Paul Whiteman, Vincent Lopez, Andre Kostelanetz and the music of Irving Berlin, Jerome Kern and George Gershwin. They further realized that since the hot variety of jazz was proving its merits not only from an artistic but from a box-office standpoint as well, they had better pull in their horns and call time out for a little mediation. Ever since the last war, they remembered, there had been frequent predictions of the doom, the inevitable death of jazz—such music was but a fad, a reaction from the war, and was fit only for musical adolescents anyhow. Jazz, nevertheless, had kept growing in stature and importance, until finally it could not be denied. Where art-qualities were concerned, the music of King Oliver, Louis Armstrong and Sidney Bechet had become more significant than that of Whiteman, Lopez, Wayne King and Meredith Willson.

Yet among jazz critics and fans there currently exists a raging argument not about jazz itself, but about what kind of jazz is the real jazz, the best jazz, the only jazz. The principal participants have been the writers and editors of *Metronome* as against the writers and editors of *The Jazz Record, The Record Changer* and *Jazz Quarterly*. The adherents of the *Metronome* group have championed the modern big-band swing style; its opponents, small-band jazz. This division of interest has not been precise, but in the main the two schools of thinking have paired themselves off in the categories of big-band modern, small-band traditional. Over the question of which of these is the better jazz, angry words have flowed, words that only added to the confusion in jazz criticism which for ten years had been growing to larger and larger proportions. It is time, we believe, for the boys on the jazz front to take stock of themselves, to become aware of their own contradictions and resolve them. Only in this way can they solidify the gains which thus far have been made on the national jazz scene through more widespread understanding and acceptance.

Proof that these confusions have been engendered in the ranks of jazz itself is evident in the fact that the champions of, for example, modern big-band swing *do* write about New Orleans, Nicksieland and Dixieland jazz—and call it jazz. They claim only that it is bad jazz played by misguided musicians. There is complete agreement that the music of a Sammy Kaye, a Kay Kyser, a Phil Harris or a Guy Lombardo is *not* jazz; it is only within the realm of what admittedly is jazz that there is argument about which is the genuine, undiluted, pure product. Eddie Condon, no doubt, would rather listen to Benny Goodman than to Ted Lewis, as would Harry James prefer Woody Herman to Lawrence Welk. Similarly, that staunch supporter of New Orleans Jazz, Bill Russell, although he might do plenty of beefing about its "impure" qualities, could listen to a Bob Crosby Dixieland version of *Muskrat Ramble* above a Paul Whiteman rendition—while simultaneously insisting that the Bunk Johnson interpretation was the greatest of all, the only true jazz.

With so many journalistic writers about jazz and so few critics —true critics such as Charles Edward Smith, Roger Pryor Dodge, Reed Dickerson and Walter Sidney, for example—it is not surprising to find that the reasons advanced for the so-called devitalization of jazz are such superficial and contradictory ones as (1) too little regard for what the academicians call form; (2) disregard of the melodic; (3) too much attention to melody; (4) not enough improvisation, that is, too much concern with "paper" scores; (5) too much commercialization; etc., etc.

For ten full years the vast majority of printed words concerned, supposedly, with an aesthetic-critical appraisal of jazz has addressed itself to the question: *how* should jazz be played if it is to be called good or excellent or great? As a corollary, the argument further concerns itself with the number of men in a band. It seems that if, following the New Orleans school, a three-horn front line of trumpet, trombone and clarinet, backed by a nice relaxed but vigorous rhythm section, plays that interweaving kind of jazz with solos interspersed here and there—if jazz is performed that way and by such a combination, it's not only great jazz but the only jazz. The big-band moderns, on the other hand, want plenty of instrumentalists so the arrangers can go to work and produce something really terrific that will knock everybody for a loop—and what harmonies! That New Orleans and Dixieland stuff, they continue, is all right—it might have been great in its day—but now the musicians and arrangers know so much more and are so much more proficient technically that they need bigger groups with which to work so their ideas can find fuller expression. In short, one school insists that New Orleans jazz is the genuine article, while the Nicksielanders (the musicians who gather at Nick's in New York for sessions, a cross section of whom appear on Eddie Condon's Blue Network broadcasts) are an abomination; the other coterie puts its faith in new techniques, new instrumentation, "improved" knowledge of harmony and instrument, claiming that the older, more traditional methods are a horrible anachronism out of the dead past.

Further, the so-called styles bearing the tab "Chicago" and "Kansas City" have come in for their share of adherents too. Why there has not been more clamor in behalf of a New York, Memphis, St. Louis, Los Angeles and Detroit style—since each of these cities contributed to jazz—is explainable only on the grounds that no writers who grew up in these urban centers have taken up the cudgel. The term "hybrid" has been hurled at performers as diverse as Teddy Wilson and Raymond Scott, while the two-beat Dixieland style has been defended as firmly as it has been attacked by equally fanatic believers in the four-beat Negro style —hailed as the type of jazz that no white musician can *really* play. Categorical statements have become the stock-in-trade of the jazz writer. At every point in his "criticism," when the reader expects him to prove that this is jazz and this is not, he reverts to phrases such as "this sends me," "it's terrific," "out of this world," "he plays with heat," "gutbucket chorus," "barrelhouse intonation," etc., etc. These descriptive terms, of course, are acceptable in themselves, but they do not define good jazz. Such a vocabulary hardly can form the basis for aesthetic criteria.

What happens when the same standards of measurement used by jazz writers are applied to symphonic music and musicians? The critics of so-called serious music would not risk ridicule by comparing the *ideal* of the symphony to the *ideal* of the quartet. There has, for example, never been any question about the grandeur and dignity, *as music*, of the late Beethoven quartets—no opinion to the effect that these pieces written for but four instruments were not really classical music, but just old traditional outmoded forms. In fact, there is agreement that the last six of his quartets surpass, *as music,* some of his symphonies such as the First, Second, Fifth and Eighth. But, if bigness and complexity equal greatness, then, to be sure, the more the jazz orchestra can approximate the symphony in size and in the elaborateness of notated scores, the better the jazz. This kind of thinking has rendered fanatic several otherwise excellent virtuosi-leaders. What Artie Shaw set in motion with his thirty-two piece band (which included sixteen strings) has been topped by Tommy Dorsey, with forty-two men. We may well expect that if a showman-leader such as Glenn Miller returns from his A.A.F. adventures in music he may decide that to reffirm his bid for fame and greatness he'll need fifty-two men, whereupon Shaw or Harry James or Dorsey or Gene Krupa will enter the competition and raise the ante to sixty-two, seventy-two, eighty-two—well, why stop there? Why not go on and beat the symphony orchestras and then jazz will be bigger and greater and better and more complex than the symphony and classical music. There's real accomplishment!

The critical doctrine that bigness and complexity are directly related to greatness is one that has been debunked over and over again, but apparently one that the journalists of jazz have not heard of. Neither have they comprehended that a small-sized group is capable of producing jazz artistically as fine and as deep, as intense and as broad as is an aggregation of a hundred men—and that includes symphony orchestras. The greatest jazz we have ever heard anywhere, which, incidentally also is the best contemporary music of *any* kind we have heard, was performed by a trio consisting of soprano saxophone, piano and drums! We do not, however, argue here that only small groups can make great jazz or that jazz written for large orchestras cannot also be great. Just as we do not claim that the sonata or trio or quartet in classical music is either superior or inferior to the full symphony in its potentialities for great music, so with jazz it is not a matter of by whom or how the music is played, or how many musicians are involved in its performance. Each grouping, each instrumentation is the proper and ideal vehicle for certain musical ideas and emotional attitudes. Depending on what the writer or performer wishes to project through his ideas and emotional attitudes, each group best can be adapted to them, each in its own way.

Tradition or modernity, simplicity or complexity, bigness or smallness—these are no critera in themselves What jazz, what recordings, then, merit the banner of great *music?* What is an aesthetically defensible criterium of judgment? It is this: The *emotional values* expressed by the artist (performer or composer) through the medium of music. The emotional values and attitudes of the artist, of course, stem directly from his own and others' experiences in our own time. Those attitudes in the jazzman reflect directly the attitudes in society itself; no music, no matter by what name it is called or in what time it was written and and played, no music can do *more* than that. If the jazzman's values and attitudes are recognized by his audience and it responds to them, he is fulfilling the same function and attaining the same artistic stature as his fellow-artist in the realm of so-called serious music. Jazz now is at loggerheads with itself (the dispute among the different schools) not because jazz, but because society has stopped flowing. The new emotional content, not only of jazz, but of all art-forms, will be derived from the relationships that obtain between men after the war: that content will determine the new form and the new emotional attitude of jazz and of all the arts.

Let it be understood here and now that when we speak of jazz we speak only of the best; that when we refer to emotional values, attitudes and content we refer to sincerely and clearly conceived and articulated values and attitudes. The attitude, however, may be either conscious or instinctive—and with most jazz it happens to be instinctive. We rule out the drool and drivel, the soupy sentimentality; we do not regard the sheer escape-music of jazz any more worthy of attention than the ditto of symphonic music. The great masses of people respond to escape-art, hence it is easy to understand the popularity of the sweet band. The highly popular swing band, too, offers escape, even if the escape its listeners seek is that of more jitters, more excitement, more pressure, since that is their reaction to contemporary life. It is no accident that a musician like Harry James becomes increasingly undignified and lush in his romanticism as he makes more and more money. Artie Shaw's music often lies on the borderline between heartfelt romanticism and the lush sentimentality of escape and dreams.

Actually, there is more kinship between Pee Wee Russell and Duke Ellington than between the two New Orleans-born hornmen, Irving Fazola and Red Allen. The fact that Ellington writes for and conducts a large orchestra has no bearing whatsoever on the fact that his emotional attitude (decadent) is very similar to that of Russell's, who has rarely played in a big band and whose reputation rests on what virtually amounts to his free-lance solo activities. Their kinship is deep despite the fact that Ellington's cocktail-lounge weariness is poles apart from Russell's outright dirtiness. Although Fazola and Allen were born in the same generation and in the same city, nevertheless their approach to life —through music—is different: Fazola delineates the Blues attitude, Allen the Protest. They cannot both be dubbed "New Orleans style" performers any more than King Oliver and Earl Hines (who played during their best days in Chicago) can be categorized as counterparts of the white Austin High musicians who erroneously have been connected with a style which does not exist at all, the "Chicago" style.

Alcide Pavageau
(bass)
Jim Robinson
(trombone)
Tubby Hall
(drums)
Alphonse Picou
(clarinet)

Distinguished New Orleans musicians. Picou originated High Society. Pavageau & Robinson photos by William Russell; Picou by Bechet.

Wade Whaley
(clarinet)
Bob Lyons
(bass)
Eddie Miller
(tenor)
Buster Wilson
(piano)

Distinguished New Orleans musicians. Whaley and Wilson photos by Standard Oil Co.; Lyons by William Russell; Miller by Down Beat.

Lawrence Marrero
(banjo)
Nappy Lamare
(guitar)
Ed Garland
(bass)
Red Allen
(trumpet)

Distinguished New Orleans musicians. Garland photo by Standard Oil; Marrero by William Russell· Lamare by Down Beat; Allen by Ferstel.

The New Orleans Rhythm Kings at Friars Inn, Chicago, 1923. They gave Chicago its first real taste of post-war white jazz, both in person and on records. Their frequent trips to New Richmond, Indiana, to record for the Gennett label resulted in excellent sales of the discs throughout the Middle-West. Left to right: trombonist Georg Brunis (then spelled Brunies), trumpeter Paul Mares, drummer Ben Pollack, clarinetist Leon Rappolo, pianist Mel Stitzel, altoist Volly De Faut, banjoist Lew Black, bassist Steve Brown. Photo by George Hoefer.

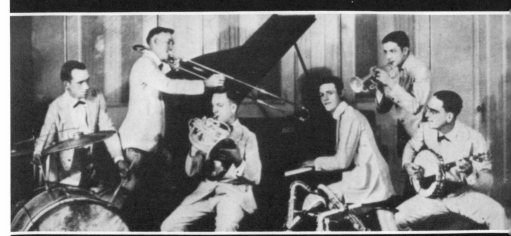

The Norman Brownlee Band in New Orleans, 1920. After Jack Laine, the Original Dixielanders and The Louisiana Five, this was the white jazz group which next nurtured the hot tradition. Left to right: Alonzo Crombie, George Barth, Bill Braun, Norman Brownlee, Emmett Hardy and Billy Eastwood. Cornetist Hardy is the "great" man in this outfit. Like Bix, he succumbed to an early death (age 22); unlike Bix Beiderbecke he left no recordings to settle the arguments: some musicians claim he was greater than Bix. Photo by National Jazz Foundation.

The Original Dixieland Band in New Orleans, 1914. These youngsters grew up under the inspiration of Jack (Papa) Laine, carried his spirit northward to Chicago, then throughout the world. Left to right: Tony Sbarbaro, Eddie Edwards, Nick LaRocca, Alcide (Yellow) Nunez, Harry Ragas. The presence of Nunez on clarinet (not Larry Shields) gives credence and verification to the authenticity of the split-up between LaRocca and Nunez in Chicago late in 1914, when Nunez joined The Louisiana Five. Photo by Fred Williams & Jazz Foundation.

The balance of this short chapter is but an effort to sketch in and suggest the main currents (the emotional attitudes) which jazz has taken during the half century since New Orleans first heard the music known as hot jazz.

We do not contend:

That each and every jazzman can be pigeonholed within the confines of *one* emotional attitude.

That every jazz record can be classified as belonging to but *one* emotional attitude.

That all jazz—or all music of any kind—can be grouped according to its emotional values and attitudes, since some of it is completely barren of any genuine emotional attitude.

That the listing of either music or performer in any given emotional attitude thereby passes judgment on its or his art-quality or acceptability as art or artistry.

We do emphasize:

That an instrumentalist may reflect one emotional attitude at one time or on one recording, quite another attitude at some other time or on some other recording.

That each jazzman whom we have classified below is so grouped because *predominantly* his attitude was of one type—an authentically contemporary one.

That within the space of a jazz recording not only one, but two or more emotional attitudes may be portrayed.

That some jazz which can be labeled commercial—having the jazz flavor but expressing no genuine emotion—is quickly assimilated, best forgotten and has no enduring art-value.

That in all five emotional-attitude groupings which we have made, only that jazz and those jazzmen competent to express such attitudes sincerely have been included.

That the examples we cite—the best only—are considered as among the most artistic performers and the finest jazz, artistically: our groupings do not imply or suggest a lack of art or artistry;

quite the contrary, they include the jazz musically most moving—and no other.

That not only jazz, but all music of the past and present, reflects the artist's emotional attitude toward society.

We specifically emphasize:

That we agree with Otto Cesana that "music is emotion—if it isn't emotion it isn't music."

That we are dealing exclusively with genuine emotion; that the spurious variety easily can be detected.

Emotional attitude I: THE BLUES. Here is simple, direct, personal sadness, without posturing or posing, without the lugubrious or the fantastic The Blues of jazz are not the dramatic, almost self-pitying sadness of a Wagnerian Siegfried moaning because he has been unable to slay his quota of dragons for the week, but the sadness of remembrances past, of living life as it presents itself each day, remembering the sadness, too, of friends and of the deep darkness of the unconscious.

In no jazzman, of course, does this emotional tendency (or any other) appear unmixed; yet above all others, one tendency does persist and predominate. Among the Blues instrumentalists a strong quality of lyricism invariably appears, but does not dominate. Clarinetists Irving Fazola and Johnny Dodds exemplify this mixture: Fazola on *Milk Cow Blues* and *Jazz Me Blues* (Bob Crosby—Decca) and *Clarinet Blues* (Jess Stacy—Varsity); Dodds on *Once in a While, Savoy Blues, Hotter Than That* (Louis Armstrong—Okeh), *Drop That Sack* (Lil's Hot Shots—Vocalion) and *Wild Man Blues/Melancholy* (Dodds—Brunswick). Since, merely because it is the Blues attitude, there is an implication of Protest in it, that the Blues guitarist Charlie Christian should include the Protest in his outlook is not surprising. The Christian chorus in *The Shiek* (Benny Goodman Sextet—Columbia) stands out prominently Blues in an otherwise Romantic piece.

Considering complete compositions, records as a whole, a predominantly Blues approach with elements of Protest and Lyric combined are to be heard in discs such as these: the Muggsy Spanier Bluebirds of *Dippermouth, Relaxin' at the Touro, Someday Sweetheart, Livery Stable Blues;* the Spike Hughes English Deccas of *Sweet Sorrow Blues* and *Fanfare;* the King Oliver Vocalion of *Sugar Foot Stomp;* the Bob Crosby Decca of *Dogtown Blues;* and the Bunny Berigan Victor of *Davenport Blues.* For Blues with an overtone of Decadent: *Winin' Boy Blues* (Jelly Roll Morton—Bluebird). A Blues-Lyric without the protest: *Davenport Blues* (Charleston Chasers—Columbia). Blues with little or no admixture of other attitudes; *Rainbow Blues* (Jerry Jerome—Asch); *Zuddan* (Ruben Reeves—Vocalion); *Muggles, Got No Blues, Two Deuces, Skip the Gutter* (Louis Armstrong—Okeh).

Among the other characteristically Blues instrumentalists are Jack Teagarden, Joe Marsala, Woody Herman and Jelly Roll Morton.

Emotional attitude II: THE ROMANTIC. The essence of individualism: the ego giving out over all. This attitude is characterized by big, lugubrious, fabulous sweeps of sound; the outlook is one of breadth, picturesqueness, a reassertion of the imagination and sentiment (but not sentimentality, at which level it deteriorates to artistic insignificance). The music which reflects this attitude is expansive, full of buoyant, happy tones and dramatic pauses and arpeggios.

Performers in the Romantic vein are profuse: Lionel Hampton and Red Norvo, Lawrence Brown and Tommy Dorsey, Joe Smith and Billie Butterfield, Fats Waller and Mary Lou Williams —to name but a few. To these add a trio of outstanding performers: Louis Armstrong, Benny Goodman, Artie Shaw, whose recorded examples are many. Here are some samplings: Shaw's *Yesterdays* (suggesting a hint of decadence), *Concerto for Clarinet, Sometimes I Feel Like a Motherless Child* (a strong blend of Blues) and *Nocturne;* Goodman's *Benny Rides Again, Sugar Foot Stomp, The Sheik, Poor Butterfly, The Man I Love,* and with Mel Powell on Commodore, *The World Is Waiting for the Sunrise;* Armstrong's *Save It Pretty Mama* and *Monday Date.* The entire platter of *Drop That Sack* (Lil's Hot Shots), with the exception of the piano chorus which registers no emotion, fairly gushes forth the Romantic; even Johnny Dodds' Blues chorus almost breaks through its lyricism to become romantic. Muggsy Spanier's *Big Butter and Egg Man* hits the same stride and is an excellent example for determining the sound-qualities of the Romantic attitude toward life. (Most of Spanier's trumpeting however, falls into the emotional outlook of Protest.) The French-Gypsy guitarist, Django Reinhardt (on *St. Louis Blues,* for example) serves as a contrast to Charlie Christian, the former being a Romantic and therefore a good basis for the contrasting approaches on this instrument.

Although much of Bunny Berigan's trumpeting is Lyric, his best-known recording, *I Can't Get Started/Prisoner's Song* on Victor is typically Romantic, with an exuberant, ego-filling tone that is quite unlike the lyricism of his *In the Dark* or *Candlelight.*

Emotional attitude III: THE LYRIC. A very thin line, but nevertheless a discernible one, exists between the Romantic and the Lyric approach to life through music. To grasp the Lyric thoroughly the samples cited must be closely studied with reference to the Romantic. A highly personal expression is the Lyric—a singing, a brilliant soaring of the spirit portraying the simple joy of life and living, with the notes sharp and clear; but restrained, though not restrained in intensity. Rather, the music comes out like water flows restrained but intense through a nozzle. A tenderness, too, never maudlin, but singing a quiet, confident song—this is an integral part of the lyricist and his music.

Red Nichols is one of the greats who expresses the Lyric attitude; so are Edmond Hall (with mixtures of Blues and Protest), Sidney Bechet (ditto), Bix Beiderbecke, Chu Berry, Barney Bigard, Les Robinson, Cootie Williams, Don Redman. Many of the Nichols platters contain excellent samplings: the second chorus on the Louisiana Rhythm Kings' *Lady Be Good*; *Panama/Margie* by the Five Pennies, which has a punch and confidence bordering on Protest; while *Clarinet Marmalade* (both by Five Pennies and Fletcher Henderson—Columbia) contain, over and above the dominant Lyric, Protest tinged with Blues. Sidney Bechet on *Dear Old Southland* mixes his lyricism with a heavy tinge of Blues; the same is true of Armstrong's *Savoy Blues* and *Knee Drops*, while his *Once in a While* sings out wonderfully with just sheer joy. Both Robinson and Bigard play that way too on *Someday Sweetheart* (Capitol Jazzmen); Chu Berry hits the same pace in *Limehouse Blues* (Wingy Manone).

Emotional attitude IV: THE DECADENT. Deterioration and decline of the personal spirit, with neurotic overtones. This emotional reaction to life veers in two directions: (1) lush resignation —a resolution downward to plaintive resignation, with consequent lessening of the intensity of life by softness and lethargic relaxation: the artist is pulled away from the usual tensions of life; (2) the utter inability to adjust—a plunge directly into more intensity in an effort to break through to an impossible adjustment, resulting in white-heat intensity.

Frank Teschemacher is the supreme example of the latter direction; trumpeters Jimmy McPartland and Bill Davison blow out notes of the same calibre. The music of Duke Ellington and his protégé-arranger, Billy Strayhorn, falls in both directions: plaintive resignation is found in *Passion Flower* (Johnny Hodges —Bluebird), *Moon Mist* and *Blue Serge* (Ellington—Victor); a Protest-plunge in the powerful *Ko Ko* (Ellington—Victor). It is startling to recall that the same Hodges who plays *Passion Flower* with such green-tinged fervor is the performer who likewise portrays the sheer lyricism of *On the Sunny Side of the Street* (Lionel Hampton—Victor). Pee Wee Russell's lush resignation is perfectly portrayed in *The Last Time I Saw Chicago* and in *Basin St. Blues* (Condon—Commodore), though almost all his choruses display Lyric overtones, often in striking contrast. The Billy Banks disc of *Margie* offers a striking contrast (Decadent vs. Lyric) to the Nichols version.

Emotional attitude V: THE PROTEST. Direct, precise, clipped, here is an angry, sometimes vicious, attack on life, somewhat analogous to the literature of social protest. It is for the most part an unconscious expression of the artist's reaction to his everyday living conditions.

Muggsy Spanier, Red Allen, Greeley Walton and Jay C. Higginbotham are among the instrumentalists who dominantly adhere to the attitude of Protest. Just as there are heavy overtones of Protest in the Spanier Blues recordings, so in *At the Jazz Band Ball, Riverboat Shuffle* and *Eccentric*, Spanier and his whole band lash out against life, but not without a mixture of Blues and Lyric. The Luis Russell Vocalion platter of *Ease on Down* features two standout Protest choruses: Higginbotham on trombone, Walton on tenor. Higginbotham and Allen played that way side by side on many of Russell and Blue Rhythm Band recordings. Edmond Hall's *Seein' Red* (Blue Note) beautifully exemplifies the clean, sharp clarity of Protest in Hall's clarineting, which invariably suggests a Blues overtone.

The foregoing have been no more than sketches, indicating what we believe to be the main currents of jazz—the emotional attitudes into one of which all the great instrumentalists tend to fall. If there is a feeling among jazzmen and jazz lovers that old forms are exhausted, if the name bands grope for new arrangements to express things they anticipate rather than feel now, while even the boys at Nick's nightly realize through their horns the further implications of what they have played before, we do not mourn the end of jazz. We believe these things simply signify that the attitudes of the past will no longer sustain while society itself is shifting, and that they will be resolved as men resolve their own relationships into new forms. Meanwhile, they are expressed daily in music by everything from trios to large orchestras.

So brief a sketch could hardly hope to lay bare all the subtle overlappings of so richly various an expression as jazz, which almost matches society's own complexity. We do hope, however, that the consideration of such an approach will help clarify the critical air and resolve some of the disputes which are vitiating jazz criticism and blocking its wider public appreciation by presenting the reading public confusion in place of explanation.

Chapter IV

Wartime Hints for Collectors

by GEORGE HOEFER

LOOKING back, I think it is safe to say that a wise collector buys his records when they are issued." If you read ESQUIRE'S 1944 JAZZ BOOK, you'll remember this as the last sentence in the chapter on collectors, and I repeat it here to emphasize its prime importance. Wartime conditions have underscored the truth of this warning a hundredfold. Whatever good jazz records are issued seem to be gobbled up so fast that it takes an alert collector to obtain them and it has resulted in records only a month old appearing on auction lists. This condition, of course, will not continue many months more, but, nevertheless, the fact that the record companies regularly delete discs from their catalogues is argument enough that platters must be bought as they appear. The Basie Deccas which were so common only a few years ago have become "regulars" in the auction lists. In the same category, are the Bob Crosby Dixieland Deccas and the 1937-38 Goodman Trios and Quartets.

One night about a half dozen years ago while sorting out a pile of old jazz items I was accosted by a rather perplexed roommate. He tossed a new copy of the Crosby Band's *Dogtown Blues* onto a pile saying, "Put that in your collection so that twenty years from now you won't be hunting all over the country for a beaten-up copy." Today, six years later, it is necessary to pay a premium for this record if you can find it listed on an auction list.

Pre-war jazz record collectors frantically accumulated such vintage items as Okehs by Armstrong's Hot Five and Gennetts by King Oliver's Creole Jazz Band on their original labels. Jazz discophiles specialized on these 1920-30 recordings, usually seeking the solo work of some star instrumentalist. The junk shop forager had neither the time nor the money to go into a legitimate record store and buy a current release over the counter.

Now, however, the majority of collectors concentrate on more recent issues. The collector of 1945 is receiving auction lists that contain not only records made six years ago but some waxed a mere month past. The classics of the twenties on original labels have almost disappeared entirely from these lists. When an Oliver or Armstrong original does happen to show up on an auction list the competition is keen and the bidding is high. The neophyte record collector of the future will have to be satisfied by filling his shelves with reissues if he desires to have a complete representative and historical collection.

The foregoing paragraph is not to be construed as a discouragement to the hot record collector who still persists in combing through the musty wax piles in junk shops. Startling discoveries are still being made by the collectors who refuse to give up their searching. A year or so ago John Reid of Cincinnati walked into a shop on Camp Street in New Orleans and pulled not one but two (four sides) original QRS piano solo records by Earl Hines out of a pile of wax not two blocks away from the building where the outstanding Crescent City collector, Orin Blackstone, was busy city editing the New Orleans *Times-Picayune*.

Out in the Northwest last summer Monte Ballou of Portland, Oregon, located a copy of a fabulous King Oliver disc. Several years ago the New York collector Dick Rieber found an old dealer's catalogue put out by the Gennett company and in it were listed two King Oliver Creole Band records that had never turned up. In fact, this catalogue listing was the only evidence that the records had ever been made and there was no proof that they had ever actually been pressed up. Monte Ballou must have received quite a thrill when he came upon a copy of King Oliver's *Zulu Ball* and *Workingman's Blues*—one of the records listed in that catalogue. The other record has yet to be found and there are undoubtedly additional copies of *Zulu Ball* somewhere.

A New Jersey discophile recently located the first record Duke Ellington's band ever recorded. It was on the obscure Blu-Disc label and its authenticity was substantiated by Ellington himself who requested it be brought to his apartment where he could study the disc. These stories have been cited in an endeavor to show that a persistent quest can still be rewarded. In the main, however, hot record collecting has become much more restricted than it has been in the past.

Let us look at some of the causes for the changes and restrictions in collecting hot. There is a record shortage due to the war just as there are shortages in all commodities. The world conflict has even caused a scarcity of records made twenty years ago. This comes about due to the fact that shortly after Pearl Harbor the supply of shellac from the South Pacific was cut off by the Japanese. In order to allay this shortage, a plan was devised to call in all available old records for melting down to extract the shellac. There is no doubt but what a great many keenly sought after jazz records went into the reclaiming vats at the large record plants. Many of the junk shop dealers disposed of large stacks of records by selling them in bulk to the record manufacturers. This has thrown the emphasis on current waxings.

The small jazz recorders have given rise to quite a library of noncommercial jazz recordings. These sides are made without the confining restrictions made by the larger companies—therefore better records for the jazz student result. There have been more than enough jazz record buyers to purchase all the records these independents have been able to produce with the current limitation imposed by the lack of materials and pressing facilities.

The current reaction to my column *The Hot Box* in *Down Beat* Magazine has indicated that many new converts to good jazz music constantly are being made. This 1945 ESQUIRE JAZZ BOOK will undoubtedly make many new additions to the fold of jazz enthusiasts if the response to the 1944 book is any criteria. Last year's book went all over the world to collectors in almost every country as well as to numerous American collectors in the various services. The boys are hearing jazz on V-discs and surprisingly enough are retaining an avid interest in music. There is beginning to be quite a potent interest in jazz developing in South America and they are forming Rhythm Clubs regularly down there. Australia is showing an active interest which has been aided and abetted by our own jazz fans who have been down there on war duty. This expanding appreciation of jazz music will make a potent record market once the war is over.

Many collectors in the services are still actively collecting in spite of considerable restriction. Some of them are bidding on the current mail record auctions and having the records sent directly to their homes here. Quite a few of the more arduous still hunt platters wherever they might find themselves. For instance, Robert Sales of Louisville, now a warrant officer in the Army, located a record shop in Charleroi, Belgium, where he purchased seventy-eight records by French, Dutch and Belgian jazz bands. He also managed to obtain thirteen records on the French Swing label in Paris shortly after the liberation. He is most proud of finding Fletcher Henderson's famous waxing of *Fidgety Feet* on the French Brunswick label. Ed Hartwell of Chicago reported finding the Ellington *Creole Rhapsody* on Disco Grammofono S 10373 *Rapsodia Creola*. Keith Lees, an English collector in the R.A.F. stationed in India, sent to the United States a series of

Indian Columbias featuring Teddy Wetherford playing six piano solos recorded in India. Wetherford was once Erskine Tate's pianist but has been abroad for over fifteen years.

The probable brisk activity in reissuing after the war will offer a new problem to the discerning collector. When an old record is reissued on a current label with a different record number it will be quite easy to determine which is the original and which is the reissue. However, recently Victor and some of the older independents have reissued records on their labels with the old record number applying to the original. This will prove confusing to some of the label collectors who wish to make certain they are getting an original. The new Victors and Bluebirds do not have the label printing in the usual familiar gold leaf. Therefore the recent rerelease will be identified by printing in a much lighter color. First edition Blue Notes recorded before the war were released on labels using a color scheme of blue and yellow. They are now rereleasing some of the original sides on a blue and white label.

As there are now record companies specializing in jazz recording, there are also jazz magazines and columns interested in reviewing this particular type of music. The new collector will find sources where he can find out what is good jazz. *Esquire* monthly features two full pages of critical and informative jazz discussion. Jazz record reviews can be found in *Down Beat, Metronome, The Needle, Jazz Quarterly* and in many regular popular magazines and papers. Collectors may advertise their wants and records for disposition in *The Record Changer, The Needle* and *Recordiana*. These three publications serve as mediums of exchanging, selling or buying the catalogue or out-of-print records.

How will scientific development affect record collecting? The most outstanding progressive feature will be the use of vinylite for records after the war. This material has been used exclusively for radio transcriptions up to the present. It is a high-grade material giving high fidelity, has a fine surface and is light. Also being flexible and nonbreakable it has advantages over the regular wax plate. Record executives prophesy wide use of this fine reproducing texture when things again become normal. One of the small independents, Session Records, already has released a set of records on vinylite. These were the Jimmy Yancey-Mama Yancey piano solos and blues vocals. A set of three twelve-inch records sold for eight dollars and a half, bringing the cost to about two eighty-five per record. After the war it is expected this cost will come down to the regular record price.

The other major development is not quite ready according to the record engineers. This is wire recording which offers the possibility of continuous records of complete sessions and concerts. The Steiner-Davis company has done some experimenting along these lines. They have put on wire their seven released records. They have a spool for each pair of sides which measures one inch in diameter and one and a half inches in length, weighing one half a pound. However, in wire recording it has been found the fidelity is flat. In order to get true fidelity comparable to a disc record it is necessary to use a length of wire which would be too bulky to be generally practical. The wartime use of wire recording has been with voices which do not require the fidelity as does music. Fidelity on wire can be obtained by not trying to crowd the wire into the space practical for use in home reproduction. Time will iron out the bugs and this type of reproduction may be generally used, but not immediately after the war.

Several other possibilities are still in experimental stages. There is sound track reproduction which is now up in the air due to the inability to erase the dust problem. Punch paper recording has possibilities that have hardly been touched as yet. There is the general feeling of not wanting to junk existing methods which always tends to slow up new developments.

Chapter V

Esquire's All-American Band

by ESQUIRE'S BOARD OF EXPERTS

Whether he be intensely curious or mildly interested, every reader here will find judgments passed which inevitably will lead to discussion and controversy. That is healthy; may such reaction continue to be strong and vigorous. No other portion of the 1944 JAZZ BOOK roused so much out-and-out crossing of critical swords as did the chapter pertaining to the experts' choices. I have no doubt that such again will be the case and in anticipation of this I must strongly emphasize the limitations which the rules of the balloting placed upon all the experts. The reader who finds trends, opinions and choices with which he disagrees may find that under the same restrictions as those imposed upon the experts, he too may have been hard put to select greats in each of the instrumental divisions. In short, I plead here for careful consideration of the exact stipulations under which each expert expressed his choices.

We asked for the naming of "outstanding performers in each division, artists to be chosen for their individual ability, without regard for their ability to work with each other in a band." Then, we insisted that "selections be based on *current performances*," with the further warning: "do not vote for musicians whose work you have not heard sufficiently during 1944 to judge their present stature." We believe that this was a fair qualification in spite of the fact that it may have worked a hardship on some of the experts. As one of them commented, "the experts are apt to judge more fairly, firsthand, not by hearsay or sentimentality." Some of them, in their comments on the choices (pages 52-91), named musicians whom the rigid rules had excluded. In this manner, they felt, they could better justify having deleted some of their special favorites from their All-American choices—where the favorites would have appeared had it not been for the rule concerning current performances.

A third choice in each division encompassed New Stars, "the newer artists who have not yet had the recognition they deserve and who have had relatively little prominence in jazz" during the past several years. In order to preserve the spirit and intent of this grouping, we were forced to eliminate the names of all musicians who, although perhaps unrecognized by a large public, nevertheless cannot be considered "new" when one considers the length of their activity as musicians. This included such jazzists as George Lewis, Wade Whaley, Ed Garland, Baby Dodds, none of whom are new any more than Sidney Bechet is new. Had there been an Esquire All-American Jazz Band in the early days, these men might well have earned places on the roster. As it is, several did garner enough ballots to bring them to fourth place on their respective instruments. What we hope to accomplish with our New Stars grouping is the furtherance of young, new, deserving talent, not merely a reminder that greats of other days who may yet be great today did not, in their own time, receive the prestige and wide national acclaim which, without question, they would have received had there been *Jazz Informations, Down Beats, Jazz Quarterlys, Jazz Record Books, HRS Rags, Hot Discographies, Yearbooks* and *Esquire* All-Americans during the first three decades of our century. But we also hope that whoever is great, young *or* old, will continue to hold the attention of the experts on whose hands we have entrusted this responsibility. To maintain our New Star intentions, we will permit no winner in that division to be voted for again as a New Star, although he may legitimately receive votes for All-Americans. This, we feel, should lend a certain inspiration to jazz tyros.

The tabulation of points for each individual musician (found in full on pages 93-108) was arrived at on the following basis: three points for a "greatest soloist" first place vote; two points for a second choice; one point for a New Star. In cases where one expert named a musician as first or second choice and another chose the same musician as a New Star, that man was placed in both the All-American and New Star tabulation, with only one point being allowed for each vote in the latter category. A "no choice" indicates that the expert felt that no musician he had heard measured up to his standards of judgment.

In the choices of favorite records, no expert was allowed to name discs for which he supervised the recording. This eliminated some favorites of Hammond, Lim, Feather, Dexter, Smith, Thiele, and was considered unfair by Williams, who refrained from naming his favorite records.   –P. E. M.

ESQUIRE'S ALL-AMERICAN
JAZZ BAND

Gold Award

Cootie Williams, *trumpet*
Jay C. Higginbotham, *trombone*
Johnny Hodges, *alto saxophone*
Coleman Hawkins, *tenor saxophone*
Benny Goodman, *clarinet*
Teddy Wilson, *piano*
Al Casey, *guitar*
Oscar Pettiford, *string bass*
Sidney Catlett, *drums*
Red Norvo, *vibraharp*

This past year Benny Goodman disbanded his orchestra; appeared with a Quartet at a jazz concert in New Orleans; made numerous radio guest appearances; and formed a Quintet including Red Norvo, Teddy Wilson and Sid Weiss, which is featured in the Billy Rose musical, The Seven Lively Arts. Now in his eleventh year as a national jazz figure, he again received a strong majority approval (16 experts out of 22) from Esquire's Board as the greatest clarinetist, maintaining the wide margin which he held in '44. Down Beat photo by Ray Rising.

Teddy Wilson has never stopped studying, never has hesitated to engage in activities which he felt would improve his playing. This, combined with his unquestionable natural talent, has resulted in his high position among present-day jazz pianists. Clean, precise and devoid of fancy frills, Wilson's piano stylings may be compared to the sheer simplicity of American skyscraper architecture. Not only did Teddy help to make the Goodman Trio and Quartet an artistic achievement, but he helped the cause of better race relations as well. Down Beat photo.

This recent photo, taken in Hollywood in June, 1944, shows Louis Armstrong with his bride. The trumpeter-vocalist-leader has spent much time in the movie capital in recent years; in 1944 he appeared in Jam Session for Columbia and in Hollywood Canteen for Warner Brothers and is scheduled for yet more cinematic endeavors. Although Esquire's experts failed to name Louis to a trumpet-winning position, he was easy victor as male vocalist in the All-American Gold Award Band, just as he was in '44. Dave Dexter, Jr., photo by Charlie Mihn.

Louis Armstrong, *vocal*
Mildred Bailey, *vocal*
Duke Ellington, *arranger & band*
Buck Clayton *(Armed Forces)*, *trumpet*

Silver Award

Roy Eldridge, *trumpet*
Lawrence Brown, *trombone*
Benny Carter, *alto saxophone*
Lester Young, *tenor saxophone*
Edmond Hall, *clarinet*
Art Tatum, *piano*
Oscar Moore, *guitar*
Slam Stewart, *string bass*
Dave Tough, *drums*
Harry Carney, *baritone saxophone*
Joe Turner, *vocal*
Billie Holiday, *vocal*
Billy Strayhorn, *arranger*
Count Basie, *band*
Willie Smith *(Armed Forces)* *alto saxophone*

New Stars

Dizzy Gillespie, *trumpet*
Bill Harris, *trombone*
Herbie Fields, *alto saxophone*
Flip Phillips, *tenor saxophone*
Aaron Sachs, *clarinet*
Eddie Heywood, *piano*
Remo Palmieri, *guitar*
Chubby Jackson, *string bass*
Specs Powell, *drums*

Ray Nance, *violin*
Eddie Vinson, *vocal*
Anita O'Day, *vocal*
Johnny Thompson, *arranger*
Lionel Hampton, *band*
Mel Powell *(Armed Forces) piano*

DAN BURLEY—writer for the Associated Negro Press, Continental Features and the New York *Amsterdam Star-News.*

> Trumpet: Harry James, Charlie Shavers, Frank Humphries. Trombone: Jay C. Higginbotham, Trummy Young, J. J. Johnson. Alto: Tab Smith, Johnny Hodges, Earl Bostic. Tenor: Georgie Auld, Ben Webster, Flip Phillips. Clarinet: Benny Goodman, Buster Bailey, Rudy Rutherford. Piano: Count Basie, Johnnie Guarnieri, Marlowe Morris. Guitar: Oscar Moore, Tiny Grimes, Teddy Walters. Bass: Oscar Pettiford, John Kirby, John Simmons. Drums: Jo Jones, Gene Krupa, Max Roach. Other Instr: Lionel Hampton, Red Norvo, Jimmy Smith. Male vocal: Louis Jordan, Joe Turner, Wynonie Harris. Female vocal: Georgia Gibbs, Mildred Bailey, Ann Cornell. Arranger: Benny Carter, Duke Ellington, Fred Norman. Orchestra: Lionel Hampton, Count Basie, Herbie Fields. Armed Forces: Buck Clayton, Kenneth Kersey, Mel Powell.

With the individual ability of the musician the prime consideration, I'm convinced that James can still play great jazz although he has gone almost completely commercial. Shavers has brilliance of tone, the ability to think way ahead of the melody, and has depth in what he plays. Humphries, huge counterpart of an earlier Armstrong, combines rare qualities in his work. Higginbotham has mastered every trick of his instrument and can take solos with faultless grace. Trummy's novelty, his slyness in slipping in riffs, makes him outstanding. Johnson plays mighty fine jazz consistently.

Tab Smith has inventiveness, sweetness of tone, rare musicianship and exceptional taste in phrasing. Hodges is still the mighty man of the alto, but is typed by his medium. Bostic interprets with perception, plays with authority. Among tenor saxmen, Auld has forged to the front because of his ability to recreate, to impart newness to his performances. His assurance is startling. Webster is still the superb solist. Phillips is full of exciting new ideas. Goodman remains head and shoulders above contemporary clarinetists. Bailey is consistently good—rich creativeness culled from a fertile imagination. Rutherford has demonstrated fine all-around musicianship.

Basie is still the greatest soloist among pianists. Playing in the thirds and fifths pattern, he does things to jazz. Guarnieri is a comer. He executes with sureness and has a delicate touch. Marlowe Morris is one of those truly great pianists knocking at the door. Moore has soul; he plays with a rich earthiness that touches kindred strings in the heart. The playing of Tiny Grimes has both quality and body. Walters has the innate ability to imitate, yet blend in his own ideas. Pettiford is the ideal bassist in that he makes his instrument completely the medium. Kirby has steadiness, craftsmanship and flowing rhythmic punch. Simmons combines deftness of touch, a sparkling sense of nicety in his passages. Hampton is a dynamic, driving force always creating—without equal on the vibes. Next best, Norvo's solos are fundamentally sound jazz.

Jordon is the greatest folk singer on the horizon today. Carter puts something into his arrangements that transforms ordinary tunes into rare gems.   —DAN BURLEY

TEN FAVORITE RECORDS:

Benny Carter: *Scandal in A Flat*. King Cole: *I Can't See for Looking*. Duke Ellington: *Blue Serge*. Benny Goodman: *Pick-A-Rib*. Lionel Hampton: *Homeward Bound*. Buddy Johnson: *Boogie Woogie's Mother-in-Law*. Louis Jordan: *Is You Is or Is You Ain't*. Meade Lux Lewis: *Honky Tonk Train*. Glenn Miller: *Tuxedo Junction*. Artie Shaw: *Begin the Beguine*.

MAL BRAVEMAN—writer for *Orchestra World*.

> Trumpet: Cootie Williams, Roy Eldridge, Dizzy Gillespie. Trombone: Jay C. Higginbotham, Lawrence Brown, Tommy Pederson. Alto: Johny Hodges, Benny Carter, no choice. Tenor: Coleman Hawkins, Lester Young, Don Byas. Clarinet: Benny Goodman, Edmond Hall, Aaron Sachs. Piano: Art Tatum, Earl Hines, Eddie Heywood. Guitar: Al Casey, Freddie Greene, Teddy Walters. Bass: Oscar Pettiford, Milton Hinton, no choice. Drums: Joe Jones, Sidney Catlett, George Jenkins. Other Instr: Red Norvo, Lionel Hampton, no choice. Male vocal: Louis Armstrong, Cab Calloway, no choice. Female vocal: Billie Holiday, Mildred Bailey, no choice. Arranger: Duke Ellington, Fletcher Henderson, Dizzy Gillespie. Orchestra: Count Basie, Duke Ellington, no choice. Armed Forces: Buck Clayton, Mel Powell, no choice.

Each of the individuals chosen for first place perform with the most intense feeling for jazz. Their section work is technically perfect, their solos deep from the heart and mind, a tonic for fellow musicians. With no hesitation at all, I cast a first-place vote for three artists who reign supreme as masters of their respective instruments: Goodman, Tatum and Coleman Hawkins; each seems gifted with an unlimited supply of ideas. When playing with a full band, this triumvirate executes fine jazz in a relaxed, almost effortless manner; when stimulated by the spirit of individual competition, they perform with unsurpassable drive and inventiveness.

Choosing the remaining first-place winners demanded much more time and thought. Cootie Williams is superb both on open and muted horn. He wields his trumpet with ease for fast tempos, slow blues and jazz interpretations of pop tunes. Higgy performs with spirited drive; he expertly executes difficult breaks and daring passages. Hodges has been and is one of the main reasons for the success of Ellingtonia; his smooth-riding alto sax weaves patterns of unrestrained beauty. Casey and Pettiford join the rhythm section because of their potent backing of soloists and their own tasteful, well-toned solo work. Then comes Joe Jones to drive the band with his impeccable rhythm and delicate cymbal work. Norvo wheels in his xylophone (or vibes) to add solos of beauty.

Armstrong and Holiday sing with deep feeling, using to emotional advantage both their physical and mental capacities. Billie's phrasing is unequaled. The Basie band is now as good as it ever was and better than others. It is rich in expressive soloists, has fine section work and is driven by the best rhythm combination in any band. Ellington arranges to suit the individual talents and idiosyncrasies of each man in his band. Jazzmen now are playing what Duke wrote years ago. If khaki-clad Buck Clayton blew the bugle calls at camp, the boys would fall asleep peacefully to a beautiful, muted rendition of taps, wake up merrily to a jumpin' reveille.

Eldridge, Young, Hines, Catlett, Hampton and Calloway are inclined to be a little too exhibitionistic and Duke's band just ain't what is used to be—that's why they're second choices. But each newcomer is an enthusiastic jazzman.

—MAL BRAVEMAN

TEN FAVORITE RECORDS:

Chu Berry: *Blowing Up a Breeze.* Chocolate Dandies: *Smack.* Duke Ellington: *Conga Brava, Mood Indigo.* Benny Goodman: *Benny Rides Again, Vibraphone Blues.* Lionel Hampton: *Singin' the Blues.* Coleman Hawkins: *Honeysuckle Rose.* Red Norvo: *Blues in E Flat.* Teddy Wilson: *What a Little Moonlight Can Do.*

INEZ CAVANAUGH—contributor to *Metronome, Band Leaders, Crisis.*

Trumpet: Louis Armstrong, Bill Coleman, Joe Thomas. Trombone: Lawrence Brown, Benny Morton, Tyree Glenn. Alto: Johnny Hodges, Benny Carter, Herbie Fields. Tenor: Coleman Hawkins, Lester Young, Flip Phillips. Clarinet: Benny Goodman, Barney Bigard, Aaron Sachs. Piano: Art Tatum, Teddy Wilson, Herman Chittison. Guitar: Oscar Moore, Al Casey, Remo Palmieri. Bass: Slam Stewart, Bob Haggart, Al Hall. Drums: Cozy Cole, Gene Krupa, Specs Powell. Other Instr: Red Norvo, Harry Carney, Ernie Caceres. Male vocal: King Cole, Louis Armstrong, Al Hibbler.

Female vocal: Billie Holiday, Mildred Bailey, Betty Roché. Arranger: Duke Ellington, Eddie Sauter, Brick Fleagle. Orchestra: Duke Ellington, Red Norvo, Eddie Heywood. Armed Forces: Buck Clayton, Joe Bushkin, Eddie Bert.

My interest in and close association with jazz and the men who play it began some 20 years ago, when I bought a copy of King Oliver's *Tin Roof Blues*. Two nights later I managed to wrangle my way (at 14) into the Lincoln Gardens where I first heard Armstrong. Sharp, strong, sure and beautiful, his trumpet tones hung in the air and completely possessed one. Hurdling the gropings of his contemporaries, Louis evolved a style and tone as yet unequaled and to me "Pops" is still tops!

While still young, I was privileged to hear Tatum. Even in those days, it was evident that here was sheer genius. Tatum lived down the block and many a night found this erstwhile youngster listening instead of doing school chores. Tatum, Wilson and amazing Herman Chittison are to my ear the Big Three of the ivories. Chittison's lighter-than-air technique and exciting ideas demand recognition and acclaim.

Bill Coleman nosed out Cootie on my list. I was hearing again the beautiful simplicity and heart-breaking purity of his phrasing and tone. Today, Bill plays the same exciting, driving trumpet I heard back in the thirties at Mexico's "cutting contests" when Harlem was in flower. My third trumpet choice, Joe Thomas, is an excellent example of how outstanding musicians get "lost." Benny Carter, the world's greatest all-around musician, jumped out of his chair and put the needle back on hearing Thomas' trumpet ring out on Tatum's *Stomping at the Savoy*.

"Who's that?" asked Benny.

Was it possible?

"That's Joe Thomas—he played in *your* band for several months at the Savoy!"

Norvo, sensitive and sure, is one of the greatest musicians today and consistently brings to light such sterling jazzmen as Eddie Bert, Aaron Sachs, Remo Palmieri and Flip Phillips.

Those of us fortunate enough to have been around New York have been fully aware of the artistry of Eddie Heywood, Al Hall, Slam Stewart, Ernie Caceres and other jazzmen who have recently gained recognition via recordings and radio.

In the vocal department, Billie Holiday and Mildred Bailey reign supreme, Betty Roché being the only likely contender.

—INEZ CAVANAUGH

TEN FAVORITE RECORDS:

Louis Armstrong: *When Your Lover Has Gone.* Count Basie: *Lester Leaps In.* King Cole: *Sweet Lorraine.* Duke Ellington: *Subtle Lament.* Benny Goodman: *Blues in My Flat.* Billie Holiday: *Strange Fruit.* Willie (The Lion) Smith: *What Is There To Say.* Fats Waller: *I'm Gonna Sit Right Down and Write Myself a Letter.* Teddy Wilson: *Don't Blame Me.* Lester Young: *Sometimes I'm Happy.*

DAVE DEXTER, Jr.—editor of *The Capitol* and author of many articles in jazz magazines.

Trumpet: Muggsy Spanier, Cootie Williams, Dizzy Gillespie. Trombone: Lawrence Brown, Jack Teagarden, J. J. Johnson. Alto: Benny Carter, Johnny Hodges, no choice. Tenor: Coleman Hawkins, Eddie Miller, Bumps Myers. Clarinet: Benny Goodman, Barney Bigard, Heinie Beau. Piano: Teddy Wilson, Pete Johnson, Stan Wrightsman. Guitar: Carl Kress, Dave Barbour, Hy White. Bass: Art Shapiro, Sid Weiss, Eugene Ramey. Drums: Jo Jones, Zutty Singleton, Baby Lovett. Other Instr: Red Norvo, Harry Carney, Willard Brown. Male vocal: Jack Teagarden, Joe Turner, Walter Brown. Female vocal: Mildred Bailey, Rosetta Tharpe, Peggy Lee. Arranger: Duke Ellington, Benny Carter, Stan Kenton. Orchestra: Duke Ellington, Benny Carter, Stan Kenton. Armed Forces: Babe Russin, Buck Clayton, Jay McShann.

Unless one is hopelessly biased in one's appreciation of jazz and jazzmen, it is impossible to compile a list of the "greatest musicians" and "greatest records" without appending some sort of a qualification. There are today not one or two great men on every instrument, but rather, scores of capable artists who are contributing something unique. Jazz has improved with the years and the men who pioneered the art—with rare exceptions—are completely outclassed by those who, more recently, have blown their way into prominence.

The musicians whom I have selected are possibly no more talented than many of their contemporaries. It just happens that they impress and "move" me more forcibly. All are in complete command of their instruments, all are original as to style, all possess the "heart" required of true jazzmen. In short, my nominees are those who thrilled Dexter most during 1944. But how many others I'd like to include!

A few words regarding the "New Stars" are in order. Gillespie, White, Walter Brown and Miss Lee have performed with various bands and are included herewith because I feel that each deserves greater recognition. Johnson, Myers and Willard Brown (baritone sax) are extremely able sidemen with the incomparable Benny Carter and destined for prominence. Beau is young, white and fly. He, Wrightsman, Lovett and Ramey are comparatively unknown and deserving of the acclaim accorded many others less capable. Private McShann is a young pianist who sooner or later, after V-day, will take his place alongside the Wilsons, Basies and Tatums.

Stan Kenton is so far ahead of every other "new" leader in the field that his music zooms over the heads of the public like a supercharged P-40. A superb pianist, Kenton also is a phenomenal arranger. His scores are harmonically and rhythmically ingenious —in some respects as complex as Ellington's—and the coming years surely will prove his worthiness.

Of my list of records only this need be added: it is not possible to choose ten favorites. My selections are merely representative of the best and were I requested to select 500 sides I should still insist that my list be accepted as "representative." Jazz today is an adult art which connot be broken down into a narrow "best" channel.

—DAVE DEXTER, JR.

TEN FAVORITE RECORDS:

Count Basie: *Doggin' Around*. Benny Carter: *Melancholy Lullaby*. Bob Crosby: *Sugar Foot Strut*. Duke Ellington: *any record*. Benny Goodman: *Sometimes I'm Happy*. Johnny Hodges: *Day Dream*. Andy Kirk: *Moten Swing*. Norvo-Bailey: *Garden of the Moon*. Bessie Smith: *Gimme a Pigfoot*. Teddy Wilson: *What a Little Moonlight Can Do*.

LEONARD G. FEATHER—co-editor *The Rhythm Section* (*Esquire*); assistant editor *Metronome;* record reviewer *Look;* author of many articles in jazz magazines.

Trumpet: Cootie Williams, Roy Eldridge, Jesse Miller. Trombone: Jay C. Higginbotham, Lawrence Brown, Bill Harris. Alto: Benny Carter, Pete Brown, Herbie Fields. Tenor: Coleman Hawkins, Georgie Auld, Arnette Cobbs. Clarinet: Benny Goodman, Edmond Hall, Aaron Sachs. Piano: Art Tatum, King Cole, Milton Buckner. Guitar: Oscar Moore, Remo Palmieri, Mary Osborne. Bass: Oscar Pettiford, Slam Stewart, Chubby Jackson. Drums: Cliff Leeman, Dave Tough, Alvin Burroughs. Other Instr: Stuff Smith, Red Norvo, Ray Nance. Male vocal: Joe Turner, Lips Page, King Cole. Female vocal: Billie Holiday, Anita O'Day, Dinah Washington. Arranger: Duke Ellington, Billy Strayhorn, George Handy. Orchestra: Duke Ellington, Woody Herman, Lionel Hampton. Armed Forces: Kenneth Kersey, Mel Powell, Gerald Wiggins.

My selections are based on fact, not fancy. I took particular care to choose musicians on the basis of their current work. I have not allowed myself to be influenced sentimentally by their historical or geographical background, or by their performances in previous years. In other words, my choices reflect a realistic view of the 1944 jazz scene.

My choices are all "musicians' musicians" who have the unanimous respect and admiration of contemporary fellow jazzmen. That speaks worlds for them in itself, for I would rather take a consensus of musicians' opinion than critics anytime. You won't find a clarinetist in a thousand who'll dispute Goodman's supremacy, nor a pianist who will belittle the genius of Tatum. The same goes for almost everyone on my first team. In my second team I supplanted Armstrong by Eldridge because, after hearing Louis at every rehearsal and performance during the All-American rally last January, I'm convinced (as were all the other All-Americans at the time) that Louis no longer has the alertness or the physical ability to keep pace with many younger stars, though he still plays some beautiful stuff from time to time. I wasn't at all sure what to do about Fields and Auld, since both of them might well have had my vote in the alto, tenor and new band divisions. I finally voted for them once each.

Woody Herman's band is one that I never expected to be voting for in any poll. Departing almost completely from his earlier semi-Dixieland style, he now has a driving, jumping band with great arrangements by Dave Matthews, Eddie Sauter and Ralph Burns and a raft of amazing individual stars such as Phillips, Jackson, Harris, Tough, Hyams.

To sum up my selections, I'd say that they are based on ten years of constant listening to jazz through all media—records, radio, night clubs, theatres, dances—and in bands of every shape, size and color. They are based on the premise that jazz is not divided into white and colored, or Dixieland and arranged, or big band and small band, or New Orleans and modern. Jazz is simply divided into good and bad. If you've ever studied, written and played jazz, that's one of the truths you hold to be indivisible.

—LEONARD FEATHER

TEN FAVORITE RECORDS:

King Cole: *Sweet Lorraine*. Duke Ellington: *The Flaming Sword, Crescendo and Diminuendo in Blue*. Benny Goodman: *I Cried for You*. Coleman Hawkins: *The Man I Love*. Billie Holiday: *Fine and Mellow*. Jimmie Lunceford: *Uptown Blues*. Art Tatum: *Wee Baby Blues*. Fats Waller: *Buck Jumpin'*. Teddy Wilson: *Just a Mood*.

ROBERT GOFFIN—author of *Aux Frontieres du Jazz* and *Jazz: From the Congo to the Metropolitan*.

Trumpet: Louis Armstrong, Muggsy Spanier, Johnny Windhurst. Trombone: Georg Brunis, Sandy Williams, Ray Coniff. Alto: Johnny Hodges, Benny Carter, George Johnson. Tenor: Al Sears, Gene Sedric, Bumps Myers. Clarinet: Benny Goodman, Edmond Hall, Aaron Sachs. Piano: Teddy Wilson, Mary Lou Williams, Herman Chittison. Guitar: Al Casey, Eddie Condon, Remo Palmieri. Bass: Slam Stewart, Al Morgan, no choice. Drums: Sidney Catlett, Gene Krupa, no choice. Other Instr: Red Norvo, Sidney Bechet, Ernie Caceres. Male vocal: Louis Armstrong, Willie Dukes, Walter Pichon. Female vocal: Billie Holiday, Pearl Bailey, no choice. Arranger: Duke Ellington, Billy Strayhorn, no choice. Orchestra, Lionel Hampton, Miff Mole, Max Kaminsky. Armed Forces: Willie Smith, Jimmy McPartland, Mel Powell.

This would have to be an unrehearsed jam band. A few days' rehearsal would only serve to reduce the men's inspiration and enthusiasm; they would be better off left to their own initiative. A band can work two ways: improvise on themes everyone knows, or prepare carefully, like Ellington. To select a list of names for the second method would be a purely hypothetical job. The other alternative, therefore, meets the occasion and an improvising group is indicated. Any intermediary solution would be doomed from the start.

If genius be the consummation of an art, then Armstrong is still the master of jazz and only those who believe a copy can be as good as the original will deny this. I almost voted for Charlie Shavers in second place, but a rehearsal of Muggsy's changed my mind. I heard young Windhurst in Boston and believe you will hear more of him. Brunis remains the most effective trombonist. Sandy Williams can play some beautiful stuff when he wants to. Coniff may develop into a true master. The altos are self-explanatory. Hawkins retains tenor supremacy, but there are many youngsters giving him competition. I have selected three men who could be classed in any order. There is no commentary needed for the clarinets.

On piano, Tatum remains the outstanding technician, but his style is a little cold for an improvising group. I prefer Wilson or Mary Lou Williams; perhaps such an ace as Chittison would fit in best. The selections on guitar, bass and drums speak for themselves. Norvo's profound and intelligent feeling for jazz gives him supremacy in the miscellaneous instruments. Bechet, other opinions to the contrary, retains his place in the picture and Caceres is developing into a star of considerable importance on baritone sax.

Hampton seems to have the power of trancelike frenzy necessary to every good jazz orchestra. This is the true basis of all improvisation. My best kicks have come from the groups of Miff Mole at Nick's and Max Kaminsky at the Pied Piper. I know the merits and faults of both of them too well to expect perfection, but even the way they are, they're still the best that's around.

—ROBERT GOFFIN

TEN FAVORITE RECORDS:

Louis Armstrong: *West End Blues, Shine, Confessin'*. Chicago Rhythm Kings: *I've Found a New Baby*. Chocolate Dandies: *Got Another Sweetie Now*. Duke Ellington: *It Don't Mean a Thing*. Mound City Blue Blowers: *Hello Lola*. New Orleans Rhythm Kings: *Shimme-Sha-Wabble*. Original Dixieland Band: *Tiger Rag*. The Wolverines: *Shimme-Sha-Wabble*.

JOHN HAMMOND—author of many articles on jazz, both in jazz magazines and those of more general circulation.

Trumpet: Bill Coleman, Cootie Williams, Emmett Berry. Trombone: Vic Dickenson, Jay C. Higginbotham, Fred Beckett. Alto: Lem Davis, Johnny Hodges, Eddie Vinson. Tenor: Lester Young, Bumps Myers, Eugene Ammons. Clarinet: Benny Goodman, Edmond Hall, Rudy Rutherford. Piano: Teddy Wilson, Count Basie, Jimmy Jones. Guitar: Freddie Greene, Al Casey, Mundell Lowe. Bass: Israel Crosby, John Simmons, Red Callender. Drums: Jo Jones, Cozy Cole, Specs Powell. Other Instr: Harry Carney, Red Norvo, Peter Graham. Male vocal: Joe Turner, Big Bill Broonzy, T-Bone Walker. Female vocal: Mildred Bailey, Helen Humes, Evelyn Knight. Arranger: Phil Moore, Sonny Burke, Johnny Thompson. Orchestra: Count Basie, Eddie Heywood, Cootie Williams. Armed Forces: Buck Clayton, Dick Davis, Willie Anderson.

With at least half of the great musicians of the country in the Armed Forces, it is no easy matter to make out a list of one's favorites in the year 1944. And it is particularly tough for a critic who has been hearing principally the work of GI musicians from coast to coast, and not a fraction of the civilian instrumentalists that it's been his custom to encounter.

There are many of us jazz "experts" now in the Army who feel that the *Esquire* poll is rather unduly slighting the thousands of fine virtuosi in the Army by eliminating them from consideration in all classifications but one. I, for one, have heard some fabulous new stars in various Army units that easily dwarf their civilian competition, but the rules of this poll are being scrupulously adhered to with only one exception—the name of Private Mundell Lowe, guitarist of the 398th ASF Band now stationed in the Pacific area.

With a few exceptions, this list of preferences is pretty much the same as the one submitted last year. Since the incomparable Buck Clayton has assumed the prefix Corporal, Bill Coleman becomes the favored civilian who combines depth of feeling, tone and technical facility most completely for these ears. Vic Dickenson is so easily the outstanding trombonist of the day that one's failure to include him in last year's list is all the more shameful. Hall is emotionally the more satisfying clarinetist, but Goodman's complete mastery of the instrument in both realms of music makes him at least the debatable first choice. Failure to list Bumps Myers in last year's poll was an unpardonable oversight which is herewith being atoned for. Honesty compels the naming of James Mundell Lowe, a young Mississippian who once played briefly with Jan Savitt and is by far the most exciting guitar find since Charlie Christian. Magnificent in ensemble and stupendous in solos, his is the most exciting talent encountered in years.

Returning to the question of musicians in the Armed Forces, there are literally dozens of names that could be listed. The three that we pull out are Clayton, Dick Davis who was fine in civilian life as tenorman with the Sunset Royals, and Willie Anderson, a phenomenal young pianist who is also a whiz at valve trombone, guitar, bass and trumpet.

—JOHN HAMMOND

TEN FAVORITE RECORDS:

Louis Armstrong: *West End Blues*. Chocolate Dandies: *Dee Blues*. Ida Cox: *Coffin Blues* (Paramount). Duke Ellington: *Lazy Rhapsody*. Earl Hines: *Blues in Thirds* (QRS). Meade Lux Lewis: *Honky Tonk Train* (Paramount). Bessie Smith: *Young Woman Blues, Baby Doll*. Art Tatum: *Wee Baby Blues*.

GEORGE HOEFER—author of *The Hot Box*, a regular *Down Beat* feature, and contributor to jazz magazines.

Trumpet: Max Kaminsky, Cootie Williams, Jesse Miller. Trombone: Jack Teagarden, Jay C. Higginbotham, Tommy Pederson. Alto: Benny Carter, Johnny Hodges, Johnny Board. Tenor: Coleman Hawkins, Dave Matthews, Charlie Venturo. Clarinet: Barney Bigard, Edmond Hall, no choice. Piano: Earl Hines, Jess Stacy,

Floyd Bean. Guitar: Hy White, Les Paul, Bobby Sherwood. Bass: Milton Hinton, Chubby Jackson, John Levy. Drums: Dave Tough, Sidney Catlett, Alvin Burroughs. Other Instr: Red Norvo, Sidney Bechet, Max Miller. Male vocal: Jack Teagarden, Louis Armstrong, Eddie Vinson. Female vocal: Mildred Bailey, Billie Holiday, Peggy Lee. Arranger: Benny Carter, Jimmy Hilliard, Ralph Burns. Orchestra: Duke Ellington, Count Basie, no choice. Armed Forces: Vido Musso, Jay McShann, no choice.

Jazz expression has a dual quality. The primary requisite for an outstanding jazz musician is the ability to create within himself musical ideas that set him apart from other musicians. Secondarily, in order fully to express these same musical ideas, it is necessary for the topflight jazzist to possess technique on his chosen instrument. Fine jazz is not produced by a player who has terrific ideas and the feeling but not the ability to express himself musically. Nor does fine jazz result when an impeccable technician is barren of original ideas and tends to repeat the same banal phrases.

Given a jazz musician with creative talent and musical technique, the determination of his status among his contemporaries on the same instrument resolves itself into a matter of taste and appreciation on the part of the listening critics. I am firmly of the opinion that extreme emphasis on either jazz feeling or jazz technique is not good. The former has produced some wild and unmusical results; the latter has resulted in some stultified music.

Hence, my selection, chosen from performances heard during 1944, are based on the following requirements: (1) creative ability and feeling for jazz expression; (2) musical technique and mastery of instrument; (3) my own individual preference of style.

There may be some surprises in store for the readers of my record collectors' column, but the above general explanation should suffice. Permit me to add that I find worthy music from Buddy Bolden's day to the 52nd Street era.

Kaminsky's playing is both incisive and lyrical with a rich tone; Cootie's driving and versatile; Jesse Miller's abandoned. Mr. Tea's blues style clinches my number one vote from the sometimes relaxed and sometimes frantic Higginbotham. Carter's versatility rates him higher than Hodges, while Board verges on the phenomenal. Coleman Hawkin's mastery is conclusive, but Matthews has been pushing him hard. While Bigard is an indisputable star, Hall's work on recordings clearly demonstrates his greatness; Lewis maintains the superb New Orleans tradition. Hines can't miss, having that undefinable quality of true genius.

—GEORGE HOEFER

TEN FAVORITE RECORDS:

Louis Armstrong: *West End Blues*. Benny Carter: *My Buddy*. Chicago Rhythm Kings: *There'll Be Some Changes Made*. Bob Crosby: *I'm Prayin' Humble*. Duke Ellington: *Black and Tan Fantasy* (Okeh). Lionel Hampton: *On the Sunny Side of the Street*. Coleman Hawkins: *My Blue Heaven*. Luis Russell: *Ease on Down*. Muggsy Spanier: *Dipper Mouth Blues*. Jack Teagarden: *Muddy River Blues*.

JAX (JOHN LUCAS)—record reviewer and Research Editor for *Down Beat*.

Trumpet: Sidney de Paris, Muggsy Spanier, Dizzy Gillespie. Trombone: Vic Dickenson, Georg Brunis, Bill Harris. Alto: Johnny Hodges, Boyce Brown, Herbie Fields. Tenor: Coleman Hawkins, no choice, Flip Phillips. Clarinet: Edmond Hall, Mezz Mesirow, Aaron Sachs. Piano: Earl Hines, Jess Stacy, Eddie Heywood. Guitar: Al Casey, Eddie Condon, Teddy Walters. Bass: Israel Crosby, no other choices. Drums: Sidney Catlett, Dave Tough, Specs Powell. Other Instr: Eddie South, Red Norvo, no choice. Male vocal: Joe Turner, Bing Crosby, Eddie Vinson. Female vocal: Rosetta Tharpe, Mildred Bailey, Savannah Churchill. Arranger: Billy Strayhorn, Dave Matthews, no choice. Orchestra: Duke Ellington, no other choices. Armed Forces: Buck Clayton, Bud Freeman, Mel Powell.

In the Spring of 1944 this group of New Orleans musicians broadcast from San Francisco over a West Coast network for the Standard Oil Company of California. The occasion was Standard Oil's radio series on American music, several programs of which were devoted to genuine New Orleans jazz. Front, left to right: clarinetist Wade Whaley, guitarist Bud Scott, bassist Ed Garland; rear, trombonist Kid Ory, trumpeter Mutt Carey, drummer Zutty Singleton, pianist Buster Wilson. Jazz fan Bill Colburn stands next to Zutty. Standard Oil photo.

In the Summer of 1944 these New Orleans musicians were playing in home territory, at the San Jacinto Club in the Crescent City. Bill Russell made some recordings of the outfit which have drawn high praise from those few who have been privileged to hear them. Left to right: trombonist Jim Robinson, trumpeter Bunk Johnson, clarinetist George Lewis, drummer Baby Dodds, bassist Alcide Pavageau (Slow Drag) and banjoist Lawrence Marrero. Like the above group, these old-timers showed startling vitality on recordings. Photo by William Russell.

Sidney Bechet
(clarinet)

Bunk Johnson
(trumpet)

Richard M. Jones
(piano)

Distinguished New Orleans musicians: after more than thirty years, this trio carries forward great traditions. Johnson photo by Russell.

George Lewis
(clarinet)

Zutty Singleton
(drums)

Johnny Dodds
(clarinet)

Distinguished New Orleans musicians: Dodds' recordings live on. Lewis photo by Wm. Russell; Zutty by Standard Oil; Dodds by Baby Dodds.

Irving Fazola
(clarinet)

Barney Bigard
(clarinet)

Freddie Keppard
(trumpet)

Distinguished New Orleans musicians: Fazola has become the greatest white blues clarinetist (Down Beat photo); Keppard by Bill Johnson

At best, the selection of such lists remains a rather thankless task, a purely arbitrary matter. Some choices would naturally be but the favorites of a moment, varying frequently according to the individual's tastes and moods. An enthusiasm for the present may indeed seem almost incomprehensible in the future. Today's pet may become tomorrow's peeve. Some men, on the other hand, demand constant recognition. Most of the musicians of my first and second choices fall into such a category. They were good in the thirties, they are still good today and they undoubtedly will be good even in the fifties.

It will be noticed that my first-choice list is comprised entirely of Negro musicians, my second wholly of white. This is only as it should be, for my preferences incline decidedly in favor of colored jazzmen. To me, white jazz signifies Dixieland or Chicago or something in between, absolutely nothing else. New Orleans, of course, is jazz itself. Although at times I like Davey's drumming better than Big Sid's, the Negro wins my vote easily in every other instance. Except for Vinson and Mel Powell, my New-Stars list includes nobody whom I consider genuinely promising.

Had I heard Armstrong and Pops Foster in 1944, I am convinced that they would replace de Paris and Crosby respectively on my first list. Dickenson just managed to ease out Higginbotham, as Hines did J. P. Johnson. Teagarden, Rod Cless and Joe Sullivan would deserve spots on my second list, I am sure, if I had heard samplings of their recent work.

I suppose I must explain the "no-choice" blanks I left in my ballot. With Freeman and Eddie Miller both in service, there is no other white tenorman around who plays the kind of sax I most admire. The same can be said for white bass players, now that Bernstein and Shapiro are in uniform. I declined to pick a white orchestra for the simple reason that, since the Bob Crosby band dispersed, I have found none anywhere worthy to take its place.

Let me nominate an even dozen as the outstanding recording

artists of 1944 hot jazz (alphabetically): Count Basie, Georg Brunis, Sidney Catlett, Cozy Cole, Sidney de Paris, Vic Dickenson, Johnnie Guarnieri, Edmond 'Hall, Coleman Hawkins, Earl Hines, James P. Johnson and Lester Young.

—JAX (JOHN LUCAS).

TEN FAVORITE RECORDS:

Armstrong-Dorsey: *Dipper Mouth* (Decca). Sidney Bechet: *Wild Man Blues*. Eddie Condon: *Someday Sweetheart* (Decca). Bill Davison: *That's a Plenty*. Gene Gifford: *New Orleans Twist*. Edmond Hall: *Royal Garden Blues*. Lionel Hampton: *On the Sunny Side of the Street*. Mezz Mezzrow: *Apologies*. Jelly Roll Morton: *West End Blues*. Zutty Singleton: *King Porter Stomp*.

HAROLD JOVIEN—reviewer and writer on jazz for Associated Negro Press; contributor to jazz magazines.

Trumpet: Cootie Williams, Roy Eldridge, Shorty Sherock. Trombone: Jack Teagarden, Jay C. Higginbotham, Ford Canfield. Alto: Johnny Hodges, Charlie Barnet, Ray Degeer. Tenor: Coleman Hawkins, Georgie Auld, Flip Phillips. Clarinet: Benny Goodman, Barney Bigard, no choice. Piano: Earl Hines, King Cole, no choice. Guitar: Les Paul, Hy White, Remo Palmieri. Bass: Eugene Ramey, Jimmy Middleton, John Levy. Drums: Dave Tough, Gene Krupa, no choice. Other Instr: Red Norvo, Stuff Smith, Max Miller. Male vocal: Louis Jordan, Jack Teagarden, Eddie Vinson. Female vocal: Mildred Bailey, Billie Rogers, Thelma Carpenter. Arranger: Billy Strayhorn, Dave Matthews, Ralph Burns. Orchestra: Duke Ellington, Woody Herman, Hal McIntyre. Armed Forces: Jay McShann, Willie Smith, George Barnes.

Although the *Esquire* poll presents an obvious limitation in requesting judgment of musicians according to current performances—thus in certain cases ruling out perennial jazz favorites—there is a looming advantage. The experts are apt to judge more fairly, first hand, not by hearsay or sentimentality, keeping this important poll from becoming stagnant through the simple process of eliminating the probability of the same musicians winning repeatedly. However, there is this inescapable fact. With travel restriction and the two-year record ban, musicians confining their playing to one section of the country are penalized. Therefore, had I had the opportunity to hear them play in recent months, I might very well have chosen, in preference to those whom I did select, jazzmen such as Armstrong, Les Robinson, Emmett Berry, Bill Harris, Jack Jenney, Shavers, Fazola, Bechet, Les Young, Casey, Bunn, Pettiford or Zutty.

Starting with the rhythm-pulse of the band, I named Ramey for his tremendous drive and endless energy, Middleton for his speed, execution and tone, Tough for his relaxed and perfect beat, Krupa for the spectacular. Les Paul is an expert technician, an inspiration to any section, while White is solidly there all the time. As my choice for ace of all jazz musicians, Hines can't miss here. Cole's versatility edged out Tatum. Mildred Bailey's airshow reveals she's still singing in her wonderful "without-effort" style.

Cootie possesses ideas and a quality unmatched by any other trumpeter; Roy I take for ceaseless drive and powerhouse. In a similar vein is Barnet's furious playing. Combine the finest qualities in jazz and you've got Goodman, Hodges, Hawkins, Teagarden, Higginbotham and Bigard. Auld, one of those playing in the Hawkins tradition, frequently reveals such intent feeling that he should be placed next to the master himself. Norvo's persistent undercurrent of subtle jazz thrills, his superb musicianship and originality rank him high. Smith rates for his renewed spirit and spontaneity. For witty, happy blues Jordan is in; Teagarden for the slow, easygoing moods.

Among the unrecognized and newcomers, a varied but versed group: Sherock, fine on conception and execution; Canfield and Degeer, worthy of more attention. Phillips and Palmieri, really inspiring. Levy for his rhythmic backing *and* soloing. Miller for his fast pace, harmonic ideas.

—HAROLD JOVIEN

TEN FAVORITE RECORDS:

Louis Armstrong: *Confessin'*. Charlie Barnet: *Ring Dem Bells*. King Cole: *Sweet Lorraine*. Duke Ellington: *Echoes of Harlem, Across the Track Blues*. Benny Goodman: *The Sheik*. Fletcher Henderson: *Big John's Special*. Hines-Bechet: *Stompy Jones*. Don Redman: *Chant of the Weed* (Brunswick). Art Tatum: *Wee Baby Blues*.

MIKE LEVIN—contributing editor, *Down Beat*.

Trumpet: Cootie Williams, Max Kaminsky, no choice. Trombone: Benny Morton, Lawrence Brown, no choice. Alto: Benny Carter, Johnny Hodges, no choice. Tenor: Ben Webster, Coleman Hawkins, no choice. Clarinet: Benny Goodman, Edmond Hall, no choice. Piano: Teddy Wilson, Art Tatum, no choice. Guitar: Al Casey, Leonard Ware, Remo Palmieri. Bass: Al Hall, Oscar Pettiford, no choice. Drums: Specs Powell, Sidney Catlett, no choice. Other Instr: Red Norvo, Harry Carney, no choice. Male vocal: Bing Crosby, Louis Jordan, Frankie Laine. Female vocal: Mildred Bailey, Billie Holiday, no choice. Arranger: Johnny Thompson, Eddie Sauter, no choice. Orchestra: Duke Ellington, Red Norvo, no choice. Armed Forces: Artie Bernstein, Willie Smith, no choice.

Now I can defend my choices, tomorrow perhaps not. Good music is as much a function of the man listening to it as the player creating it. If I have a terrific hangover, even Bailey may not be able to boff me out of my blues. Tastes change depending on what you've heard before and what you've had for dinner.

Williams' haunting muted solos are overshadowed only by his technique and the poignance of his open horn work. Kaminsky, a thoroughly schooled musician, plays with driving energy and fluent ideas. Morton can do almost anything on a horn. Brown is a slow starter—but once he hits, there comes a mouthful of trombone. Exactly constructed, completely unified, and played with a dainty touch, Carter fills every requirement for great soloist and all-around musician. Hodges legatoed phrasings have characterized the Ellington band for years. There may be beefing about putting Webster ahead of Hawkins; but despite Hawk's tremendous grasp of harmonic variation, I still think Webster is more consistent and doesn't commit the breaches of taste that Hawk occasionally does. Though his playing is often frigid and tasteless, I still think that BG can be tops. The same goes for Hall's virile style.

Teddy over Tatum for one reason—taste. Tatum is fast, filled with ideas, but Teddy is filled with tone and restraint, and that I like better. If you remember Fats Waller's small band, then you remember Casey's guitarings. Ware rates because of his humorful, easy style and his weird, full changes on rhythm work. Both Hall and Pettiford stay in tune and have good beats—that's enough from any bassman. There are drummers who play with bands and then there is a minute handful like Powell, who not only back every riff to the hilt, but can play lightly for small and powerfully for big bands. "Big Sid" can give a deep, driving beat as can few other drummers besides Dave Tough.

For a musician with a sense of discrimination who can listen to a soloist and unerringly pick the right man for a band, I give you Red Norvo—he's the best we have. Carney's big-toned, soft, strikingly phrased baritone, besides yielding wonderful solos, is a Rock of Gibralter to the Ellington reeds.

—MIKE LEVIN

TEN FAVORITE RECORDS:

Louis Armstrong: *Struttin' with Some Barbecue*. Mildred Bailey: *Someday Sweetheart*. Commodore All-Stars: *Embraceable You*. Duke Ellington: *Reminiscing in Tempo*. Jimmie Lunceford: *Dream of You*. Red Norvo: *Remember*. New Orleans Feetwarmers: *Sweetie Dear*. Eddie South-Stephane Grappelly: *Variation on Bach D Minor Concerto*. Muggsy Spanier: *Sister Kate*. Teddy Wilson: *Miss Brown to You*.

HARRY LIM—contributor to jazz magazines; organizer of many jam sessions.

> Trumpet: Roy Eldridge, Charlie Shavers, Joe Thomas. Trombone: Benny Morton, Jay C. Higginbotham, Bill Harris. Alto: Benny Carter, Johnny Hodges, Tab Smith. Tenor: Coleman Hawkins, Lester Young, Don Byas. Clarinet: Benny Goodman, Edmond Hall, Aaron Sachs. Piano: Teddy Wilson, Art Tatum, Billy Taylor. Guitar: Oscar Moore, Teddy Walters, Remo Palmieri. Bass: Slam Stewart, Milton Hinton, Al Hall. Drums: Sidney Catlett, Jo Jones, J. C. Heard. Other Instr: Harry Carney, Lionel Hampton, Ray Nance. Male vocal: Louis Armstrong, Joe Turner, Eddie Vinson. Female vocal: Mildred Bailey, Billie Holiday, Dinah Washington. Arranger: Duke Ellington, Eddie Sauter, Johnny Thompson. Orchestra: Count Basie, Duke Ellington, no choice. Armed Forces: Willie Smith, Kenneth Kersey, Harold Baker.

I think this yearly poll by Esquire is an excellent means by which to come to certain standards in the judging of musicians and jazz. Tastes differ among the jazz cognoscenti, and as so many people say, that's what makes it interesting. But before the question of taste enters, there should be a rule that a musician who is included in the poll shall have the technique to express himself more than adequately. It's all very well to say that it's the "soul" that counts and musicians might have gotten away with just soul a few years ago, but in these days of rapidly advancing modern ideas in jazz, there has to be a lot more than feeling. I wouldn't want to vote for a man who plays with feeling and practically no technique, nor would I want to vote for a musician who plays with a lot of technique and no feeling, but I would definitely vote for a man who plays with both feeling and technique, and there are definitely a few guys in the latter category even a rabid "New Orleans style" jazz fan would vote for without fear that the hallowed "tradition" he talks about so much shall be harmed.

My choices this year don't differ much from last year's. The New Star division should have been instituted last year and this division should also include some older jazzmen who somehow haven't gotten the breaks they deserve. A case in point is trumpeter Joe Thomas, who is very much admired by fellows like Eldridge and Emmett Berry for his beautiful, clear tone and impeccable phrasing in the Armstrong tradition.

Also, the separation between alto and tenor has proven to be necessary, I think, because many experts last year had to omit their second favorite alto or tenor. I should have included Lester Young last year if it weren't for that 1944 limitation because I sincerely believe that Lester is the only really great tenorman who has come up since Hawkins.

As for the favorite records, this is certainly a very difficult limitation with which to comply. I'm sure the real jazz fan has at least 500 favorite records. I would have included some of the Keynote sides I have been supervising, but here *Esquire* stepped in and said "no go." So I don't think anyone ought to take that "ten favorites" division too seriously; certainly nobody should take my choices too seriously. —HARRY LIM

TEN FAVORITE RECORDS:

> Louis Armstrong: *West End Blues*. Duke Ellington: *Ko Ko, Ducky Wucky*. Benny Goodman: *Sometimes I'm Happy*. Coleman Hawkins: *Body and Soul*. Eddie Heywood: *I Cover the Waterfront*. Johnny Hodges: *Junior Hop*. Red Norvo: *Dance of the Octopus*. Teddy Wilson: *When You're Smiling, What a Little Moonlight Can Do*.

PAUL EDUARD MILLER—co-editor *The Rhythm Section* (*Esquire*); author of *Yearbook of Swing, Yearbook of Popular Music;* editor, ESQUIRE'S JAZZ BOOK.

> Trumpet: Cootie Williams, Red Allen, Eddie Roane. Trombone: Benny Morton, Jay C. Higginbotham, Ford Canfield. Alto: Benny Carter, Les Robinson, Boots Mussulli. Tenor: Coleman Hawkins, Dave Matthews, Flip Phillips. Clarinet: Benny Goodman, Edmond Hall, Hank D'Amico. Piano: Johnny Guarnieri, Teddy Wilson,

Stan Wrightsman. Guitar: Les Paul, Tommy Kay, Remo Palmieri. Bass: Milton Hinton, Jimmy Middleton, Chubby Jackson. Drums: Dave Tough, Sidney Catlett, Alvin Burroughs. Other Instr: Sidney Bechet, Harry Carney, Max Miller. Male vocal: no choices. Female vocal: Mildred Bailey, no other choices. Arranger: Paul Jordan, Zilner Randolph, Ralph Burns. Orchestra: Red Allen, Louis Jordan, Jimmy Hilliard. Armed Forces: Vido Musso, Willie Smith, Mike Simpson.

Expressiveness and the facility for expressiveness: these constitute the prime requisites for great jazz instrumentalists. Great jazz music demands a further qualitative postulate: that it articulately portray an awareness of what is being said by both the music and musician. It is not entirely a question of whether jazz has too little feeling or too much technique, since there is a point at which technique alone becomes useless and intuitive feeling *per se* becomes helpless. The essential *quality* of the feeling—its depth, breadth, intensity, clarity—comprises the distinguishing marks of great jazz. It is the job of jazz criticism to determine its art-value on such a basis of judgment.

I can hardly advance, at this late date, new reasons for choosing jazzists of the calibre of Williams, Morton, Carney, Goodman, Wilson, Hawkins, Mildred Bailey and Catlett.

Allen and Higginbotham still cut loose with the blues in the best jazz tradition; their band, thought rough and informal, attains magnificent heights when it concentrates on what they best can play—the blues. Roane, truly a new star, contributes much to the more precise, but equally great, Louis Jordan band—which likewise is best on the blues. To the Hilliard band, a studio group worth wide attention, Canfield brings his specialty, a plunger style *à la* Tricky Sam, but also fast, clean, open bell playing. Give Robinson a chance to solo more and he'll surprise everyone; Guarnieri this past year proved what a good jazzist can do when given the opportunity to show his real talents. Freshness, a new vigor—these qualities may be applied to Matthews, Hall, Mussulli, Wrightsman, Tough, Kay, Jackson, Burroughs, Middleton and Bechet.

Yes, Bechet. He is a true giant, always fresh, vigorous, always renewing his art from the deep springs of his heart. I like to think of Max Miller when I mention Bechet. Max (no kin of mine) is one of my special favorites; I'll stack him against anyone on vibes with the confidence he'll surpass. His piano playing, too, unique and unacademic as it is, possesses that full, sure jazz flavor—a perfect setting for the melodic lines of Bechet's soprano and clarinet.

I wholeheartedly enjoyed the bewildering problems posed by choosing ten records: for me "favorite" means great and that's the way I selected them.   —PAUL EDUARD MILLER

TEN FAVORITE RECORDS:

> Sidney Bechet: *Dear Old Southland*. Bunny Berigan: *Davenport Blues*. Bob Crosby: *Dogtown Blues*. Duke Ellington: *Ko Ko*. Spike Hughes: *Sweet Sorrow Blues*. King Oliver: *Sugar Foot Stomp* (Vocalion), *West End Blues* (Victor). Ruben Reeves: *Zuddan*. Artie Shaw: *Two in One Blues*. Erskine Tate: *Stomp Off Let's Go*.

J. T. H. MIZE—head of music department at Rye (New York) high school, where he has been conducting classes in jazz.

> Trumpet: Louis Armstrong, Johnny Austin, Royce Janszen. Trombone: Jack Teagarden, Jay C. Higginbotham, Al Lepol. Alto: Johnny Hodges, Claude Lakey, Vernon Mayfield. Tenor: Coleman Hawkins, Dave Matthews, Jesse Webb. Clarinet: Benny Goodman, Edmond Hall, no choice. Piano: Peck Kelley, Earl Hines, no choice. Guitar: Teddy Bunn, Al Casey, no choice. Bass: Fitz Fitzgerald, no choice, Lynn Mano. Drums: Buddy Rich, Sidney Catlett, William Shirley Davis. Other Instr: Lionel Hampton, Red Norvo, Emilio Caceres. Male vocal: Louis Armstrong, Bon Bon, Don Cannon. Female vocal: Billie Holiday, Ella Mae Morse, Anita O'Day. Arranger: Jack Chapman, Duke Ellington, Charlie Mitchell. Orchestra: Duke Ellington, Lionel Hampton, Stan Kenton. Armed Forces: Sy Oliver, Bobby Byrne, Weldon Scheel.

Space limitation prompts devotion of comments primarily to adjudication justification of the New Stars; the stature and abilities of the All-American choices appears obvious.

Armstrong's proper and peerless placement is incontestable —it is one of the few musical *facts*. Austin plays a wild and uninhibited style, unexcelled for sheer excitement and exhibited emotionalism. He fully exploits the decuple scale and makes frequent rhapsodic excursions into exotic modes. Janszen's is veritably an admixture of Dixieland trumpet sonority and carnival tone-timbre coupled with something of the flowing New Orleans clarinet conception, all blended into a unique product. Lepol exploits the full range of his instrument and evinces a superior technique in projecting his keenly subtle jazz conception. Lakey has been buried in the frequently saccharine Harry James band for too long; his highly superior ability in playing mellow alto is too seldom heard. Mayfield is nothing less than sensational on both alto and trumpet. Webb is the possessor of a large, throbbing and thrilling tone, an acute ear which permits his duplicating random styles, and a judgment and selection which is very discriminatory. Prognostication: eventual Armstrong-Goodman stature.

To be an active and objective audience to Kelley's pianistics for repeated performances can result only in the admission of his superiority in versatility, flexibility and musical breadth over *any* pianist. Fitzgerald is well known to the better musicians, but he always returns to Houston to play small-band jazz for peanuts and aesthetics. Mano has facile technique coupled with sharp conception of full bass playing, including a most intelligent and tasteful use of his French-type bowing. With a plethora of splendid recorded examples, absolving tasteless exhibitionisms, Rich can hardly be deprived of first consideration as a "keeper of the takt" and an inspiring and inspired drummer. Davis, from the University of Mississippi, has always, but only with Southern recognition, played well.

Caceres is a candidate for one of America's "overlooked musicians." His recordings and present performances demonstrate the possibilities of a primarily feminine and somewhat sterile instrument.   —J. T. H. MIZE

TEN FAVORITE RECORDS:

Red Allen: *Body and Soul.* Louis Armstrong: *Sleepy Time Down South* (Okeh). Duke Ellington: *C Jam Blues.* Benny Goodman: *Benny Rides Again.* Edmond Hall: *Profoundly Blue.* Billie Holiday: *No Regrets.* Coleman Hawkins: *Body and Soul* (Bluebird). Jack Jenney: *Stardust.* Mound City Blue Blowers: *One Hour.* Artie Shaw: *Concerto for Clarinet.*

GEORGE T. SIMON—editor-on-leave, *Metronome.*

Trumpet: Cootie Williams, Roy Eldridge, Cat Anderson. Trombone: Lawrence Brown, Vernon Brown, Theodore Donnelly. Alto: Johnny Hodges, Ben Smith, Bill Shine. Tenor: Coleman Hawkins, Al Sears, Charlie Venturo. Clarinet: Benny Goodman, Jimmy Lytell, Buddy De Franco. Piano: Teddy Wilson, Art Tatum, Bill Clifton. Guitar: Al Casey, Oscar Moore, Remo Palmieri. Bass: Oscar Pettiford, Jimmy Middleton, Chubby Jackson. Drums: Dave Tough, Gene Krupa, Max Roach. Other Instr: Red Norvo, Lionel Hampton, Ray Nance. Male vocal: Woody Herman, Red McKenzie, Benny Goodman. Female vocal. Ella Fitzgerald, Anita O'Day, Liz Tilton. Arranger: Eddie Sauter, Johnny Thompson, Eddie Finkel. Orchestra: Duke Ellington, Woody Herman, Lionel Hampton. Armed Forces: Eddie Miller, Lou McGarity, Harry Divito.

Rather than make this primarily a defense of my selections (which wouldn't hold any water with people who disagree with me, anyway), I'd like to talk a bit about my non-selections too. Seems that a lot of people I wanted to vote for weren't eligible because (a) they were in the Armed Forces and couldn't be heard, or (b) because I was in the Armed Forces and so couldn't hear them.

In the first category I've already listed my favorite trombonists, Lou McGarity, and my favorite tenorman, Eddie Miller, both of whom, peculiarly enough, are now in the last category. Same goes among bassists, where my favorite is Artie Bernstein and where Trigger Alpert should have come, and for arrangers, where Sy Oliver enters with a big "of course." On the border line among the firing liners were Buck Clayton, Mel Powell and Ray McKinley.

In the second group comes Jack Teagarden, one of my all-time favorites on any instrument, but whom you have to run out to Hollywood to hear; Irving Fazola, my second favorite clarinetist, who went home for a rest; and Buddy Rich, just a wonderful drummer I haven't heard since his Marine release.

Some of my selections, I realize, need some explanation, both for the uninitiated as well as for those who've already paid their dues. Anderson is the brilliant trumpeter who's been playing most of the jazz and lead for Hampton's band. Brown is the same Vernon who sparked Goodman's James-Krupa-Elman band and who has now been playing wonderfully whenever somebody in the New York radio studios thinks that maybe there ought to be a jazz trombone passage somewhere after all. Donnelly plays wonderfully loose jazz, in the Higginbotham vein but with less clichés. Sears is that booting tenorman. Venturo is one of the most thrilling new musicians I've heard in years. Ben Smith plays more like Hodges than anyone I've heard. Shine is an altoman with amazing ideas, copied from nobody. Like Lytell, Clifton is also hidden in the studios, but there's no pianist who has thrilled me more with the deep soul and powerful beat. Middleton is probably the closest to Bernstein extant. Tough, who gets the most simple, direct and moving beat of them all is my choice over Krupa, probably the greatest all-around drummer.   —George Simon.

TEN FAVORITE RECORDS:

Louis Armstrong: *Mahogany Hall Stomp.* Duke Ellington: *Cotton Tail, Steppin' Into Swing Society.* Johnny Hodges: *Day Dream.* Kansas City Six: *Pagin' the Devil.* Mound City Blue Blowers: *I Can't Believe That You're in Love with Me.* Red Norvo: *Remember.* Mel Powell: *The World Is Waiting for the Sunrise.* Muggsy Spanier: *Sister Kate.* Teddy Wilson: *Miss Brown to You.*

CHARLES EDWARD SMITH—editor, *Jazz Record Book;* co-editor, *Jazzmen;* frequent contributor to jazz and general magazines on jazz subjects.

> Trumpet: Louis Armstrong, Max Kaminsky, no choice. Trombone: Georg Brunis, Jay C. Higginbotham, no choice. Alto: Johnny Hodges, Pete Brown, no choice. Tenor: Coleman Hawkins, Eddie Miller, no choice. Clarinet: Pee Wee Russell, Edmond Hall, no choice. Piano: Joe Sullivan, James P. Johnson, no choice. Guitar: Al Casey, Carl Kress, no choice. Bass: George Foster, Bob Haggart, no choice. Drums: George Wettling, Zutty Singleton, no choice. Other Instr: Sidney Bechet, Red Norvo, no choice. Male vocal: Louis Armstrong, James Rushing, no choice. Female vocal: Billie Holiday, Mildred Bailey, no choice. Arranger: Duke Ellington, Mary Lou Williams, no choice. Orchestra: Duke Ellington, Max Kaminsky, no choice. Armed Forces: Bill Davison, Joe Bushkin, no choice.

Since the last *Esquire* poll the critics have, as they used to say, locked wheels in true New Orleans fashion. Armstrong, who's no older than the present century, has been described as a has-been and some of the righteous folk have been saying that Bunk Johnson is the gospel. As to the last, I've no doubt that Bunk is great. Further than that I can't go, since I've heard very few of his recordings. But the issue is bigger than critical hairsplitting might make it seem. The so-called jazz of yesteryear is still around and kicking or the obituary would not be repeated so frequently.

Which leads one to believe I'm for it. Well, I am, in that New Orleans style is fundamental to jazz, both as to band and solo work. In my choices I didn't make up rules and look for men to fit them. I chose some of my favorite jazzmen and it so happens that most of them have the qualifications one finds in the best New Orleans musicians and, indeed, eight of them are from New Orleans.

Taking his weak moments and all, Hawkins is still our best man on tenor. But that doesn't hold, for me, when he's noodling around the harmonies. There are many fine trumpets, some of whom are capable of astonishing technical feats, but Louis is still the king. His style has less complexity than it had during the late twenties. In its directness it sometimes recalls the Hot Five Days. But Louis is not reviving the style of his youth. On the contrary, he has never lost what was fundamental to it, the intense swing, the mellow tone and his sureness of feeling out of the melodic line. Kaminsky plays with terrific push and, like Muggsy and a few others, can still play old tunes as well as new and make both sound good. Both of my trombonists are good in ensemble work. Brunis has a gutty New Orleans tailgate style, Higgy is explosive and virtuoso, both swing beautifully and both play trombone parts which, strangely enough, many trombonists fail to do. Hodges is far ahead in his field, not merely because of fine tone and swing, impeccable technique and beautiful melodic ideas, but because he is one of the few really fine altos in ensemble work.

—CHARLES EDWARD SMITH

TEN FAVORITE RECORDS:

Louis Armstrong: *Potato Head Blues, Mahogany Hall Stomp.* Duke Ellington: *The Gal from Joe's.* Wingy Manone: *Panama* (Bluebird). Jelly Roll Morton: *Black Bottom Stomp, The Pearls* (Victor). Ma Rainey: *Jelly Bean Blues.* Bessie Smith: *You've Been a Good Ole Wagon.* Jimmy Yancey: *Jimmy's Stuff.*

FRANK STACY—New York editor of *Down Beat.*

> Trumpet: Cootie Williams, Bill Coleman, Dizzy Gillespie. Trombone: Lawrence Brown, Vic Dickenson, Bill Harris. Alto: Benny Carter, Johnny Hodges, Johnny Bothwell. Tenor: Coleman Hawkins, Ben Webster, Herbie Fields. Clarinet: Benny Goodman, Edmond Hall, Buddy De Franco. Piano: Art Tatum, Teddy Wilson, Eddie Heywood. Guitar: Al Casey, Oscar Moore, Zeb Julian. Bass: Slam Stewart, Israel Crosby, no choice. Drums: Sidney Catlett, Gene Krupa, Specs Powell. Other Instr: Red Norvo, Lionel Hampton, Ray Nance. Male vocal: Josh White, Eddie Vinson, King Cole. Female vocal: Billie Holiday, Mildred Bailey, Anita O'Day. Arranger: Billy Strayhorn, Ben Homer, Stan Kenton. Orchestra: Duke Ellington, Count Basie, Boyd Raeburn. Armed Forces: Willie Smith, Mel Powell, Sam Donahue.

It seems a needless preamble to say that none of my choices intend to deprecate other musicians but simply reflect my own prejudices and an unfathomable quality called taste. Just as futile is explaining why I picked men like Williams, Brown, Carter and the like. Either their names speak for themselves or I can't imagine how you ever happened to pick up this book. More to the point, I think, is a brief discussion of the New Stars—the young musicians who stand for jazz today, who are plotting its changes and advances, and with whose work, it may be, you're not quite so familiar.

On trumpet, no other new name leaps so quickly to mind as that of Gillespie. Possessor of an erratic horn style, there's little doubt but what he is setting the pace for today's young trumpeters with his frantic search for new ways of expression. Harris has thorough command of his instrument, uses imaginative ideas and plays with an enthusiasm far too often lacking among most of his contemporaries. Bothwell's consistently fine musicianship warrants his being placed on any all-star list of newcomers. His clean melodic line is featured on limpid ballads that suggest Hodges' *Day Dream.* Probably no other young tenorman is so admired and so deplored as Herbie Fields. His tone is fat and blasting; his style outlandishly mad and spotty; his manner of playing, with arms akimbo and knees held alternately high in the air while he reaches for an impossible note, is the jitterbugs' delight but anathema to the pompous jazz lover. De Franco's work struck me as being almost flawless; his tone and ideas smack neither of Goodman nor Rappolo, but are uniquely his own and altogether excellent. Heywood's piano and band were an oasis in a desert of schmaltz last year at Downtown Café Society. For my taste, his piano is often too tricky, too slick, but his command of the keyboard and fertility of ideas easily bring him to the fore. A lover of atonal effects, Julien plays a beautifully intricate guitar that is literally out of the world. It is for his facility on the violin and for the freshness he brings to jazz that Nance wins my vote. Cole, with his soft-voiced, nostalgic, jazz-impregnated ballad-vocals, is available on the nearest juke box. O'Day is so good, so thoroughly a jazz singer, that it's all a little surprising.   —FRANK STACY

TEN FAVORITE RECORDS:

> Count Basie: *Swinging the Blues*. Benny Carter: *Fable of a Fool*. Duke Ellington: *Reminiscing in Tempo, Sloppy Joe, Giddybug Gallop*. Bobby Hackett: *Embraceable You*. Coleman Hawkins: *Body and Soul*. Johnny Hodges: *Day Dream*. Red Norvo: *I Surrender Dear*.

ROBERT THIELE—editor of *Jazz*.

> Trumpet: Cootie Williams, Yank Lawson, Ray Nance. Trombone: Dickie Wells, Jack Teagarden, no choice. Alto: Benny Carter, Johnny Hodges, Herbie Fields. Tenor: Coleman Hawkins, no choice, Flip Phillips. Clarinet: Benny Goodman, Barney Bigard, no choice. Piano: Earl Hines, Jess Stacy, Eddie Heywood. Guitar: Freddie Greene, Al Casey, Teddy Walters. Bass: Oscar Pettiford, Bob Haggart, Chubby Jackson. Drums: Dave Tough, George Wettling, Max Roach. Other Instr: Harry Carney, Red Norvo, Ray Nance. Male vocal: Louis Armstrong, James Rushing, no choice. Female vocal: Billie Holiday, Mildred Bailey, Betty Roché. Ar-

Xylophonist-vibraharpist Red Norvo and vocalist Mildred Bailey frequently have teamed together to create good jazz. Both on recordings and in person, when they both worked in the Norvo band of the middle thirties, they produced a soft, subtle kind of jazz, the kind which Red performs so beautifully on his instrument and which Mildred sings with a rich expressiveness, a warmth, a tasteful phrasing such as no other woman jazz vocalist has been able to surpass. Norvo currently is appearing in the revue, The Seven Lively Arts. Down Beat photo.

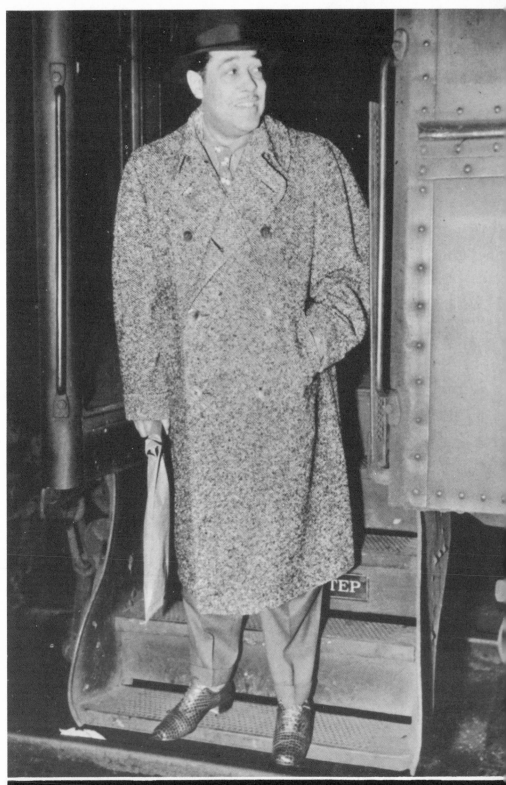

Never before in his twenty-two years as a leader-composer has Duke Ellington gained such wide prestige and public acknowledgment. Among other things, he was the only musician to win a first in two different divisions of Esquire's All-American Jazz Band: the experts rated him both as leader of the greatest band and the best arranger-composer. Since five other members of his organization likewise were accorded positions on the winning bands, it seemed fitting to feature his group at Esquire's 1945 All-American Jazz Concert in Los Angeles.

ranger: Duke Ellington, Benny Carter, no choice. Orchestra: Duke Ellington, Benny Carter, no choice. Armed Forces: Buck Clayton, Artie Bernstein, Shelley Manne.

Within these space limitations it is utterly impossible to write about the 40 selections I have made, so I decided to write about three instruments only: trumpet, clarinet and drums. Trumpet and clarinet, because my taste for these has changed immeasurably since last year; drums because it gives me an opportunity to write about a musician who is the greatest of all jazz drummers.

Last year I voted for Armstrong as Number One; unfortunately, I haven't heard Louis play during 1944, and to be perfectly honest and follow the rules, I chose Cootie instead. He has developed into one of the great all-around trumpeters. His remarkable growl style is as exciting as ever; his imagination seems endless; he plays with plenty of guts, with a broad tone, in relaxed interpretations. In recent months I have become exceedingly familiar with Lawson's brilliant trumpet stylings. As intense as Cootie, yet Yank's playing is inspired by the old New Orleans jazz style, the style I like to call real jazz. Yank is superior to other white "Dixieland" trumpeters because of his fertile imagination, his ability to lead an ensemble with drive and simplicity, particularly when playing the blues.

Many years ago I considered Goodman's playing to be without equal. Then, through plain stupidity and musical ignorance, I lost all pleasure in hearing Goodman play. Today I sincerely feel that Benny, along with Hawkins and Armstrong, is one of the "Big Three" of jazz improvisation. His staggering instrumental technique enables him to improvise intricate choruses of perfect form with plenty of confidence. His tone is brilliant and pure, so polished and tender at times, but never birdie-like. Benny Goodman is jazz.

Jazz musicians rely on the steady tempo, the variety of accents and tricks used by the drummer to stimulate the soloist or ensemble. The steadiest of all drummers is Dave Tough. He drives a trio or a 16-piece orchestra persistently and sensitively at all times. He has exquisite taste, using cymbals and brushes exceptionally well. He has never attained great popularity with the public for the one reason that he is not a showman. He is a musician who never "knocks himself out" by groaning or having his hair fall over his face. Little Davey is *the* drummer—so relaxed, so subtle, and so much swing.   —BOB THIELE

TEN FAVORITE RECORDS:

Louis Armstrong: *Potato Head Blues, Savoy Blues.* Eddie Condon: *Strut Miss Lizzie.* Duke Ellington: *Conga Brava, It's Glory.* Benny Goodman: *Blues in My/Your Flat, Sometimes I'm Happy.* Fletcher Henderson: *Yeah Man.* Bessie Smith: *Young Woman Blues.* Frankie Trumbauer: *Riverboat Shuffle.*

BARRY ULANOV—editor of *Metronome.*

Trumpet: Roy Eldridge, Cootie Williams, Dizzy Gillespie. Trombone: Lawrence Brown, Dickie Wells, J. J. Johnson. Alto: Benny Carter, Johnny Hodges, Georgie Auld. Tenor: Arnette Cobbs, Coleman Hawkins, Bob Dukoff. Clarinet: Benny Goodman, Edmond Hall, Rudy Rutherford. Piano: Art Tatum, King Cole, Milton Buckner. Guitar: Oscar Moore, Al Casey, Remo Palmieri. Bass: Oscar Pettiford, Red Callender, Chubby Jackson. Drums: Specs Powell, Sidney Catlett, Max Roach. Other Instr: Red Norvo, Lionel Hampton, Ray Nance. Male vocal: King Cole, Joe Turner, Peanuts Holland. Female vocal: Mildred Bailey, Billie Holiday, Betty Roché. Arranger: Billy Strayhorn, Duke Ellington, George Handy. Orchestra: Duke Ellington, Lionel Hampton, Georgie Auld. Armed Forces: Kenneth Kersey, Willie Smith, Gerald Wiggins.

In my first and second choices for solo positions I have tried to select two solid units. As a matter of fact, the New Stars I chose would comprise a formidable band too, compact, united by tastes, temperaments and techniques. Furthermore, I think, any combination of these musicians, firsts, seconds or tyros, would add up to first-rate jazz.

There are great things happening in jazz today. A young art form is coming to its maturity with all the grace and technical distinction that one might expect of this country's finest creative expression. Jazz soloists, composers, singers, arrangers are all possessed by some feeling for the growth and change in their art. Some, a small but vigorous minority, fight this growth and change, hewing crudely, rudely, but steadfastly to outworn traditions and outmoded sounds. This group is questionable aesthetically and on purely technical musical grounds. They have lost touch with their time; their fingers have grown weak and weary on their horns. The great majority of jazzmen, on the other hand, fight continually to go ahead, to absorb technical advances, to create new sound patterns within the abiding rhythmic and improvisatory traditions of jazz. It is from this great majority that I have chosen my soloists.

Most of my choices, though perhaps controversial, are self-explanatory. Not much needs to be said at this point in jazz history, in support of the rich talents of Eldridge, Williams, Brown, Wells, Carter, Hodges, Hawkins, Goodman, Tatum, Cole, Norvo, Hampton, etc., etc.

Cobbs is the brilliant tenorman who not only blows with the furious fervor which characterizes the playing of every member of the Hampton band, but presents stimulating, out-of-the-way musical ideas as well. His solos are beautifully constructed and wonderfully varied in dynamics, too. There isn't space enough to comment on all the New Stars, but I should like to single out Johnson, Dukoff, Palmieri, Nance and Wiggins for special mention, as soloists of remarkable ingenuity, with full command of their instruments. I chose Strayhorn over Ellington, not only to call attention to this gifted musician, but also to point out the fact that no other composer-arranger has been able to absorb and recreate the glistening facets of the Ellington style so convincingly and then to add something of his own devising as well.

—BARRY ULANOV

TEN FAVORITE RECORDS:

Count Basie: *Texas Shuffle.* Duke Ellington: *Ko Ko, All Too Soon, Chelsea Bridge.* Benny Goodman: *Clarinet á la King, Good Enough to Keep, World Is Waiting for the Sunrise.* Coleman Hawkins: *The Man I Love.* Red Norvo: *Smoke Dreams.* Artie Shaw: *Concerto for Clarinet.*

GEORGE AVAKIAN—M/Sgt, Infantry, U.S. Army, now serving in Southwest Pacific area; editor Columbia's Hot Jazz albums; contributor to jazz magazines.

Trumpet: Bunk Johnson, Mutt Carey, Benny Strickler. Trombone: Kid Ory, Jim Robinson, George Lugg. Alto: no choices. Tenor: no choices. Clarinet: George Lewis, Bud Jacobson, Wade Whaley. Piano: James P. Johnson, Art Hodes, Buster Wilson. Guitar: Lawrence Marrero, Bud Scott, no choice. Bass: Pops Foster, Squire Girsback, Ed Garland. Drums: Baby Dodds, Zutty Singleton, Joe Grauso. Other Instr: Sidney Bechet, Harry Carney, no choice. Male vocal: Louis Armstrong, no other choices. Female vocal: New Star choice only, Estella Yancey. Arranger: Lu Watters, Eddie Condon, no choice. Orchestra: Bunk Johnson, Kid Ory, Max Kaminsky. Armed Forces: Turk Murphy, Bill Davison, Dick Cary.

Esquire has asked us to choose "the greatest soloists" on each instrument in making our 1945 selections, although it seemed to me that after last year's *Esquire* concert anyone should have realized that tossing together a batch of prima donnas (Armstrong and Wilson excepted) just wasn't going to produce anything but a frightful hash of applause-begging, every-man-for-himself exhibitionism (Armstrong and Wilson excepted).

My idea of jazz is New Orleans ensemble music, so once again I'm picking men who can play well *together.* The new balloting rules permit me to leave out such impedimenta as saxophones, so I have kept the classic front line of trumpet, trombone and clarinet. I seriously considered eliminating pianists, too, because the George Lewis Climax records reverted so successfuly to this old New Orleans custom, occasioned by the fact that so much early jazz was played out of doors.

I believe that the men I have chosen for my two bands require no individual discussion. Hear them and you hear jazz.

I'd rather say something of the many splendid musicians I've had to leave out. Armstrong simply wouldn't be as effective with these groups today as Bunk or Mutt Carey, but I would want no one else to sing with either band. It's hard to omit Brunis and Spanier, neither of whom I heard during the year, and it seems strange not to have Condon down for guitar. There are several clarinetists I like; Ellis Horne, Omer Simeon or Wade Whaley undoubtedly would fit into the second band just as well as the remarkable Bud Jacobson, and I want to promise Pee Wee Russell and Rod Cless several beers when I return to Julius's.

I repeat, I'm sticking to New Orleans jazz, where sheer ability and inspiration of the musicians and the quality of their spontaneous music are the factors that count, not arrangers and manuscripts. Nevertheless, Lu Watters has made brilliant arrangements of a great many of the best jazz tunes for the guidance of his Yerba Buena band, following the general style, I should say, of King Oliver's Creole Jazz Band. Condon, of course, doesn't use paper, but he is certainly one of the most energetic and successful organizers jazz has known, and there have been dozens of sessions and records which are as truly Condon's as the Ellington band's output is Duke's. In the orchestral division, Bunk Johnson's band played in New Orleans last summer, Ory's was organized for Orson Welles' CBS show on the West Coast and Kaminsky's made the Pied Piper the best jazz spot in New York.

—George Avakian

TEN FAVORITE RECORDS:

Louis Armstrong: *Muskrat Ramble, Ory's Creole Trombone.*
George Lewis: *Careless Love, Climax Rag.* Miff Mole: *Shimme-
Sha-Wabble.* Jelly Roll Morton: *Steamboat Stomp, Kansas City
Stomp.* King Oliver: *Canal St. Blues, I Ain't Gonna Tell Nobody,
Mabel's Dream* (Okeh).

WILLIAM RUSSELL—co-editor and contributor to *Jazzmen, The Jazz
Record Book;* author of many articles in jazz magazines.

Trumpet: Bunk Johnson, Kid Shots Madison, no choice. Trombone: Jim Robinson, Kid Ory, no choice. Alto: no choices. Tenor:
no choices. Clarinet: George Lewis, no other choices. Piano: no
choices. Guitar: Lawrence Marrero, Arthur Budd Scott, no choice.
Bass: Alcide Pavageau, Ed Garland, no choice. Drums: Baby Dodds,
no other choices. Other Instr: no choices. Male vocal: Louis Armstrong, no other choices. Female vocal: no choices. Arranger: no
choices. Orchestra: Bunk Johnson, no other choices. Armed Forces:
no choices.

In compliance with the conditions imposed by the rules of this
poll, I have limited my selections to musicians I have been able to
hear extensively during 1944. Since the ballot specified *jazz* musi-
cians, and since the word jazz was not spelled with $$ signs, I did
not feel compelled to choose stars just because their names were
up in the bright lights. Rather, I have picked men solely on their
musicianship and their individual ability. Most of them are rela-
tively unknown nationally, but the music they have played this
year is the most thrilling in my experience.

Bunk Johnson is blowing the most powerful trumpet I have
ever heard and his tone remains as beautiful as ever. The terrific
force with which he drives down the blues or fast stomps is un-
surpassed. In wealth of ideas and creative ability he surpassed any
musician I have been privileged to know in three decades. Ever
since I first heard George Lewis two years ago he has been my

favorite clarinetist. His lyrical style is as fresh and unspoiled as ever, his driving energy unequaled.

Jim Robinson wouldn't last long under Toscanini, but he can outswing any jazz trombonist I know. He has the roughness and abandon indispensable to real jazz. Lawrence Marrero, who plays several string instruments but prefers banjo, is a rhythm section by himself. Although he has received little national recognition, his rhythmic punch has added so much life to every orchestra in which I've heard him, it would be impossible to leave him out of my all-star lineup. Slow Drag (as Pavageau is known) I had never heard until last year. His amazing tone and forcefulness place him in the front rank of jazz bassists. The choice of Dodds requires no explanation to anyone who has ever heard him play. One need say only that he is playing as wonderfully as ever—deserving of any all-time, all-star lineup.

All of these musicians not only are masters of the jazz idiom on their particular instruments, but have exceptional knowledge of jazz band ensemble. The ability to play with others is a most important part of the individual musician's worthiness.

WILLIAM RUSSELL

TEN FAVORITE RECORDS:

Louis Armstrong: *Gully Low Blues, Wild Man Blues, Potato Head Blues, Put 'Em Down Blues*. Bunk Johnson: *Moose March, Panama, St. Louis Blues, Weary Blues*. King Oliver: *I Ain't Gonna Tell Nobody, Snake Rag*.

EUGENE WILLIAMS—editor of the late *Jazz Information*.

Trumpet: Bunk Johnson, Mutt Carey, no choice. Trombone: Jim Robinson, Kid Ory, no choice. Alto: no choices. Tenor: no choices. Clarinet: George Lewis, Wade Whaley, no choice. Piano: no choices. Guitar: Lawrence Marrero, Arthur Budd Scott, no choice. Bass: George Foster, no other choices. Drums: Baby Dodds, no other choices. Other Instr: no choices. Male vocal: Louis Armstrong, no other choices. Female vocal: no choices. Arranger: no choices. Orchestra: no choices. Armed Forces: no choices.

Experts' polls in general seem to me neither sound nor useful. The selection of a team of "All-American Jazz Stars" might as well be entrusted to a circle of sports columnists as to such a group of "jazz experts"—and the team, once selected, might as well be expected to perform in the Yankee Stadium as in a concert hall.

It is curious to be asked to name outstanding "jazz stars" in company with persons whose definition of jazz basically is different from mine, and some of whom have been conducting a campaign *against* what I consider to be jazz.

But since I have been asked, it seems better to vote than not to vote.

Bunk Johnson is my only unqualified first choice—the greatest trumpeter and greatest jazz musician I have ever heard. After Bunk, the best trumpeter I know is Mutt Carey; but I'm sure that Armstrong (whom I have voted for only as a singer) can play great jazz trumpet anytime he wants to.

For the rest, I have named one or two players of every instrument which belongs in a jazz band, except the piano; in the last few years I have not heard any pianists whom I could mention among my other choices.

Except in the trumpet class, my selections are not firsts and seconds. Each of the men named is a fine musician, and—except that Bunk is incomparable—there is no advantage in expanding personal preferences into critical comparisons.

Robinson, Lewis and Marrero were unknown, except in New Orleans, until the '40's; and there may be many equally notable musicians still to be uncovered.

I have not voted for New Stars, but if they had been active in 1944 I could have mentioned men like trombonist Turk Murphy, clarinetists Bob Helm and Ellis Horne, pianist Paul Lingle, trumpeters Lu Watters and Ben Strickler—young musicians, most of them, who know their first responsibility is to emulate the spirit and the form of the great jazzmen without presuming to "improve" on them.

My votes are for the New Orleans Negro musicians who created jazz and who remain almost its only authentic exponents. So my selections would fit together in a band, even though they were chosen for their individual ability.

Take Bunk or Mutt, or both of them, and any trombone, clarinet and rhythm section from the men listed; put them in a dance hall, playing their own music; and pipe it into whatever concert hall you like. You will hear something very unlike an All-American "jam session"—a New Orleans jazz band playing the real jazz.

—EUGENE WILLIAMS

TEN FAVORITE RECORDS: No choices.

THE FAVORITE RECORDS OF ESQUIRE'S EXPERTS

IN THE choice of favorite recordings, the divergence of taste among the experts was far greater than that in the choice of musicians. A total of 175 title-performer combinations was named. Only nine discs received the approval of three or more experts; of these only *West End Blues* had the approval of four experts. Here are the nine favorites:

WEST END BLUES. Okeh 8597 and 41078; reissued on Vocalion 3204, Okeh 3204, Columbia 36377. *Louis Armstrong and his Hot Five:* Louis Armstrong, trumpet; Fred Robinson, trombone; Jimmy Strong, clarinet; Earl Hines, piano; Zutty Singleton, drums; Mancy Cara, banjo.

POTATO HEAD BLUES. Okeh 8503; reissued on United Hot Clubs of America 59-60, Columbia 35660. *Louis Armstrong and his Hot Seven:* Louis Armstrong, trumpet; Kid Ory, trombone; Johnny Dodds, clarinet; Baby Dodds, drums; Peter Briggs, brass bass; Johnny St. Cyr, guitar; Lil Hardin, piano.

WEE BABY BLUES. Decca 8526. *Art Tatum and his Orchestra:* Art Tatum, piano; John Collins, guitar; Billy Taylor, string bass; Eddie Dougherty, drums; Edmond Hall, clarinet; Joe Thomas, trumpet; Joe Turner, vocal.

KO KO. Victor 26577. *Duke Ellington and his Orchestra:* Cootie Williams, Wallace Jones, Rex Stewart, trumpets; Joe Nanton, Juan Tizol, Lawrence Brown, trombones; Johnny Hodges, Otto Hardwick, altos; Harry Carney, alto and baritone sax; Barney Bigard, clarinet and tenor sax; Ben Webster, tenor; Duke Ellington, piano; Fred Guy, guitar; Sonny Greer, drums; Jimmy Blanton, string bass.

BODY AND SOUL. Bluebird 10523. *Coleman Hawkins and his Orchestra:* Coleman Hawkins, tenor; Eustace Moore, Jackie Fields, altos; Joe Guy, Tommy Lindsey, trumpets; Earl Hardy, trombone; William Oscar Smith, string bass; Gene Rodgers, piano; Arthur Herbert, drums.

DAY DREAM. Bluebird 11021. *Johnny Hodges and his Orchestra:* Johnny Hodges, alto and soprano sax; Harry Carney, baritone sax; Cootie Williams, trumpet; Lawrence Brown, trombone; Sonny Greer, drums; Jimmy Blanton, string bass; Duke Ellington, piano.

SOMETIMES I'M HAPPY. Victor 25090. *Benny Goodman and his Orchetra:* Bunny Berigan, Nate Kazebier, Ralph Muzzillo, trumpets; Red Ballard, Jack Lacey, trombones; Benny Goodman, clarinet; Hymie Shertzer, Toots Mondello, altos; Dick Clark, Arthur Rollini, tenors; Gene Krupa, drums; George Van Eps, guitar; Frank Froeba, piano; Harry Goodman, bass.

WHAT A LITTLE MOONLIGHT CAN DO. Brunswick 7498; reissued on Columbia 36206. *Teddy Wilson and his Orchestra:* Teddy Wilson, piano; John Kirby, string bass; Cozy Cole, drums; John Truehart, guitar; Benny Goodman, clarinet; Ben Webster, tenor; Roy Eldridge, trumpet; Billie Holiday, vocal.

SWEET LORRAINE. Decca 8520. *The King Cole Trio:* King Cole, piano; Oscar Moore, guitar; Wesley Prince, string bass.

MUSICIANS' POINT TABULATION

for Esquire's All-American Jazz Band

TRUMPET

	Total Points
COOTIE WILLIAMS (8)	32

Braveman—3, Dexter—2,
Feather—3, Hammond—2,
Hoefer—2, Jovien—3,
Levin—3, Miller—3, Simon—3,
Stacy—3, Thiele—3, Ulanov—2.

ROY ELDRIDGE (5)	14

Braveman—2, Feather—2,
Jovien—2, Lim—3, Simon—2,
Ulanov—3.

LOUIS ARMSTRONG (16)	12

Cavanaugh—3, Goffin—3,
Mize—3, Smith—3.

BUNK JOHNSON (0)	9

Avakian—3, Russell—3,
Williams—3.

MUGGSY SPANIER (2)	7

Dexter—3, Goffin—2, Jax—2.

MAX KAMINSKY (2)	7

Hoefer—3, Levin—2,
Smith—2.

BILL COLEMAN (5)	7

Cavanaugh—2, Hammond—3,
Stacy—2.

MUTT CAREY (0)	4

Avakian—2, Williams—2.

CHARLIE SHAVERS (3)	4

Burley—2, Lim—2.

SIDNEY DE PARIS (0)	3

Jax—3.

HARRY JAMES (3)	3

Burley—3.

YANK LAWSON (0)	2

Thiele—2.

TRUMPET (*cont'd*)

	Total Points
RED ALLEN (0)	2

Miller—2.

KID SHOTS MADISON (0)	2

Russell—2.

JOHNNY AUSTIN (0)	2

Mize, 2.

DRUMS

SIDNEY CATLETT (17)	24

Braveman—2, Goffin—3,
Hoefer—2, Jax—3, Levin—2,
Lim—3, Miller—2, Mize—2,
Stacy—3, Ulanov—2.

DAVE TOUGH (6)	19

Feather—2, Hoefer—3,
Jax—2, Jovien—3, Miller—3,
Simon—3, Thiele—3.

JO JONES (7)	14

Burley—3, Braveman—3,
Dexter—3, Hammond—3,
Lim—2.

GENE KRUPA (0)	12

Burley—2, Cavanaugh—2,
Goffin—2, Jovien—2,
Simon—2, Stacy—2.

SPECS POWELL (2)	10

Cavanaugh—1, Hammond—1,
Jax—1, Levin—3, Stacy—1,
Ulanov—3.

BABY DODDS (0)	9

Avakian—3, Russell—3,
Williams—3.

(Bracketed figures following names indicate points received in 1944.)

DRUMS (*cont'd*)

	Total Points
Zutty Singleton (6)	6
Avakian—2, Dexter—2, Smith—2.	
Cozy Cole (9)	5
Cavanaugh—3, Hammond—2.	
George Wettling (4)	5
Smith—3, Thiele—2.	
Cliff Leeman (o)	3
Feather—3.	
Buddy Rich (o)	3
Mize—3.	

ORCHESTRA

Duke Ellington	43
Braveman—2, Cavanaugh—3, Dexter—3, Feather—3, Hoefer—3, Jax—3, Jovien—3, Levin—3, Lim—2, Mize—3, Simon—3, Smith—3, Stacy—3, Thiele—3, Ulanov—3.	
Count Basie	15
Burley—2, Braveman—3, Hammond—3, Hoefer—2, Lim—3, Stacy—2.	
Lionel Hampton	12
Burley—3, Goffin—3, Feather—1, Mize, 2, Simon—1, Ulanov—2.	
Woody Herman	6
Feather—2, Jovien—2, Simon—2.	
Bunk Johnson	6
Avakian—3, Russell—3.	
Red Norvo	4
Cavanaugh—2, Levin—2.	

ORCHESTRA (*cont'd*)

	Total Points
Max Kaminsky	4
Avakian—1, Goffin—1, Smith—2.	
Benny Carter	4
Dexter—2, Thiele—2.	
Red Allen	3
Miller—3.	
Eddie Heywood	3
Cavanaugh—1, Hammond—2.	
Miff Mole	2
Goffin—2.	
Kid Ory	2
Avakian—2.	
Louis Jordan	2
Miller—2.	

ARMED FORCES FAVORITE

Buck Clayton, trumpet (2)	20
Burley—3, Braveman—3, Cavanaugh—3, Dexter—2, Hammond—3, Jax—3, Thiele—3.	
Willie Smith, alto sax (6)	17
Goffin—3, Jovien—2, Levin—2, Lim—3, Miller—2, Stacy—3, Ulanov—2.	
Kenneth Kersey, piano (o)	10
Burley 2, Feather—3, Lim—2, Ulanov—3.	
Mel Powell, piano (2)	9
Burley—1, Braveman—2, Feather—2, Goffin—1, Jax—1, Stacy—2.	
Vido Musso, tenor sax (o)	6
Hoefer—3, Miller—3.	

ARMED FORCES FAVORITE
(cont'd)

Total Points

JAY McSHANN, piano (o)...... 6
  Dexter—1, Hoefer—2,
  Jovien—3.
ARTHUR BERNSTEIN, bass (2)... 5
  Levin—3, Thiele—2.
BILL DAVISON, cornet (o) 5
  Avakian—2, Smith—3.
JOE BUSHKIN, piano (2) 4
  Cavanaugh—2, Smith—2.
BABE RUSSIN, tenor sax (1) 3
  Dexter—3.
TURK MURPHY, trombone (o).. 3
  Avakian—3.
SY OLIVER, arranger (o) 3
  Mize—3.
EDDIE MILLER, tenor sax (o) ... 3
  Simon—3.
LOU McGARITY, trombone (2) 2
  Simon—2.
BUD FREEMAN, tenor sax (o) ... 2
  Jax—2.
JIMMY McPARTLAND, trumpet (o) 2
  Goffin—2.
DICK DAVIS, tenor sax 2
  Hammond—2.
BOBBY BYRNE, trombone (o)... 2
  Mize—2.

ARRANGER

DUKE ELLINGTON 30
  Burley—2, Braveman—3,
  Cavanaugh—3, Dexter—3,
  Feather—3, Goffin—3,
  Lim—3, Mize—2, Smith—3,
  Thiele—3, Simon—2.

ARRANGER (cont'd)

Total Points

BILLY STRAYHORN 16
  Feather—2, Goffin—2, Jax—3,
  Jovien—3, Stacy—3, Simon—3.
BENNY CARTER 10
  Burley—3, Dexter—2,
  Hoefer—3, Thiele—2.
EDDIE SAUTER 9
  Cavanaugh—2, Levin—2,
  Lim—2, Simon—3.
JOHNNY THOMPSON 7
  Levin—3, Simon—2,
  Lim—1, Hammond—1.
DAVE MATTHEWS 4
  Jax—2, Jovien—2.
PAUL JORDAN 3
  Miller—3.
LU WATTERS 3
  Avakian—3.
PHIL MOORE 3
  Hammond—3.
JACK CHAPMAN 3
  Mize—3.
ZILNER RANDOLPH 2
  Miller—2.
MARY LOU WILLIAMS 2
  Smith—2.
FLETCHER HENDERSON 2
  Braveman—2.
BEN HOMER 2
  Stacy—2.
SONNY BURKE 2
  Hammond—2.
JIMMY HILLIARD 2
  Hoefer—2.
EDDIE CONDON 2
  Avakian—2.

OTHER INSTRUMENTS

Total
Points

RED NORVO vibraharp (15) 44
Burley—2, Braveman—3,
Cavanaugh—3, Dexter—3,
Feather—2, Goffin—3,
Hammond—2, Hoefer—3,
Jax—2, Jovien—3,
Levin—3, Mize—2,
Simon—3, Smith—2, Stacy—3,
Thiele—2, Ulanov—3.
HARRY CARNEY, baritone sax (2) 19
Avakian—2, Cavanaugh—2,
Dexter—2, Hammond—3,
Levin—2, Lim—3,
Miller—2, Thiele—3.
LIONEL HAMPTON, vibra-
harp (15) 16
Burley—3, Braveman—2,
Lim—2, Mize—3, Simon—2,
Stacy—2, Ulanov—2.
SIDNEY BECHET, soprano sax (6) 13
Avakian—3, Goffin—2,
Hoefer—2, Miller—3,
Smith—3.
STUFF SMITH, violin (0) 5
Feather—3, Jovien—2.
EDDIE SOUTH, violin (3) 3
Jax—3.

PIANO

TEDDY WILSON (5) 24
Cavanaugh—2, Dexter—3,
Goffin—3, Hammond—3,
Levin—3, Lim—3, Miller—2,
Simon—3, Stacy—2.
ART TATUM (17)............ 21
Braveman—3, Cavanaugh—3,
Feather—3, Levin—2, Lim—2,

PIANO (*cont'd*)

Total
Points

ART TATUM (17) (*cont'd*)
Simon—2, Stacy—3,
Ulanov—3.
EARL HINES (7) 16
Braveman—2, Hoefer—3,
Jax—3, Jovien—3, Mize—2,
Thiele—3.
JESS STACY (4) 6
Hoefer—2, Jax—2, Thiele—2.
KING COLE (2) 6
Feather—2, Jovien—2,
Ulanov—2.
JOHNNY GUARNIERI (2) 5
Burley—2, Miller—3.
JAMES P. JOHNSON (0) 5
Avakian—3, Smith—2.
COUNT BASIE (1) 5
Burley—3, Hammond—2.
JOE SULLIVAN (3) 3
Smith—3.
PECK KELLEY (0) 3
Mize—3.
MARY LOU WILLIAMS (3) 2
Goffin—2.
PETE JOHNSON (0) 2
Dexter—2.
ART HODES (2) 2
Avakian—2.

FEMALE VOCAL

MILDRED BAILEY (15) 38
Burley—2, Braveman—2,
Cavanaugh—2, Dexter—3,
Hammond—3, Hoefer—3,
Jax—2, Jovien—3, Levin—3,
Lim—3, Miller—3, Smith—2,
Stacy—2, Thiele—2,
Ulanov—3.

FEMALE VOCAL (*cont'd*)

Total
Points

BILLIE HOLIDAY (23) 32
Braveman–3, Cavanaugh–3,
Feather–3, Goffin–3,
Hoefer–2, Levin–2, Lim–2,
Mize–3, Smith–3, Stacy–3,
Thiele–3, Ulanov–2.

ANITA O'DAY (0) 6
Feather–2, Mize–1,
Simon–2, Stacy–1.

ROSETTA THARPE (0) 5
Dexter–2, Jax–3.

ELLA FITZGERALD (4) 3
Simon–3.

GEORGIA GIBBS (0) 3
Burley–3.

PEARL BAILEY (0) 2
Goffin–2.

HELEN HUMES (0) 2
Hammond–2.

BILLIE ROGERS (0) 2
Jovien–2.

ELLA MAE MORSE (0) 2
Mize–2.

GUITAR

AL CASEY (11) 31
Braveman–3, Cavanaugh–2,
Goffin–3, Hammond–2,
Jax–3, Levin–3, Mize–2,
Simon–3, Smith–3, Stacy–3,
Thiele–2, Ulanov–2.

OSCAR MOORE (10) 19
Burley–3, Cavanaugh–3,
Feather–3, Lim–3, Simon–2,
Stacy–2, Ulanov–3.

GUITAR (*cont'd*)

Total
Points

REMO PALMIERI (0) 10
Cavanaugh–1, Feather–2,
Goffin–1, Jovien–1,
Levin–1, Lim–1, Miller–1,
Simon–1, Ulanov–1.

LAWRENCE MARRERO (0) 9
Avakian–3, Russell–3,
Williams–3.

LES PAUL (2) 8
Hoefer–2, Jovien–3,
Miller–3.

FREDDIE GREEN (4) 8
Braveman–2, Hammond–3,
Thiele–3.

TEDDY WALTERS (0) 6
Burley–1, Braveman–1,
Jax–1, Lim–2, Thiele–1.

ARTHUR BUDD SCOTT (0) 6
Avakian–2, Russell–2,
Williams–2.

HY WHITE (0) 6
Dexter–1, Hoefer–3,
Jovien–2.

CARL KRESS (1) 5
Dexter–3, Smith–2.

EDDIE CONDON (0) 4
Goffin–2, Jax–2.

TEDDY BUNN (7) 3
Mize–3.

DAVE BARBOUR (0) 2
Dexter–2.

TINY GRIMES (0) 2
Burley–2.

TOMMY KAY (0) 2
Miller–2.

LEONARD WARE (0) 2
Levin–2.

TROMBONE

Total
Points

JAY C. HIGGINBOTHAM (0).... 23
Burley–3, Braveman–3,
Feather–3, Hammond–2,
Hoefer–2, Jovien–2, Lim–2,
Miller–2, Mize–2, Smith–2.

LAWRENCE BROWN (8) 21
Braveman–2, Cavanaugh–3,
Dexter–3, Feather–2,
Levin–2, Simon–3,
Stacy–3, Ulanov–3.

JACK TEAGARDEN (13) 13
Dexter–2, Hoefer–3,
Jovien–3, Mize–3, Thiele–2.

BENNY MORTON (1) 11
Cavanaugh–2, Levin–3,
Lim–3, Miller–3.

JIM ROBINSON (0) 8
Avakian–2, Russell–3,
Williams–3.

VIC DICKENSON (2) 8
Hammond–3, Jax–3,
Stacy–2.

GEORG BRUNIS (7) 8
Goffin–3, Jax–2, Smith–3.

KID ORY (0) 7
Avakian–3, Russell–2,
Williams–2.

DICKIE WELLS (2) 5
Thiele–3, Ulanov–2.

SANDY WILLIAMS (0) 2
Goffin–2.

TRUMMY YOUNG (0) 2
Burley–2.

VERNON BROWN (0) 2
Simon–2.

STRING BASS

Total
Points

OSCAR PETTIFORD (6) 20
Burley–3, Braveman–3,
Feather–3, Levin–2,
Simon–3, Thiele–3,
Ulanov–3.

SLAM STEWART (3) 14
Cavanaugh–3, Feather–2,
Goffin–3, Lim–3, Stacy–3.

MILTON HINTON (5) 10
Braveman–2, Hoefer–3,
Lim–2, Miller–3.

POPS FOSTER (0) 9
Avakian–3, Smith–3,
Williams–3.

ISRAEL CROSBY (3) 8
Hammond–3, Jax–3,
Stacy–2.

CHUBBY JACKSON (0) 7
Feather–1, Hoefer–2,
Miller–1, Simon–1,
Thiele–1, Ulanov–1.

JIMMY MIDDLETON (0)........ 6
Jovien–2, Miller–2, Simon–2.

BOB HAGGART (2) 6
Cavanaugh–2, Smith–2,
Thiele–2.

AL HALL (0) 5
Cavanaugh–1, Levin–3,
Lim–1.

EUGENE RAMEY (0) 4
Dexter–1, Jovien–3.

FITZ FITZGERALD (0) 3
Mize–3.

ALCIDE PAVAGEAU (0) 3
Russell–3.

JOHN SIMMONS (0) 3
Burley–1, Hammond–2.

Under the supervision of Dave Dexter, Jr., these men recorded four sides for Capitol's excellent New American Jazz album. Front row, left to right: the late Jimmie Noone, Billy May, Zutty Singleton, Dave Barbour; behind them, in the same order, Artie Shapiro, Joe Sullivan, Jack Teagarden, Dave Matthews. It was the last record date on which Noone played before his death; his clarineting was a standout, together with the vocalizing and tromboning of Teagarden. Matthews turned in a superb tenor solo on Solitude. Capitol photo by Charlie Mihn.

Backstage at Chicago's Regal Theatre, in the late summer of 1944, a group of six New Orleans musicians came to greet another native of their home town—Louis Armstrong. With a big, warm smile Louie greeted them with "What's this, man, a reunion?" It was. Left to right: Baby Dodds, Stanley Williams, Red Allen, Richard M. Jones, Armstrong, Al Wynn, Tubby Hall. All are, or have been, leaders. Dodds, Allen, Wynn, Hall have worked with Louie; Jones is directly responsible for Louie's appearance on Okeh records. Photo by Jim Ferstel.

The Esquire All-American Jazz Band Concert at the Metropolitan Opera House, New York City, January 18, 1944: a gala occasion for jazz. A sellout, with hundreds turned away, the box-office proceeds of over six hundred thousand dollars in the form of War Bonds were contributed by the audience to the cause of victory. Billie Holiday (right), 1944 winner in the female vocal division, sings with accompaniment by Roy Eldridge (left), pianist Art Tatum, bassist Oscar Pettiford, as Trombonist Jack Teagarden watches in the immediate background.

The Esquire Concert again: singer Mildred Bailey (left), who won the 1945 Gold Award over last year's winner (Holiday), consults with pianist Art Tatum, preparatory to her heartfelt rendition of Squeeze Me, which brought a wave of approval from the audience. Next to Oscar Pettiford is guitarist Al Casey, while the man behind the drums (not visible on the picture) is Big Sid Catlett—all of them being two-time Gold Award winners. The Metropolitan Opera never before had been honored for the presentation of such uniquely American music.

Vibraharpists Lionel Hampton and Red Norvo engaged in a duo that literally rocked the rafters. The number began with each player using his own set of vibes, but when Lionel hit his instrument so hard that he put it out of commission, he joined Red and they both used his vibes. Roy Eldridge tips his trumpet heavenward as tenorman Coleman Hawkins adds his bit to the spontaneous proceedings. Just to the right of Norvo's arm sits Louis Armstrong, who played a dual role at the concert, winning both the trumpet and vocal spots. Esquire photos.

STRING BASS (*cont'd*)

Total Points

RED CALLENDER (4) 3
Hammond—1, Ulanov—2.

SQUIRE GIRSBACK (0) 2
Avakian—2.

AL MORGAN (5) 2
Goffin—2.

JOHN KIRBY (4) 2
Burley—2.

ED GARLAND (0) 2
Russell—2.

SID WEISS (2) 2
Dexter—2.

ALTO SAXOPHONE

JOHNNY HODGES (10) 42
Burley—2, Braveman—3,
Cavanaugh—3, Dexter—2,
Goffin—3, Hammond—2,
Hoefer—2, Jax—3, Jovien—3,
Levin—2, Lim—2, Mize—3,
Simon—3, Smith—3, Stacy—2,
Thiele—2, Ulanov—2.

BENNY CARTER (8) 33
Braveman—2, Cavanaugh—2,
Dexter—3, Feather—3,
Goffin—2, Hoefer—3,
Levin—3, Lim—3, Miller—3,
Stacy—3, Thiele—3, Ulanov—3.

PETE BROWN (2) 4
Feather—2, Smith—2.

LEM DAVIS (0) 3
Hammond—3.

TAB SMITH (0) 3
Burley—3.

LES ROBINSON (0) 2
Miller—2.

CHARLIE BARNET (0).......... 2
Jovien—2.

ALTO SAXOPHONE (*cont'd*)

Total Points

BOYCE BROWN (0) 2
Jax—2.

CLAUDE LAKEY (0) 2
Mize—2.

BEN SMITH (0) 2
Simon—2.

CLARINET

BENNY GOODMAN (24) 48
Burley—3, Braveman—3,
Cavanaugh—3, Dexter—3,
Feather—3, Goffin—3,
Hammond—3, Jovien—3,
Levin—3, Lim—3, Miller—3,
Mize—3, Simon—3, Stacy—3,
Thiele—3, Ulanov—3.

EDMOND HALL (5) 27
Braveman—2, Feather—2,
Goffin—2, Hammond—2,
Hoefer—2, Jax—3, Levin—2,
Lim—2, Miller—2, Mize—2,
Smith—2, Stacy—2, Ulanov—2.

BARNEY BIGARD (8) 11
Cavanaugh—2, Dexter—2,
Hoefer—3, Jovien—2,
Thiele—2.

GEORGE LEWIS (0) 9
Avakian—3, Russell—3,
Williams—3.

PEE WEE RUSSELL (2) 3
Smith—3.

WADE WHALEY (0) 3
Avakian—1, Williams—2.

BUSTER BAILEY (0) 2
Burley—2.

JIMMY LYTELL (0) 2
Simon—2.

CLARINET (*cont'd*)

Total
Points

MEZZ MESIROW (o) 2
Jax—2.

BUD JACOBSON (1) 2
Avakian—2.

TENOR SAXOPHONE

COLEMAN HAWKINS (17) 45
Braveman—3, Cavanaugh—3,
Dexter—3, Feather—3,
Hoefer—3, Jax—3, Jovien—3,
Levi—2, Lim—3, Miller—3,
Mize—3, Simon—3, Smith—3,
Stacy—3, Thiele—3, Ulanov—2.

LESTER YOUNG (2) 9
Braveman—2, Cavanaugh—2,
Lim—2, Hammond—3.

BEN WEBSTER (3) 7
Burley—2, Levin—3, Stacy—2.

GEORGIE AULD (o) 7
Burley—3, Feather—2,
Jovien—2.

DAVE MATTHEWS (o) 6
Hoefer—2, Miller—2, Mize—2.

AL SEARS (o) 5
Goffin—3, Simon—2.

EDDIE MILLER (o) 4
Dexter—2, Smith—2.

BUMPS MYERS (o) 4
Dexter—1, Goffin—1,
Hammond—2.

ARNETTE COBBS (o) 4
Feather—1, Ulanov—3.

EUGENE SEDRIC (1) 2
Goffin—2.

MALE VOCAL

LOUIS ARMSTRONG (11) 31
Avakian—3, Braveman—3,

Cavanaugh—2, Goffin—3,
Hoefer—2, Lim—3, Mize—3,
Russell—3, Smith—3,
Thiele—3, Williams—3.

JOE TURNER (7) 17
Burley—2, Dexter—2,
Feather—3, Hammond—3,
Jax—3, Lim—2, Ulanov—2.

JACK TEAGARDEN (3) 8
Dexter—3, Hoefer—3,
Jovien—2.

LOUIS JORDAN (1) 8
Burley—3, Jovien—3,
Levin—2.

KING COLE (o) 8
Cavanaugh—3, Feather—1,
Stacy—1, Ulanov—3.

EDDIE VINSON (2) 6
Hoefer—1, Jax—1, Jovien—1,
Lim—1, Stacy—2.

BING CROSBY (2) 5
Jax—2, Levin—3.

JAMES RUSHING (2) 4
Smith—2, Thiele—2.

WOODY HERMAN (o) 3
Simon—3.

JOSH WHITE (2) 3
Stacy—3.

RED McKENZIE (o) 2
Simon—2.

LIPS PAGE (o) 2
Feather—2.

CAB CALLOWAY (2) 2
Braveman—2.

BIG BILL BROONZY (o) 2
Hammond—2.

WILLIE DUKES (1) 2
Goffin—2.

BON BON (o) 2
Mize—2.

BAND TABULATION FOR FAVORITE RECORDS

LOUIS ARMSTRONG:

West End Blues 4; Potato Head Blues 3; Mahogany Hall Stomp, Confessin' 2; Savoy Blues, Gully Low Blues, Wild Man Blues, Put 'Em Down Blues, Muskrat Ramble, Ory's Creole Trombone, Dipper Mouth (with J. Dorsey), Shine, Struttin' with Some Barbecue, Sleepy Time Down South (one each).

COUNT BASIE:

Texas Shuffle, Swinging the Blues, Doggin' Around, Lester Leaps In (one each).

SIDNEY BECHET:

Dear Old Southland, Stompy Jones, Sweetie Dear, Wild Man Blues (one each).

BENNY CARTER:

Scandal in A Flat, My Buddy, Fable of a Fool, Melancholy Lullaby (one each).

CHICAGO RHYTHM KINGS:

I've Found a New Baby, There'll Be Some Changes Made (one each).

CHOCOLATE DANDIES:

Dee Blues, Got Another Sweetie Now, Smack (one each).

KING COLE TRIO:

Sweet Lorraine 3; I Can't See for Looking (one).

EDDIE CONDON:

Someday Sweetheart, Strut Miss Lizzie (one each).

BOB CROSBY:

I'm Prayin' Humble, Dogtown Blues, Sugarfoot Strut (one each).

DUKE ELLINGTON:

Ko Ko 3; Reminiscing in Tempo, Cotton Tail, Conga Brava 2; The Gal from Joes, Echoes of Harlem Across the Track Blues, Lazy Rhapsody, Ducky Wucky, Crescendo and Diminuendo in Blue, The Flaming Sword, Subtle Lament, Mood Indigo, Black and Tan Fantasy (Okeh), Blue Serge, All Too Soon, Chelsea Bridge, It's Glory, Sloppy Joe, Giddybug Gallop,

C Jam Blues, Steppin' into Swing Society, It Don't Mean a Thing If It Ain't Got That Swing (one each).

BENNY GOODMAN:

Sometime I'm Happy 3; Blues in Your/My Flat 2; The Shiek, Benny Rides Again, Clarinet à la King, Vibraphone Blues, I Cried for You, Pick-a-Rib, Good Enough to Keep, The World Is Waiting for the Sunrise (one each).

EDMOND HALL:

Royal Garden Blues, Profoundly Blue (one).

LIONEL HAMPTON:

On the Sunny Side of the Street 2; Homeward Bound, Singing the Blues (one each).

COLEMAN HAWKINS:

Body and Soul 3; The Man I Love 2; My Blue Heaven, Honeysuckle Rose (All Stars)—one each.

FLETCHER HENDERSON:

Big John's Special, Yeah Man (one each).

JOHNNY HODGES:

Day Dream 3; Junior Hop (one).

BILLIE HOLIDAY:

Strange Fruit, No Regrets, Fine and Mellow (one each).

BUNK JOHNSON:

Moose March, Panama, St. Louis Blues, Weary Blues (one each).

GEORGE LEWIS:

Careless Love, Climax Rag (one each).

JIMMIE LUNCEFORD:

Uptown Blues, Dream of You (one each).

JELLY ROLL MORTON:

Mamie's Blues, Black Bottom Stomp, West End Blues, The Pearls, Steamboat Stomp, Kansas City Stomps (one each).

MOUND CITY BLUE BLOWERS:

One Hour, Hello Lola, I Can't Believe That You're in Love with Me (one each).

RED NORVO:

Remember 2; Smoke Dreams, I Surrender Dear, Dance of the Octopus, Garden of the Moon, Blues in E Flat (one each).

KING OLIVER:

I Aint' Gonna Tell Nobody 2; Snake Rag, Sugar Foot Stomp (Vocalion), West End Blues (Victor), Canal St. Blues, Mabel's Dream (Okeh) one each.

ARTIE SHAW:

Concerto for Clarinet 2; Two in One Blues, Begin the Beguine (one each).

BESSIE SMITH:

Young Woman Blues 2; Baby Doll, Gimme a Pigfoot, You've Been a Good Ole Wagon (one each).

MUGGSY SPANIER:

Sister Kate 2; Dipper Mouth Blues, Riverboat Shuffle (one each).

FATS WALLER:

Buck Jumpin', I'm Gonna Sit Right Down and Write Myself a Letter (one each).

TEDDY WILSON:

What a Little Moonlight Can Do 3; Miss Brown to You 2; Just a Mood, Don't Blame Me, When You're Smiling (one each).

ONE RECORD ONLY BY THESE BANDS:

Red Allen: Body and Soul. *Mildred Bailey:* Someday Sweetheart. *Charlie Barnet:* Ring Dem Bells. *Bunny Berigan:* Davenport Blues. *Chu Berry:* Blowing Up a Breeze. *Commodore All-Stars:* Embraceable You. *Bill Davison:* That's a Plenty. *Original Dixeland Jazz Band:* Tiger Rag. *Gene Gifford:* New Orleans Twist. *Bobby Hackett:* Embraceable You. *Eddie Heywood:* I Cover the Waterfront. *Earl Hines:* Blues in Thirds. *Spike Hughes:* Sweet Sorrow Blues. *Jack Jenney:* Stardust. *Buddy John-*

son: Boogie Woogie's Mother-in-Law. *Louis Jordan:* Is You or Is You Ain't. *Kansas City Six:* Pagin' the Devil. *Andy Kirk:* Moten Swing. *Tommy Ladnier and Ida Cox:* Coffin Blues. *Meade Lux Lewis:* Honky Tonk Train Blues. *Wingy Manone:* Panama. *Mezz Mezzrow:* Apologies. *Glenn Miller:* Tuxedo Junction. *Miff Mole:* Shimme-Sha-Wabble. *New Orleans Rhythm Kings:* Shimme-Sha-Wabble. *Mel Powell:* The World Is Waiting for the Sunrise. *Ma Rainey:* Jelly Bean Blues. *Don Redman:* Chant of the Weed. *Ruben Reeves:* Zuddan. *Luis Russell:* Ease on Down. *Zutty Singleton:* King Porter Stomp. *Willie (The Lion) Smith:* What Is There to Say. *Eddie South-Stephane Grappelly:* Variations on Bach D Minor Concerto. *Erskine Tate:* Stomp Off Let's Go. *Art Tatum:* Wee Baby Blues. *Jack Teagarden:* Muddy River Blues. *Frankie Trumbauer:* Riverboat Shuffle. *The Wolverines:* Shimme-Sha-Wabble. *Jimmy Yancey:* Jimmy's Stuff. *Lester Young:* Sometimes I'm Happy.

MUSICIANS' POINT TABULATION

for *Esquire's All-American New Stars*

TRUMPET

	Total Points
DIZZY GILLESPIE	5
Braveman–1, Dexter–1, Jax–1, Stacy–1, Ulanov–1.	
JESSE MILLER	2
Hoefer–1, Feather–1.	
JOE THOMAS	2
Cavanaugh–1, Lim–1.	
EMMETT BERRY	1
Hammond–1.	
SHORTY SHEROK	1
Jovien–1.	
EDDIE ROANE	1
Miller–1.	
CAT ANDERSON	1
Simon–1.	
BENNY STRICKLER	1
Avakian–1.	
FRANK HUMPHRIES	1
Burley–1.	

TRUMPET (*cont'd*)

	Total Points
RAY NANCE	1
Thiele–1.	
JOHNNY WINDHURST	1
Goffin–1.	
ROYCE JANSZEN	1
Mize–1.	

TROMBONE

BILL HARRIS	4
Feather–1, Jax–1, Lim–1, Stacy–1.	
J. J. JOHNSON	3
Burley–1, Dexter–1, Ulanov–1.	
FORD CANFIELD	2
Jovien–1, Miller–1.	
TOMMY PEDERSON	2
Braveman–1, Hoefer–1.	

TROMBONE (*cont'd*)

	Total Points
RAY CONIFF	1
Goffin—1.	
TYREE GLENN	1
Cavanaugh—1.	
THEODORE DONNELLY	1
Simon—1.	
GEORGE LUGG	1
Avakian—1.	
FRED BECKETT	1
Hammond—1.	
AL LEPOL	1
Mize—1.	

STRING BASS

CHUBBY JACKSON	6
Feather—1, Hoefer—1,	
Miller—1, Simon—1,	
Thiele—1, Ulanov—1.	
AL HALL	3
Cavanaugh—1, Levin—1,	
Lim—1.	
JOHN LEVY	2
Hoefer—1, Jovien—1.	
EUGENE RAMEY	2
Dexter—1, Jovien—1.	
JOHN SIMMONS	2
Burley—1, Hammond—1.	
ED GARLAND	2
Avakian—1, Russell—1.	
RED CALLENDER	2
Hammond—1, Ulanov—1.	
LYNN MANO	1
Mize—1.	

FEMALE VOCAL

ANITA O'DAY	4
Feather—1, Mize—1,	
Simons—1, Stacy—1.	

FEMALE VOCAL (*cont'd*)

	Total Points
BETTY ROCHÉ	3
Cavanangh—1, Thiele—1,	
Ulanov—1.	
PEGGY LEE	2
Dexter—1, Hoefer—1.	
DINAH WASHINGTON	2
Feather—1, Lim—1.	
THELMA CARPENTER	1
Jovien—1.	
LIZ TILTON	1
Simon—1.	
ANN CORNELL	1
Burley—1.	
EVELYN KNIGHT	1
Hammond—1.	
SAVANNAH CHURCHILL	1
Jax—1.	
ESTELLA YANCEY	1
Avakian—1.	

GUITAR

REMO PALMIERI	9
Cavanaugh—1, Feather—1,	
Goffin—1, Jovien—1,	
Levin—1, Lim—1, Miller—1,	
Simon—1, Ulanov—1.	
TEDDY WALTERS	5
Burley—1, Braveman—1,	
Jax—1, Lim—1, Thiele—1.	
HY WHITE	3
Dexter—1, Hoefer—1,	
Jovien—1.	
MARY OSBORNE	1
Feather—1.	
BOBBY SHERWOOD	1
Hoefer—1.	
ZEB JULIAN	1
Stacy—1.	

OTHER INSTRUMENTS

Total
Points

RAY NANCE, violin 6
Feather—1, Lim—1, Simon—1,
Stacy—1, Thiele—1,
Ulanov—1.
MAX MILLER, vibraharp 3
Hoefer—1, Jovien—1,
Miller—1.
ERNIE CACERES, baritone sax ... 2
Cavanaugh—1, Goffin—1.
WILLARD BROWN 1
Dexter—1.
JIMMY SMITH, vibraharp 1
Burley—1.
PETER GRAHAM, vibraharp 1
Hammond—1.
EMILIO CACERES, violin 1
Mize—1.

TENOR SAXOPHONE

FLIP PHILLIPS 6
Burley—1, Cavanaugh—1,
Jax—1, Jovien—1,
Miller—1, Thiele—1.
BUMPS MYERS 3
Dexter—1, Goffin—1,
Hammond—1.
CHARLIE VENTURO 2
Hoefer—1, Simon—1.
ARNETTE COBBS 2
Feather—1, Ulanov—1.
DON BYAS 2
Braveman—1, Lim—1.
EUGENE AMMONS 1
Hammond—1.
HERBIE FIELDS 1
Stacy—1.
JESSE WEBB 1
Mize—1.

TENOR SAXOPHONE (*cont'd*)

Total
Points

BOB DUKOFF 1
Ulanov—1.

ALTO SAXOPHONE

HERBIE FIELDS 4
Cavanaugh—1, Feather—1,
Jax—1, Thiele—1.
GEORGIE AULD 1
Ulanov—1.
EARL BOSTIC 1
Burley—1.
BOOTS MUSSULLI 1
Miller—1.
BILL SHINE 1
Simon—1.
JOHNNY BOTHWELL 1
Stacy—1.
VERNON MAYFIELD 1
Mize—1.
EDDIE VINSON 1
Hammond—1.
GEORGE JOHNSON 1
Goffin—1.
RAY DEGEER 1
Jovien—1.
JOHNNY BOARD 1
Hoefer—1.

MALE VOCAL

EDDIE VINSON 5
Hoefer—1, Jax—1, Jovien—1,
Lim—1, Stacy—1.
KING COLE 4
Cavanaugh—1, Feather—1,
Stacy—1, Ulanov—1.
PEANUTS HOLLAND 1
Ulanov—1.

MALE VOCAL (*cont'd*)

	Total Points
BENNY GOODMAN	1
Simon—1.	
WYNONIE HARRIS	1
Burley—1.	
WALTER BROWN	1
Dexter—1.	
T-BONE WALKER	1
Hammond—1.	
WALTER PICHON	1
Goffin—1.	
DON CANNON	1
Mize—1.	
FRANKIE LAINE	1
Levin—1.	
AL HIBBLER	1
Cavanaugh—1.	

ARRANGER

	Total Points
JOHNNY THOMPSON	4
Levin—1, Lim—1,	
Hammond—1, Simon—1.	
RALPH BURNS	3
Hoefer—1, Jovien—1,	
Miller—1.	
STAN KENTON	2
Dexter—1, Stacy—1.	
GEORGE HANDY	2
Feather—1, Simon—1.	
CHARLIE MITCHELL	1
Mize—1.	
FRED NORMAN	1
Burley—1.	
DIZZY GILLESPIE	1
Braveman—1.	
BRICK FLEAGLE	1
Cavanaugh—1.	
EDDIE FINKEL	1
Simon—1.	

ARMED FORCES FAVORITE

	Total Points
MEL POWELL, piano	6
Burley—1, Braveman—1,	
Feather—1, Goffin—1,	
Jax—1, Stacy—1.	
JAY McSHANN, piano	3
Dexter—1, Hoefer—1,	
Jovien—1.	
GERALD WIGGINS, piano	2
Feather—1, Ulanov—1.	
MIKE SIMPSON, clarinet	1
Miller—1.	
HARRY DIVITO, trombone	1
Simon—1.	
SHELLEY MANNE, drums	1
Thiele—1.	
WELDON SCHEEL, arranger	1
Mize—1.	
WILLIE ANDERSON, piano	1
Hammond—1.	
DICK CARY, piano	1
Avakian—1.	
HAROLD BAKER, trumpet	1
Lim—1.	
EDDIE BERT	1
Cavanaugh—1.	
SAM DONAHUE, tenor sax	1
Stacy—1.	
GEORGE BARNES, guitar	1
Jovien—1.	

PIANO

	Total Points
EDDIE HEYWOOD	4
Braveman—1, Jax—1,	
Stacy—1, Thiele—1.	
STAN WRIGHTSMAN	2
Dexter—1, Miller—1.	

PIANO (*cont'd*)

	Total Points
MILTON BUCKNER	2
Feather—1, Ulanov—1.	
HERMAN CHITTISON	2
Cavanaugh—1, Goffin—1.	
BILL CLIFTON	1
Simon—1.	
MARLOWE MORRIS	1
Burley—1.	
JIMMY JONES	1
Hammond—1.	
BILLY TAYLOR	1
Lim—1.	
FLOYD BEAN	1
Hoefer—1.	
BUSTER WILSON	1
Avakian—1.	

DRUMS

SPECS POWELL	6
Cavanaugh—1, Hammond—1,	
Jax—1, Levin—1, Stacy—1,	
Ulanov—1.	
MAX ROACH	4
Burley—1, Simons—1,	
Thiele—1, Ulanov—1.	
ALVIN BURROUGHS	3
Feather—1, Hoefer—1,	
Miller—1.	
WILLIAM SHIRLEY DAVIS	1
Mize—1.	
BABY LOVETT	1
Dexter—1.	
J. C. HEARD	1
Lim—1.	
JOE GRAUSO	1
Avakian—1.	
GEORGE JENKINS	1
Braveman—1.	

CLARINET

	Total Points
AARON SACHS	6
Braveman—1, Cavanaugh—1,	
Feather—1, Goffin—1,	
Jax—1, Lim—1.	
RUDY RUTHERFORD	3
Burley—1, Hammond—1,	
Ulanov—1.	
WADE WHALEY	2
Avakian—1, Williams—1.	
BUDDY DE FRANCO	2
Simon—1, Stacy—1.	
HANK D'AMICO	1
Miller—1.	
HEINIE BEAU	1
Dexter—1.	

ORCHESTRA

LIONEL HAMPTON	6
Burley—1, Feather—1,	
Goffin—1, Mize—1,	
Simon—1, Ulanov—1.	
MAX KAMINSKY	3
Avakian—1, Goffin—1,	
Smith—1.	
EDDIE HEYWOOD	2
Cavanaugh—1, Hammond—1.	
HAL McINTYRE	1
Jovien—1.	
COOTIE WILLIAMS	1
Hammond—1.	
GEORGIE AULD	1
Simon—1.	
HERBIE FIELDS	1
Burley—1.	
JIMMY HILLIARD	1
Miller—1.	
BOYD RAEBURN	1
Stacy—1.	
STAN KENTON	1
Dexter—1.	

Chapter VI

The Jazz Scene—1944

Events of the Year

Compiled by PAUL EDUARD MILLER

OCTOBER 1943

NEW YORK's Savoy Ballroom, after being closed for six months, reopens Oct. 22 with Cootie Williams' Orchestra and Savoy Sultans.

Leon Rappolo, historical jazz clarinetist, dies in New Orleans, Oct. 15, at the age of 41. Rappolo was organizer of New Orleans Rhythm Kings which played Chicago's Friar's Inn in 1922.

Muggsy Spanier organizes band in Hollywood.

Tommy Dorsey appears as guest soloist with Werner Janssen symphony orchestra at Wilshire Ebell Theatre, Hollywood.

Jack Ryan and Nate Kazebier leave Jimmy Dorsey in favor of studio work on West Coast.

In Philadelphia Woody Herman collapses from nervous exhaustion and is forced to leave the stand for ten days.

NOVEMBER 1943

Victor appeals AFM recording ban to WLB, and formal hearings begin Nov. 3.

Count Basie and band open in New York's Hotel Lincoln as first colored band to play that spot.

Benny Goodman begins teaching lecture course at Julliard School of Music. Subject: The Clarinet.

George Wettling leaves Abe Lyman to join Eddie Condon's Greenwich Village group which now includes Bob Hackett, Miff Mole, Brad Gowans, Pee Wee Russell, Art Hodes and Sterling Bose.

Frankie Carlson organizes new band.

Les Paul, gtr. and quartet, in Hollywood to do sustaining show for NBC.

Metronome Magazine denounces Harry Schooler Ballrooms (California) for discriminating against Negro talent.

Calvin Jackson, Harry James' arranger, quits band to join music staff of M-G-M.

Zutty Singleton joins T-Bone Walker band in Los Angeles.

DECEMBER 1943

Duke Ellington sells out Carnegie Hall week in advance with second engagement (December 11), premiering *New World a'Comin'*. Other concerts at Washington, D. C., Cleveland, Pittsburgh, Boston, Philadelphia and Chicago. New band members include Skippy Williams, replacing Ben Webster on tenor, Jimmy Hamilton, replacing Chauncey Haughton (inducted) and Al Hibbler, vocalist. New York newspaper critics reacting variously to jazz concerts, New York *Herald Tribune* and *Daily News* omitting even a notice, *Daily Mirror* and *World Telegram* reporting pieces not played and others showing complete ignorance of jazz music.

WLB concludes hearings on AFM dispute with recording companies. Recommend legislation.

Jack Teagarden dissolves band to settle down in Long Beach, Calif., because of his health, engaging in local one-nighters with pick-up band, including Joe Sullivan.

Clarence Hutchenrider leaves Casa Loma band because of his health.

Fats Waller, great pianist of jazz and composer of *Honeysuckle Rose, Minor Drag, Ain't Misbehavin'* and other famous tunes, dies Dec. 15, on board Santa Fe Flier in Union Station, Kansas City, at the age of 39, enroute to New York. Funeral in Harlem.

Commodore and other small companies sign new recording pacts with AFM.

Jazz Concert Society, directed by Eddie Condon begins Saturday afternoon Town Hall Jazz Concerts in New York Dec. 18, leading off with Fats Waller Memorial Concert, featuring pianists James P. Johnson and Art Hodes, trumpeter Max Kaminsky, and clarinetist Pee Wee Russell.

Benny Goodman voted King of Swing for 5th (not consecutive) time in *Down Beat* Magazine's annual band poll, Duke Ellington polling second place and Charlie Barnet third.

Gene Krupa quits Goodman band, joining Tommy Dorsey at Paramount Theatre, N. Y.

Miami, Fla. Local rules that Fletcher Henderson cannot play in Miami because of three white musicians in band.

Herbie Fields, discharged from Army, organizes new band.

Top-flight bands, including Basie, Goodman, Glenn Miller, Tommy Dorsey and Ellington, under special permission from Petrillo, make records for U. S. Army use.

Al Sears, tenor, gives up leadership of band to join Lionel Hampton.

INDUCTED IN ARMY: Jimmy Mundy, Buck Clayton (Basie), Tony Briglia (Casa Loma).

INDUCTED IN NAVY: Freddie Slack, Jack Jenney.

JANUARY 1944

Concert at the Metropolitan Opera House in New York, Jan. 18, by *Esquire* Magazine's All-American Jazz Band, selected by a board of 16 experts on jazz music.

As an adjunct to the above concert, publication of ESQUIRE'S JAZZ BOOK, celebrating the 10th year of positive support by a national non-musical magazine, of jazz music and its recognition as an American art form.

Sam Donahue takes over Artie Shaw's Navy Band, The Rangers, upon Shaw's return to West Coast.

Freddie Slack, released from Navy on medical discharge, reorganizes band.

Lee Castle, Benny Goodman trumpeter, leaves band to conduct his own.

Louis Armstrong breaks up band to assemble another, with the help of Teddy McRae.

Red Norvo reorganizes small group.

Dave Tough given medical discharge from Navy.

Radio station WNEW conducts first annual *Swing Festival Week*, Jan. 16-22, with programs by jazz musicians and critics.

Barney Bigard rejoins Freddie Slack, cancelling plans for his own band.

Clarence Hutchenrider sues Casa Loma band for accounting.

Billie Rogers, formerly with Woody Herman, appears in Chicago with her own group. Herman files complaint with Union re contract breaches by Miss Rogers.

Frankie Carlson (Woody Herman) and Shorty Sherock (Jimmy Dorsey) join Horace Heidt.

Artur Rodzinski, conductor of N. Y. Philharmonic Orchestra denounces boogie-woogie as "one of the greatest cause of delinquency among American youth today." Voices from other quarters are heard immediately, including the following: Leopold

Stokowski: "Modern American Music—boogie-woogie, jive and swing—will in time be absorbed into American art music. In fact, it has already begun." Micha Elman (violinist): "Modern swing is merely the social outlet of our city just as folk dancing goes on in the country, not all our youth go in for it, but those who do, it cannot harm." Dr. Sandor Lorand (psychologist): "This brings us to the question of whether a type of music *can* be a contributing factor in juvenile delinquency. My answer is definitely No." Maurice Lieberman (teacher): "The kind doctor (Rodzinski) may be able to satisfy his 'chorsuct' on his Berkshire farm with a lilting waltz. The world doesn't lilt today. It rocks, it staggers, it reels, it writhes, shudders and quivers—well, that's swing." Many felt Rodzinski's comments were a cheap attempt at publicity.

BOOKS ON JAZZ: *Jazz, from Congo to Met*, by Robert Goffin. ESQUIRE'S JAZZ BOOK, edited by Paul Eduard Miller. *The Story of Jazz*, by Rex Harris (culled from a series of BBC broadcasts in London).

INDUCTED IN ARMY: Bill Davidson, Maurice Purtill, Eddie Miller, Red Dorris (Stan Kenton), Skeets Herfurt.

FEBRUARY 1944

Artie Shaw receives medical discharge from Navy.

Barney Bigard leads all-white band in California, is denied membership in white musicians' union.

Lafayette Theatre in Detroit files a 500,000 dollar suit against Petrillo on stand-in orchestra dispute.

Memorial to Scott Joplin, composer of *Maple Leaf Rag*, planned by S. Brun Campbell, a friend of Joplin's now living in Venice, California.

Musicraft records announces entry in jazz field.

Bob Haggart and Billy Butterfield working for NBC Blue network.

Nappy LaMare, formerly of Bob Crosby band and Eddie Miller's Dixieland band, forms own group in Hollywood with Zutty Singleton, Joe Sullivan and Doc Rando.

Joe Rushton, bass sax, joins Horace Heidt.

Bob Zurke dies of pneumonia Feb. 16, at Los Angeles Gen'l Hospital, at the age of 33. One of the best-liked among jazz pianists, Zurke achieved wide recognition in 1936 when he played with the Bob Crosby orchestra, replacing pianist Joe Sullivan. Zurke was playing at the Hangover Club, Los Angeles, as a single.

John Kirby reorganizes band.

Wallace Jones leaves Duke Ellington, is replaced by Shelton Hemphill (from Armstrong).

Red Nichols joins Glen Gray orchestra after spending some time in defense plant.

Al Morgan joins Louis Jordan.

Sandy Williams, formerly with Henderson, Webb and Ellington, goes to work in post office.

Walter R. Price, 32, formerly with Glenn Miller and Tommy Dorsey, dies in New York City, Feb. 11.

BOOKS ON JAZZ: *This Is Jazz*, by Rudi Blesh, compiled from a series of lectures at San Francisco Museum of Art. In preparation: *Let's Listen—A. Thesaurus of American Music*, by J. T. H. Mize, school teacher and author of weekly publication on jazz used in high schools.

INDUCTED IN ARMY: Cappy Lewis, Jack Teagarden, Jr. (Jack Teagarden).

MARCH 1944

Duke Ellington, along with Béla Bartók and Igor Stravinsky of the classical domain, honored by special recitals at Boston and Harvard universities.

Flip Phillips   Bill Harris   Anita O'Day   Aaron Sachs

New Star winners: both tenorman Phillips and trombonist Harris joined the great Woody Herman band in 1944. Vocalist O'Day served the Stan Kenton band, while clarinetist Sachs made news with Norvo. O'Day photo by Charlie Mihn; Phillips & Harris by Robert Alderson.

Ray Nance   Herbie Fields   Lionel Hampton   Eddie Heywood

New Star winners: Nance for his violin, Fields for his alto, Hampton for his band, Heywood for his piano. Least known nationally are Fields, who leads his own big band; Heywood, who fronts a small group. Fields photo by Bruno of Hollywood; Heywood by Down Beat—Ivan Black.

Johnny Thompson   Eddie Vinson   Mel Powell   Specs Powell

New Star winners: arranger Thompson, now writes for Harry James; singer Vinson also adds altoing to his duties with Cootie Williams; pianist Powell plays with the Glenn Miller A.A.F. unit; drummer Specs with CBS staff. Powell photos by Down Beat, Specs by Ehrenberg.

Edmond Hall   Harry Carney   Dave Tough

These three All-American Silver Award winners not only displayed the high quality of their talents during 1944, but all three can point as well to more than ten years of name-band activities—no mean record. Tough photo by Robert Alderson; Carney photo by Irvin Glaser.

Chubby Jackson   Remo Palmieri   Dizzy Gillespie

Among the most talked about new talent of the year were these three winners in Esquire's New Stars Band. Each helped to make the band with which he worked a better-than-average musical success. Jackson photo by Robert Alderson; Palmieri photo by Carl J. Oppenheimer.

Horace Henderson discharged after year in Army, joins brother Fletcher as pianist.

Freddy Johnson returns to U. S. after two years in Nazi concentration camp.

Don Redman's band refuses to tour South because of Jim Crow practices.

Carpenter's Mate 1st Class Clifton Case (Bunny Berigan, Jan Savitt) cited for bravery in North Africa.

Capt. Glenn Miller offered seven-year contract at 20th Century-Fox.

Nappy LaMare to take over band of Eddie Miller (inducted). LaMare and Miller played in the Bob Crosby band of the thirties.

Al Sears leaves Lionel Hampton with several other Hampton men, to form own band.

Benny Goodman breaks up band in Hollywood after fracas with booking agency, MCA.

WLB decides in favor of recording companies against AFM on recording ban which they characterize as "strike" by musicians.

Orson Welles presents radio program on CBS including Jimmie Noone, Zutty Singleton, Kid Ory, Edward Garland, Buster Wilson, Bud Scott, Papa Carey. Welles reported planning movie of development of jazz.

Harry Schooler, West Coast ballroom owner, charged by jazz press of racial discrimination, goes to jail on morals count.

Stan Kenton in hospital for appendectomy.

Ted McKay, saxophonists, formerly with Bob Crosby, dies after long illness.

Muggsy Spanier in auto accident, joins Miff Mole upon recovery.

Gene Krupa files appeal on felony charge in San Francisco.

Wini Johnson leaves cast of *Early to Bed* to vocalize for Duke Ellington.

Damon Runyon, humorist, writes defense of jazz occasioned by Hearst writer's attacks on Robert Goffin's newest book.

Billy Butterfield leading own band for Blue Network.

Everett McLaughlin, tnr., and Ernie Figueroa, trp., cleared of marijuana charges in Los Angeles.

Oscar Moore, discharged by Army after few weeks' service, returns to King Cole group.

Barney Bigard premieres new band in Los Angeles.

Charlie Barnet breaks up band to take rest.

Down Beat Magazine reports Government hospitals studying effects of marijuana on musicians.

INDUCTED IN ARMY: Alan Reuss, Manzie Johnson (Don Redman), Eddie Miller.

APRIL 1944

Jimmie Noone, 48, veteran jazz clarinetist, dies suddenly on Apr. 19 at Los Angeles, where his Quartet had been featured at the Streets of Paris during the past year. He was also one of the featured musicians on the Orson Welles jazz program.

Hy White, gtr., forsakes Woody Herman for teaching profession.

Slick Jones, drs. formerly with Fats Waller, joins Louis Jordan.

Gene Sedric seriously ill in Boston Hospital.

Joe Venuti becomes music director for Duffy's Tavern radio show.

Juan Tizol, long-time Ellington trombonist and composer of *Caravan, Perdido*, et al., joins Harry James. Claude Jones replaces Tizol in Ellington organization. Dave Tough joins Woody Herman. Illinois Jacquet leaves Cab Calloway to lead own band.

Webster's New International Dictionary (second edition) produces a definition of jazz, as follows: "A type of American music, especially for dances, developed from ragtime by the introduction of eccentric noises and Negro melodies and now characterized by melodious themes and varied orchestral colorings."

Irving Fazola returns to his native New Orleans because of bad health.

Billy Eckstine forms band in New York, including Bud Johnson on sax and Dizzy Gillespie on trumpet.

Buster Bailey rejoins John Kirby.

American Youth for Democracy holds Fats Waller Memorial Concert at Carnegie Hall, Apr. 2, featuring Teddy Wilson orchestra, James P. Johnson, Count Basie orchestra, Earl Hines, Duke Ellington, Al Casey, Mary Lou Williams, Willie (The Lion) Smith, Trummy Young, Ben Webster, Sid Catlett, et al.

INDUCTED IN ARMY: Harold Baker (Ellington). MARINES: Vido Musso (Herman).

MAY 1944

Gene Krupa freed of felony charges in California.

The Needle, a new small magazine on jazz, goes to press in Jackson Heights, N. Y.

Frankie Carlson leaves Horace Heidt to work in war plant and loses tip of thumb in accident.

Tony Sbarbaro, drs. and Brad Gowans, trb., with Katherine Dunham dance group.

Billy Taylor (ex-Ellington bassman and NBC artist) joins Cootie Williams band.

Dave Hudkins, drummer, turns to hillbilly bandleading. Jack Jenney receives medical discharge from Navy.

Bill Harris, Benny Goodman trombonist organizes new group at Café Society Uptown.

Buddy Rich discharged from Marines.

Joe Haymes starts new band in California with Phil Dooley

on drums. Eddie Sauter, arranger, leaves Benny Goodman to work for Tommy Dorsey.

Barney Bigard joins Orson Welles' group on West Coast in place of Jimmie Noone, also leading own band in Los Angeles night spot.

Mildred Bailey has her own radio show for CBS, features Red Norvo, Roy Eldridge, Teddy Wilson, Remo Palmieri.

John Mitchell, returned to U. S. after being prisoner of war, joins Jimmie Lunceford as guitarist.

Basie and men in difficulty with Local 802 for playing other than as unit in New York.

Harry James opens in New York with revised lineup, including Juan Tizol, trb., Claude Lakey, alto, Alan Reuss, gtr., Ed Mihelich, bass.

National Jazz Foundation plans museum on Saratoga Street, which will be changed back to its original name of Basin Street, number 225 of which is the site of Madame Lulu White's Mahogany Hall, proposed site of Museum.

Orson Welles conducts radio memorial program of New Orleans jazz to honor the late Jimmie Noone.

Woody Herman-Billie Rogers controversy contract decided by AFM in favor of Rogers, who left Herman to go into retirement, married and reappeared with her own group, with husband as manager.

Muggsy Spanier returns to Ted Lewis band, which already boasts two other New Orleans jazzmen: Georg Brunis and Tony Parenti.

Tenorman Al Sears joins Ellington, replacing Skippy Williams.

Zutty Singleton joins Teddy Bunn in Hollywood. In Los Angeles the former Armstrong drummer, Jesse Price, forms own group.

Trumpeter Max Kaminsky opens in Greenwich Village leading Rod Cless, clar., Frank Orchard, trb., Fred Mason, pf., Mc-Grath, drs.

Charlie Venal, Boston clarinetist invalided by polio and mainspring of Boston's local jazz, dies April 26 of a cold.

Sweet bandleader Art Kassel tells press: "Jazz has created a Frankenstein monster!"—meaning hot jazz.

Henry (Hank) Biagini, 39, leader of the original Casa Loma orchestra, killed in an auto accident May 13 at Detroit. Tiny Harris, bass, injured in same crash.

Eddie Condon's Town Hall jazz concerts get Saturday afternoon radio time on the Blue Network out of New York.

Altoman Tab Smith organizes new group.

Tommy Dorsey enlarges band to 39 pieces, including 15 strings, harp and bass horn, for a concert tour.

Violinist Emilio Caceres leaves T. Dorsey to organize own band.

JUNE 1944

Albert Gandee, 44, one-time trombonist with The Wolverines, dies June 3 in an auto accident in Cincinnati.

Billie Holiday gets first movie contract from Warner Brothers.

Joe Marsala returns to Hickory House, New York, with wife Adele Girard on harp.

Jean Goldkette, famous leader of the '20's, organizes new small combination in Detroit.

Miff Mole in hospital for operation.

Esquire Magazine inaugurates regular monthly department on jazz music—*The Rhythm Section.*

Benny Goodman stars with Leopold Stokowski in new Walt Disney film-musical *Swing Street* to be released in 1945. Records sound track with hand-picked band.

Trumpeter Peanuts Holland joins Charlie Barnet. Guitarist

Tommy Kay leaves T. Dorsey to join Raymond Scott; Charlie Shavers quits Scott to lead own band.

Gene Krupa organizes new band in New York. Personnel includes Tommy Pederson, trb., Charlie Venturo, tnr., Remo Biondi, gtr.—and nine strings. Buddy Rich fills vacancy left by Krupa in T. Dorsey band.

INDUCTIONS: Jerry Wiggins (Benny Carter pianist); Nate Kazebier, former J. Dorsey trumpeter, who joined Meredith Willson Army band, in which Babe Russin blows the tenor.

JULY 1944

O'Neill Spencer, drummer (John Kirby, Blue Rythm Band) dies July 24, in New York, after two years of illness.

Tenth anniversary of *Down Beat* Magazine.

Roy Eldridge switches to large band of seven brass, five reed, four percussion.

Musicians in New York raise 1,115,088,785 dollars in one day of Fifth War Loan drive with daily concerts in Times Square. Another drive contributed 2,000,000 dollars to the purchase of a Liberty Ship to be known as the Bert Williams.

Will Marion Cook, 75, famous Negro composer and leader, dies in Harlem hospital July 19, after long illness.

Victor anounces reinstatement of 118 old jazz records previously cut out of catalogue.

Tommy and Jimmy Dorsey and Harry James join in partnership purchase of Casino Gardens Ballroom, Ocean Park, Calif. Rename spot The Colonnades.

Nappy Lamare (NBC Studio) organizes small band in Los Angeles including Matty Matlock, clar., Nick Fatool, drs.

V-Discs radio show featuring live recording sessions goes on air July 31 for benefit of Armed Services, with top name bands.

Horace Henderson joins Lena Horne as arranger and accompanist at Chez Paree in Chicago.

Sid Catlett and Eddie South get six months' contract at L.A.'s Street of Paris.

Capitol Records releases annotated album entitled *New American Jazz*.

AUGUST 1944

Cecil Mack (Richard C. McPherson), 61, composer of *Runnin' Wild*, dies Aug. 1 in New York.

Boyd Raeburn ousted from Palisades Park, N. J., by disastrous fire which destroyed entire library of orchestra.

S-D Records of Chicago becomes first recording company to put entire catalogue on wire spools providing indestructible records, retailing at a dollar ten per spool of two complete sides.

Jive Jamboree held in Shrine Auditorium, Los Angeles, jazz bands being enlisted to pull the Los Angeles Philharmonic out of its deficit.

United States Health Service tests on effects of marijuana on musicians prove that marijuana impairs musical efficiency although subjects believe their ability is improved.

Red Nichols organizes new band in L.A.

Jimmie Noone Memorial Concert, sponsored by Musicians' Congress, held at Trocadero on West Coast, 800 present netting 1,000 dollars for family.

Medical discharge: Eddie Miller, from Army.

SEPTEMBER 1944

Musicians' Congress and UCLA hold convention in Los Angeles Sept. 14—Music in Contemporary Life—for the purpose of "attempting to define the function of music in society, to evaluate its achievements in all fields of activity, to mobilize music and musicians in the present struggle to create a free world and to utilize the positive force that is music in the peace to follow." Of interest to jazz fans was the recognition of jazz music as an art form by representatives of all branches of music. Artie Shaw, chairman of jazz forum, proposes foundation for allowing talented composers and musicians to work free of economic instability.

Richard (Dick) Voynow, 44, one-time pianist with The Wolverines, dies in California after a long illness. Voynow was an executive for Deca Records at the time of his death.

Benny Goodman signs with Billy Rose to play with a quartet in the stage production, *The Seven Lively Arts,* scheduled for a December 1944 Broadway appearance.

Woody Herman hires new vibraharp discovery, Marjorie Hyams.

After medical discharge from Navy, trumpeter Yank Lawson plans organization of new band.

Bobby Hackett joins Glen Gray in Chicago. Former Stan Kenton tenorman Red Dorris forms small group on West Coast, while drummer Cliff Leeman organizes band with string quartet, three horns, three rhythm.

Joe Sherman, manager of Garrick Stage Bar, Chicago, slashed with knife on behalf of colored soldiers returning from three years overseas fighting, who claim Sherman refused them admittance to his Randolph Street pub, which has gained wide popularity and been highly successful through the use of colored musicians.

The newly organized National Jazz Foundation in New Orleans conducts highly successful jazz concert, featuring Benny Goodman Quartet with Teddy Wilson, Irving Fazola, Monk Hazel, Sidney Desvigne, Oct. 4 and 5. Sustaining membership (3 dollars per year) in the National Jazz Foundation is open to anybody. Purposes of foundation: (1) To build a Jazz Museum in

New Orleans where the historical evidences of hot music will be recorded, preserved and exhibited for all time to come. (2) To accumulate a complete and authentic fund of jazz data and history and place it at the service of writers, motion-picture studios, radio broadcasters, historians and any others who may be interested. (3) To establish a radio program on a national hook-up to acquaint the world with our aims and progress and to publish a periodical with more specific information and distribute it to members all over the world. (4) To open membership rolls to everyone, everywhere, who may be interested, and to attract to New Orleans and the museum, these members and others who may become interested.

DISCOGRAPHY OF THE YEAR

Compiled by LEONARD FEATHER

The year 1944 was the great jazz recording renaissance. So numerous were the new companies that sprang up overnight to assemble jazz waxing sessions that a complete tabulation of the year's activities would be almost impossible to achieve.

In the following pages I have attempted to list virtually all sessions made by the leading independent record companies between Oct. 1, 1943, and Oct. 1, 1944, as well as some of the rare jazz dates made by the larger companies. In many cases the records have been held in reserve for release after the war. If the records listed have been released, the catalogue number is listed immediately after the two titles issued. Other titles recorded at the same session and as yet unreleased (October 1944) are listed without any number following them. I should be grateful if any important errors of omission or commission are called to my attention.

Abbreviations: trp—trumpet; trb—trombone; tnr—tenor; pf —piano; gtr—guitar; drs—drums; clar—clarinet; bar—baritone sax; vio—violin.

AMMONS, ALBERT Rhythm Kings
Commodore, Feb. 1944. Lips Page, trp; Vic Dickenson, trb; Don Byas, tnr; Ammons, pf; Sid Catlett, drs; Israel Crosby, bass.
Jammin' the Boogie/Bottom Blues. 1516.

AULD-HAWKINS-WEBSTER Saxtet
Apollo, 5/17/44. Georgie Auld, tnr alto; Coleman Hawkins, tnr; Ben Webster, tnr and clar; Charlie Shavers, trp; Bill Rowland, pf; Hy White, gtr; Specs Powell, drs; Israel Crosby, bass.
Salt Peanuts/Porgy/Reunion in Harlem/Pick-Up Boys.

BERRY, EMMETT Orchestra
National, Sept. 1944. Emmett Berry, trp; Don Byas, tnr; Dave Rivera, pf; J. C. Heard, drs; Milton Hinton, bass.
Sweet & Lovely/White Rose Kick/Byas'd Opinions/Deep Blue Dream.

BIGARD, BARNEY Trio
Signature, 1/22/44. Barney Bigard, clar; Eddie Heywood, pf; Shelley Manne, drs.
Tea for Two/Moonglow/Step Steps Up/Step Steps Down.

BOWMAN, DAVE
Signature, 6/24/44. Piano solos.
Rosetta / You're Blasé / She's Funny That Way/Blues.

BRADLEY, WILL & his Boogie-Woogie Boys
Celebrity, 1943. Billy Butterfield, trp; Will Bradley, trb; Paul Ricci, clar; Johnny Guarnieri, pf; Billy Gussak, drs; Bob Haggart, bass.
Cryin' the Boogie Blues/Jingle Bells Boogie-Woogie. 7013. *Sugar Hill Boogie-Woogie / Lightning Boogie.* 7014.

BROWN, PETE and various combinations
Savoy, 7/11/44. Pete Brown, alto; Kenny Watts; pf; Al Casey, gtr; Eddie Nicholson, drs; Al Matthews, bass.
Bellevue for You/Pete Brown's Boogie. 522. *The Blues/Ooh-Wee.*
Keynote, 7/19/44. Joe Thomas, trp; Pete Brown, alto; Kenneth Kersey, pf; J. C. Heard, drs; Milton Hinton, bass.
It All Depends on You/It's the Talk of the Town/I May Be Wrong/That's My Weakness Now.
Savoy, 8/1/44. Pete Brown, alto & voc; Kenney Watts, pf; Herman Mitchell, gtr; Eddie Nicholson, drs; Al Hall, bass.
Lazy Day/It's Great/Boot Zoot/ The Sun's Gonna Shine in My Back Yard Some Day.
Session, 4/23/44. Pete Brown, alto; "Jim Daddy" Walker, gtr; John Levy, bass; Eddie Nicholson, drs.
Jim's Idea / Pete's Idea. 12012.

Eddie's Idea / Jim Daddy Blues.
12013.

BRUNIS, GEORG Orchestra
Commodore, 11/29/43. Bill Davison, trp; Georg Brunis, trb; Ed Hall, clar; Gene Schroeder, pf; Eddie Condon, gtr; George Wettling, drs; Bob Casey, bass.
Ugly Chile (voc. by Brunis)/
That Da-Da Strain. 546. *Tin Roof Blues/Royal Garden Blues.*

BUSHKIN, JOE & his Orchestra
Commodore, 5/24/44. Ernie Figueroa, trp; Bill Harris, trb; Jackie Simms, tnr; Joe Bushkin, pf; Specs Powell, drs; Sid Weiss, bass.
Liza/Blues/two originals.

BYAS, DON Quintet
Savoy, 7/28/44. Charlie Shavers, trp; Don Byas, tnr; Clyde Hart, pf; Jack Parker, drs; Slam Stewart, bass.
Free and Easy/Riffin' and Jivin'/ Worried n' Blue/Don's Idea.

CAPITOL JAZZMEN
Capitol, 1/7/44. Shorty Sherock, trp; Barney Bigard, clar; Eddie Miller, tnr; Les Robinson, alto; Pete Johnson & Stan Wrightsman, pf; Nappy Lamare, gtr; Nick Fatool, drs; Hank Wayland, bass.
Ain't Goin' No Place (vocal: Peggy Lee)/*That Old Feeling* (same) / *Sugar / Someday Sweetheart.* Album A-3.
Capitol, 11/16/43. Billy May, trp; Jack Teagarden trb; Dave Matthews, tnr; Jimmie Noone, clar; Joe Sullivan, pf; Dave Barbour, gtr;

Zutty Singleton, drs; Artie Shapiro, bass.
Casanova's Lament (voc. Teagarden)/*I'm Sorry I Made You Cry* (same) / *Solitude / Clambake in B Flat.* Album A-3.

CARLISLE, UNA MAE & her Orchestra
Beacon, 5/23 & 25/44. Ray Nance, trp; Bud Johnson, tnr; Una Mae Carlisle, pf & voc; J. Wilson, gtr; E. Robinson, bass; Shadow Wilson, drs.
Tain't Yours/Without You Baby. 7170. Six other sides.

CARTER, BENNY Orchestra
Capitol, 5/21/44. Benny Carter, alto, trp & arr; Porter Kilbert, Eugene Porter, Willard Brown, Hubert Myers, saxes; Karl George, John Carroll, Edwin Davis, Milton Fletcher, trp; Alton Moore, John Haughton, James J. Johnson, Batty Varsalona, trb; Gerald Wiggins, pf; W. J. Edwards, gtr; Charles Drayton, bass; Max Roach, drs.
I'm Lost. 165. *I Surrender Dear/ I Can't Get Started/I Can't Escape from You.*

CATLETT, SID and various combinations.
Session. Ben Webster, tnr (first side); Marlowe Morris, pf; Sid Catlett, drs; John Simmons, bass.
1-2-3 Blues/Found a New Baby. 10-009.
Commodore, April, 1944. Same personnel.

Memories of You/Just a Riff. 1515.

Delta, 5/1/44. Charlie Shavers, trp; Frankie Sokolow, tnr; Ed Hall, clar; Eddie Heywood, pf; Sid Catlett, drs; Oscar Pettiford, bass.
Blue Skies/Thermo-Dynamics. D-10-3 & 4.

COLE, KING Trio
Capitol, 1944. King Cole, pf; Oscar Moore, gtr; Johnny Miller, bass.
Sweet Lorraine / Embraceable You. 20009. *The Man I Love/Body and Soul*. 20010. *What Is This Thing Called Love/Prelude in C Sharp Minor*. 20011. *It's Only a Paper Moon/Easy Listening Blues*. 20012. Album 8-A.

COLE, COZY and various combinations
Keynote, 2/21/44. Joe Thomas, trp; Trummy Young, trb; Coleman Hawkins, tnr; Earl Hines, pf; Teddy Walters, gtr; Cozy Cole, drs; Billy Taylor, bass.
Just One More Chance/Blue Moon. 1300. *Father Cooperates/Through for the Night*. 1301.
Savoy, March, 1944. Ben Webster, tnr; Lamar Wright, trp; Ray Coniff, trb; Johnny Guarnieri, pf; Teddy Walters, gtr; Billy Taylor, bass; Cozy Cole, drs.
Body and Soul/Talk to Me. 501. *Jericho/Nice and Cozy*. 502.
Savoy, 6/14/44. Emmett Berry, trp; Walter "Foots" Thomas, alto & tnr; Coleman Hawkins, Eddie Barefield, tnr; Johnny Guarnieri, pf;

Cozy Cole, drs; Sid Weiss, bass.
On the Sunny Side of the Street/Jersey Jumpoff. 519. *Jump Awhile/Stomping at the Savoy*.
Savoy, 6/14/44. Coleman Hawkins, Foots Thomas, Bud Johnson, tnr; Emmett Berry, trp; Johnny Guarnieri, pf; Cozy Cole, drs; Mack Shepnick, bass.
Wrap Your Troubles in Dreams/Ol' Man River. 512.

CONDON, EDDIE Orchestra
Commodore, 12/11/43. Max Kaminsky, trp; Pee Wee Russell, clar; Lou McGarity, trb; Gene Schroeder, pf; Eddie Condon, gtr; George Wettling, drs; Bob Casey, bass.
Back in Your Own Back Yard/All the Wrongs You Done to Me. 551. *You Can't Cheat a Cheater/Save Your Sorrow*.
Commodore, 12/8/43. Max Kaminsky, trp; Pee Wee Russell, clar; Brad Gowans, trb; Joe Bushkin, pf; Eddie Condon, gtr; Tony Spargo (Sbarbaro) drs; Bob Casey, bass.
Pray for the Lights to Go Out/Mandy Make Up Your Mind/Swinging the Blues/Don't Worry.
Commodore, 12/2/43. Max Kaminsky, trp; Pee Wee Russell, clar; Benny Morton, trb; Joe Bushkin, pf; Eddie Condon, gtr; Sid Catlett, drs; Bob Casey, bass.
Basin Street Blues/Oh Katharina. 1512. *Nobody Knows You When You're Down and Out/Rose Room*.

DE PARIS BROTHERS Orchestra
Commodore, 2/5/44. Sidney de

Paris, trp; Wilbur de Paris, trb; Ed Hall, clar; Clyde Hart, pf; Specs Powell, drs; Billy Taylor, bass.
I Found a New Baby/Black and Blue. 552. The Shiek/Sunday at Ryan's.

DAVISON, WILD BILL Orchestra
Commodore, 11/27/43. Davison, trp; Georg Brunis, trb; Pee Wee Russell, clar; Gene Schroeder, pf; Eddie Condon, gtr; George Wettling, drs; Bob Casey, bass.
That's A Plenty/Panama. 1511. Riverboat Shuffle/Muskrat Ramble.
Commodore, 11/30/43. Davison, trp; Georg Brunis, trb; Ed Hall, clar; Gene Schroeder, pf; Eddie Condon, gtr; George Whettling, drs; Bob Casey, bass.
Clarinet Marmalade/Original Dixieland One Step. 549. At the Jazz Band Ball/Baby Won't You Please Come Home.

ECKSTINE, BILLY and Orchestra
De Luxe, 4/13/44. Freddy Webster, Al Killian, Shorty McConnell, Dizzy Gillespie, trp; Trummy Young, Claude Jones, Howard Scott, trb; Jimmy Powell, Wardell Gray, alto; Bud Johnson, Thomas Crump, tnr; Rudy Rutherford, bar; Clyde Hart, pf; Connie Wainwright, gtr; Shadow Wilson, drs; Oscar Pettiford, bass.
I Stay in the Mood/Good Jelly Blues. 2000.

ELDRIDGE, ROY and his Orchestra
Decca, 6/26/44. Roy Eldridge,

Gus Aiken, "Cookie" Mason, Clarence Wheelen, John Hamilton, trp; Geo. Wildon, Sandy Williams, Theodore Kelly, trb; Joe Eldridge, Samuel Lee, alto; Franz Jackson, Harold Singer, tnr; Dave McRae, bar; Tony D'Amore, pf; Sam Christoper, gtr; Les Erskine, drs; Carl Wilson, bass.
After You're Gone/I Can't Get Started/Body and Soul.

FEATHER, LEONARD, All-Stars
Commodore, 12/4/43. Cootie Williams, trp; Ed Hall, clar; Coleman Hawkins, tnr; Sid Catlett, drs; Oscar Pettiford, bass.
Esquire Bounce/Esquire Blues. 547. Mop Mop/My Ideal. 548.

FIELDS, HERBIE Orchestra
Signature, 4/14/44. Herbie Fields, alto, tnr, clar; Taft Jordan, trp; Johnny Mehegan, pf; Leonard Ware, gtr; Sid Catlett, drs; Rodney Richardson, bass.
Confessin' (voc: Taft Jordan)/
These Foolish Things/You Can Depend on Me/Blues in C Minor.

GREER, SONNY and his Rextet
Apollo, 5/16/44. Rex Stewart, cor; Lawrence Brown, trb; Harry Carney, bar; Jimmy Hamilton, clar; Marlowe Morris, pf; Teddy Walters, gtr; Sonny Greer, drs; Oscar Pettiford, bass; Brick Fleagle, arr.
Sleepy Baboon/Ration Stamp/ Kansas City Caboose / Helena's Dream.

GUARNIERI, JOHNNY Swing Seven
Savoy, 4/18/44. Billy Butterfield,

trp; Lester Young, tnr; Hank d'Amico, clar; Johnny Guarnieri, pf; Dexter Hall, gtr; Cozy Cole, drs; Billy Taylor, bass.
Basie English/Exercise in Swing. 509.*These Foolish Things/Salute to Fats.* 511.

HALL, EDMOND and various combinations
Delta, 5/1/44. Charlie Shavers, trp; Ed Hall, clar; Frankie Sokolow, tnr; Eddie Heywood, pf; Sid Catlett, drs; Oscar Pettiford, bass.
Sweet Georgia Brown/Blues in Room 920. D-10-1 & 2.
Blue Note, 11/29/43. Hall, clar; Sidney de Paris, trp; Vic Dickenson, trb; James P. Johnson, pf; Jimmy Shirley, gtr; Israel Crosby, bass; Sidney Catlett, drs.
High Society/Blues at Blue Note. 28. *Royal Garden Blues/Night Shift Blues.* 29.
Commodore, 12/18/43. Emmett Berry, trp; Ed Hall, clar; Vic Dickenson, trb; Eddie Heywood, pf; Al Casey, gtr; Sid Catlett, drs; Billy Taylor, bass.
Uptown Café Blues/Downtown Café Boogie. 1512. *Man I Love/Coquette.* 550.
Commodore, 7/11/44. Edmond Hall, clar; Teddy Wilson, pf; Trappy Trappier, drs; Billy Taylor, bass.
It Had to Be You/Caravan/ Where or When/Sleepy Time Gal.
Blue Note, 1/25/44. Edmond Hall, clar; Red Norvo, vib; Teddy

Wilson, pf; Carl Kress, gtr; Johnny Williams, bass.
Rompin in '44/Smooth Sailing. 30. *Seein' Red/Blue Interval.* 31.

HAMPTON, LIONEL Orchestra
Decca, March, 1944. Cat Anderson, Lamar Wright, Jr., Roy McCoy, Joe Morris, trp; Al Hayes, Michael Wood, Fred Beckett, trb; Earl Bostic, Gus Evans, alto; Al Sears, Arnette Cobbs, tnr; Chas. Fowlkes, bar; Milt Buckner, pf; Eric Miller, gtr; Fred Radcliffe, drs; Vernon King, bass; Lionel Hampton, vib & drs.
Hamp's Boogie-Woogie / Chop Chop. 18613. *Flying Home/Loose Wig.*

HAWKINS, COLEMAN and various combinations
Keynote, 1/31/44. Hawkins, tnr; Roy Eldridge, trp; Teddy Wilson, pf; Billy Taylor, bass, Cozy Cole, drs.
I Only Have Eyes for You/'S Wonderful. 609. *I'm in the Mood for Love/Bean at the Met.* 610.
Signature, 12/23/43. Hawkins, tnr; Eddie Heywood, pf; Shelley Manne, drs; Oscar Pettiford, bass.
Crazy Rhythm / Get Happy. 28104. *Sweet Lorraine/Man I Love.* 90001.
Keynote, 2/17/44. Hawkins, tnr; Teddy Wilson, pf; Cozy Cole, drs; Israel Crosby, bass.
Night and Day/Imagination/Cattin' at Keynote/All I Do Is Dream of You.

Delta, 7/27/44. Charlie Shavers, trp; Coleman Hawkins, tnr; Ed Hall, clar; Clyde Hart, pf; Tiny Grimes, gtr; Denzil Best, drs; Oscar Pettiford, bass.

It Had to Be You/All the Things You Are/Memories of You/Shivers/Riding on 52nd Street/Step on It.

Keynote, 5/29/44. Coleman Hawkins, tnr; Teddy Wilson, pf; Sid Catlett, drs; John Kirby, bass.

Just One of Those Things/Halleluja/Don't Blame Me/Make Believe.

Keynote, 5/24/44. Tab Smith, alto & arr; Coleman Hawkins, Don Byas, tnr; Harry Carney, bar; Johnny Guarnieri, pf; Sid Catlett, drs; Al Lucas, bass.

Louise / Three Little Words/ Sunny Side of the Street/Battle of the Saxes.

Apollo, Feb., 1944. Leo Parker, Leonard Lowry, alto; Coleman Hawkins, Don Byas, Ray Abramson, tnr; Al Johnson, bar; Dizzy Gillespie, Vic Coulsen, Ed Vanderver, trp; Clyde Hart, pf; Max Roach, drs; Oscar Pettiford, bass.

Feeling Zero/Disorder at the Border. 753. *Rainbow Mist/Woody'n You.* 751. *Yesterdays/Bu-Dee-Daht.* 752.

Signature, 12/18/43. Hawkins, tnr; Ellis Larkins, pf; Jimmy Shirley, gtr; Max Roach, drs; Oscar Pettiford, bass.

Hawkins' Barrel House (coupling below). 28101. *Lover Come Back to Me / Indiana / These Foolish Things.*

Signature, 12/8/43. Bill Coleman, trp; Hawkins, tnr; Andy Fitzgerald, clar & arr; Ellis Larkins, pf; Al Casey, gtr; Shelley Manne, drs; Oscar Pettiford, bass.

Voodte (coupling above). 28101. *How Deep Is the Ocean/Stumpy.* 28102. *Knockin' It Off.*

HEYWOOD, EDDIE and various combinations.

Signature, 5/2/44. Ray Nance, trp & vio; Don Byas, tnr; Aaron Sachs, clar; Eddie Heywood, pf; Shelley Manne, drs; Jim Simmons, bass.

How High the Moon/Sarcastic Lady/Them There Eyes/Penthouse Serenade/When We're Alone.

Commodore, Feb.-Mar., 1944. Adolphus "Doc" Cheatham, trp; Vic Dickenson, trb; Lem Davis, alto & clar; Eddie Heywood, Jr., pf; Jack Parker, drs; Al Lucas, bass.

Begin the Beguine/I Cover the Waterfront. 1514. *I Can't Believe That You're in Love with Me/Indiana/Let Me Go/Carry Me Back to Old Virginny/BlueLou/Love Me or Leave Me/Coquette/Lover Man/ Deed I Do/Save Your Sorrow for Tomorrow.*

HIGGINBOTHAM, J. C. Quintet
Session, Sep. 1944. J. C. Higginbotham, trb; Alvin Burroughs, drs; Bennie Moten, bass; General Morgan, pf; Jim Daddy Walker, gtr.

J. C. Jumps/Shorty Joe. 10013. *Confessin'/Dear Old Southland.* 12016.

HINES, EARL Trio
  Signature, 2/26/44. Hines, pf; Al Casey, gtr; Oscar Pettiford, bass.
  Honeysuckle Rose/Squeeze Me/ I've Got a Feeling I'm Falling/My Fate Is in Your Hands. In Album S-1.

HODES, ART and various combos
  Session. Art Hodes, pf; Mezz Mezzrow, clar; Danny Alvin, drs.
  Mezzin' Around / Feather's Lament. 10-007. *Milk for Mezz/Really the Blues.*
  Blue Note, 3/18/44. Max Kaminsky, trp; Rod Cless, clar; Ray Coniff, trb; Art Hodes, pf; Jack Bland, gtr; Bob Haggart, bass; Danny Alvin, drs.
  Maple Leaf Rag/Yellow Dog Blues/She's Crying for Me/Slow 'Em Down Blues.
  Blue Note, 3/22/44. Max Kaminsky, trp; Rod Cless, clar; Ray Coniff, trb; Art Hodes, pf; Jack Bland, gtr; Sid Jacobs, bass; Danny Alvin, drs.
  Doctor Jazz/Shoe Shiner's Drag/ Changes Made/Clark and Randolph.

HOLIDAY, BILLIE and her Orchestra
  Commodore, March & April, 1944. Billie Holiday, voc; Doc Cheatham, trp; Vic Dickenson, trb; Lem Davis, alto; Eddie Heywood, pf; Teddy Walters, gtr; Sidney Catlett, drs; John Simmons, bass.
  I'll Get By/I'll Be Seeing You. 553.

JACKSON, CLIFF Quartet
  Black and White, 1944. Pee Wee

Russell, clar; Cliff Jackson, pf; Jack Parker, drs; Bob Casey, bass.
  Quiet Please/Squeeze Me. 3.

JAFFE, NAT, piano solos, with Sid Jacobs, bass.
  Signature.
  How Can You Face Me/Keepin' Out of Mischief/Zonky/Black and Blue. In Album S-1.

JEROME, JERRY & His Cats and Jammers
  Asch, March, 1944. Yank Lawson, trp; Ray Coniff, trb; Jerry Jerome, tnr; Johny Guarnieri, pf; George Wettling, drs; Bob Haggart, bass.
  Arsenic and Old Face/When I Grow Too Old to Dream. 501. *Girl of My Dreams/Rainbow Blues.* 500.

JOHNSON, BUNK & New Orleans Band
  New Orleans, 7/31/44 and 8/2/ 44. Bunk Johnson, trp, and other New Orleans men.
  Tiger Rag/St. Louis Blues/When the Saints Go Marching In/Darktown Strutter's Ball/C.C. Rider/ Clarinet Marmalade/Sister Kate.

JOHNSON, JAMES P. piano solos
  Blue Note, 11/17/43.
  J. P. Boogie/Gut Stomp. 24. *Back Water Blues/Carolina Balmoral.* 25.
  Blue Note, 12/15/43.
  Improvisation on Pinetop's Boogie-Woogie/Caprice Rag. 26. *Mule Walk/Arkansas Blues.* 27. *Asch.*
  Impressions / Boogie-Woogie Stride. 1001.

Frankie Newton (left), sits in with the Max Kaminsky Band (center) at New York's Pied Piper. The three front-line hornmen—Newton, Max and clarinetist Rod Cless—have established fine reputations, as their recorded performances testify. Kaminsky, who returned in 1944 from a year in the South Pacific with Shaw's Rangers, shows up particularly well on Basin St. Blues (Condon on Commodore). Cless accomplished fine results with Muggsy Spanier's Ragtime Band. Newton's After Hour Blues (Blue Note) offers typical choruses. Photo by H. Kratovil.

This is what the trade calls a "pickup" band—one assembled for recording purposes only. The records which this group made for the Capitol label will appear under the name of Wingy Manone and his Dixielanders, since Manone held the contract. Personnel: in the front row: guitarist Nappy Lamare, trumpeter Wingy Manone, clarinetist Matty Matlock; behind them, Jake Flores and Abe Lincoln, drummer Zutty Singleton, pianist Stan Wrightsman, bassist Phil Stephens. Zutty, Wingy, Nappy are New Orleans boys. Capitol photo by Charlie Mihn.

Another pickup band, another recording date, this one organized by Leonard Feather for the Apollo label. It featured the blues-vocals of the ex-Duke Ellington singer, Betty Roche (center), who is surrounded by a group of hand-picked musicians, all of whom rate high with Esquire's experts. Left to right: tenorman Flip Phillips, a winner in the New Star division; bassist Oscar Pettiford, who repeated his Gold Award triumph of last year; violinist Ray Nance, another New Star winner; Gold-Awarder drummer Sid Catlett; veteran pianist Earl Hines.

A Joe Marsala session for Signature Records. The hornmen, left to right: clarinetist Marsala, a small-band musician of long standing; trumpeter Charlie Shavers, whose reputation has been growing; altoman Pete Brown, another leader of small bands.

Benny Morton's name-band achievements range over a period of fifteen years. His abilities include such diverse performances as the flashing staccato of I Got Rhythm (Don Redman), the soulful blues rendition of I'm Coming Virginia. Cafe Society photo.

After more than five years with the intimate John Kirby combination, Charlie Shavers has stepped into an ear-catching virtuoso role. His recording of Mountain Air with a group under his own name for the Keynote label is one of the high spots of 1944.

Two distinguished trombonists with an able guitarist. At the left is Vic Dickenson, possessor of an extraordinary plunger style. At the right is Dickie Wells, a great exponent of the blues. Green contributes heavily to the fine Count Basie rhythm section.

Signature, 12/18/43.
Blueberry Rhyme, Blues for Fats.
28105. *Old-Fashioned Love/Over the Bar.*

JOHNSON, JAMES P. Blue Note Jazzmen.
Blue Note, 3/4/44. Sidney de Paris, trp; Vic Dickenson, trb; Ben Webster, tnr; J. P. Johnson, pf; Jimmy Shirley, gtr; John Simmons, bass; Sidney Catlett, drs.
Victory Stride/Blue Mizz. 32. *After You've Gone/Joy-mentin'.* 33.

JONES, RICHARD M. Jazzmen
Session, 3/23/44. Richard M. Jones, pf; Bob Schoffner, trp; Darnell Howard, clar; John Lindsey, bass; Baby Dodds, drs.
Jazzin' Babies Blues/Canal Street Blues. 12-007. *New Orleans Hop Scoop Blues/29th and Dearborn.* 12-006.

KANSAS CITY SEVEN
Keynote, 3/20/44. Buck Clayton, trp; Lester Young, tnr; Dickie Wells, trb; Count Basie, pf; Freddie Greene, gtr; Jo Jones, drs; Rodney Richardson, bass.
Lester Leaps Again (KANSAS CITY FIVE—Young and rhythm section)/ *After Theatre Jump.* 1302. *Destination K.C./Six Cats and a Prince.* 1303.

LAWSON, YANK and various combinations
Signature, 6/7/44. Yank Lawson, trp; Will Bradley, trb; Ray Ekstrand, clar; James P. Johnson, pf; Carl Kress, gtr; Chauncey Morehouse, drs; Sid Weiss, bass.
I Found a New Baby / Jazz Me Blues/"Note" Worthy Blues/Lady Be Good.
Signature, Jan., 1944. Lawson, trp; Rod Cless, clar; Miff Mole, trb; James P. Johnson, pf; George Wettling, drs; Bob Haggart, bass.
Squeeze Me/The Sheik. 28103. *When My Dreamboat Comes Home /Blues.*

LEVY, JOHN Duo with Jimmy Jones
Session, Aug., 1944. John Levy, bass; Jimmy Jones, pf.
Improvisations (4 sides). 10011 & 10012.

LEWIS, GEORGE & New Orleans Stompers
New Orleans, 8/5/44. George Lewis, clar; Kit Shots Madison, trp, and other New Orleans men.
The Shiek/High Society/When You and I Were Young Maggie/ Everybody Loves My Baby.

LITTLE JAZZ TRUMPET ENSEMBLE
Keynote, 1/24/44. Joe Thomas, Emmett Berry, Roy Eldridge, trp; Johnny Guarnieri, pf; Cozy Cole, drs; Israel Crosby, bass.
Fiesta in Brass/I Want to Be Happy. 608. *St. Louis Blues/Don't Be That Way.* 607.

LOFTON, CRIPPLE CLARENCE piano
   solos
Session, 1944.
Streamlined Train/I Don't Know.
12-005.
The Fives/Deep End Boogie.
10005. *Early Blues/ In De Mornin'.*
10006.

LUNCEFORD, JIMMIE and his Or-
   chestra
Decca, 2/8/44. Melvin Moore,
Bob Mitchell, William Scott, trp;
John Ewing, Russell Bowles, Fer-
nando Arbello, Earl Hardy, trb;
Chauncey Jerrett, alto; Omer Sim-
eon, alto, tnr, clar; Joe Thomas,
tnr; Ernest Purce, alto, tnr, bar;
Jock Carruthers, bar, alto; Ed Wil-
cox, pf; Al Norris, gtr; Joe Marshall,
drs; Truck Parham, bass; Claude
Trenier, voc. (1).
Back Door Stuff (Parts I & II)/
*The Goon Comes On/Jeep Rhythm
/Once Too Often* (1).

MANONE, WINGY Orchestra
Capitol, 3/7/44. Matty Matlock,
clar; Nappy LaMare, gtr; Zutty Sin-
gleton, drs; Stan Wrightsman, pf;
Jake Flores, Floyd O'Brien, Abe
Lincoln, trb; Phil Stephens, bass;
Wingy Manone, trp & voc.
*Put the Tailgate Down/Besamé
Mucho/PaperDoll/I Wish I Could
Shimmy Like My Sister Kate.*

MARSALA, JOE and various combina-
   tions
Savoy, 3/23/44. Bobby Hackett,
cor; Joe Marsala, clar; Frank Or-
chard, trb; Gene Schroeder, pf;
Eddie Condon, gtr; Rollo Laylan,
drs; Bob Casey, bass.
*Tiger Rag/Clarinet Marmalade/
Joe's Blues/Village Blues.*
Signature, 7/21/44. Joe Marsala,
clar; Pete Brown, alto; Charlie Shav-
ers, pf & trp; Al Casey, gtr & drs;
Specs Powell, pf & drs; Al Mat-
thews, bass & vio; Carl Powell, bass
(last side only).
*Blues Before Dawn/Escapade/
When the Moon Comes over the
Mountain/Roses of Picardy.*

MATTHEWS, DAVE Orchestra
Capitol, 1/14/44. Dave Matthews,
alto; Les Baxter, bar; Roger Hanson,
trp; Joe Quartell, trb; Tommy
Todd, pf; Dave Barbour, gtr; Gene
Englund, bass; Henry Coleman, drs.
*Just Another Blues/Singin' the
Blues.* Voc. by the Barries & Johnny
Mercer.

MILLER, EDDIE Orchestra
Capitol, 2/4/44. Arthur (Doc)
Rando, Ray Lundale, Matty Mat-
lock, Clyde Rogers, Eddie Miller,
saxes; Abe Lincoln, Eddie Kucz-
borski, Elmer Smithers, trb; Charles
Griffard, Bob Goodrich, Bruce
Hudson, trp; Stanley Wrightsman,
pf; Nappy LaMare, gtr; Art Sha-
piro, bass, Nick Fatool, drs.
*Yesterdays/Stomp Mister Henry
Lee.* 170. *Our Monday Date/The
Hour of Parting.*

MILLER, PUNCH and his South Side
   Stompers
Session, 6/12/44. Punch Miller,

trp; Artie Starck, clar; Richard M. Jones, pf; John Lindsey, bass; Clifford "Snags" Jones, drs.
West End Blues/Sugar Foot Stomp/Muscle Shoals Blues/Boy in the Boat.

MORTON, BENNY and his Orchestra
Keynote, 5/30/44. Benny Morton, Bill Harris, Vic Dickenson, Claude Jones, trb; Johnny Guarnieri, pf; Cozy Cole, drs; Al Hall, bass.
Liza/Avalon/Where or When/Once in Awhile.

NORVO, RED and various combos
Keynote, 7/27/44. Red Norvo, vib; Aaron Sachs, clar; Teddy Wilson, pf; Remo Palmieri, gtr; Eddie Dell, drs; Slam Stewart, bass.
Seven Come Eleven/The Man I Love/Blues/untitled original.
S-D, 4/5/44. K. Norville, vib; Stuff Smith, vio; Remo Palmieri, gtr; Clyde Lombardi, bass.
Confessin'/Red's Stuff/Rehearssin'/A Fawn Jumped at Dawn.

OSBORNE, MARY & STUFF SMITH TRIO
Chicago, 5/30/44. Mary Osborne, gtr; Stuff Smith, vio; Jimmy Jones, pf; John Levy, bass.
Blues in Mary's Flat/Blues in Stuff's Flat (voc. Stuff & Mary)/*Sweet Lorraine/Six String Mama.*

PAGE, HOT LIPS and his Orchestra
Savoy, 6/14/44. Hot Lips Page, trp & voc; George Johnson, Floyd

"Horsecollar" Williams, alto; Don Byas, tnr; Clyde Hart, pf; Sid Catlett, drs; John Simmons, bass.
Uncle Sam Blues/Paging Mr. Page. 520. Dance of the Tambourine/I Keep Rollin' On.

PETTIFORD, OSCAR
Delta, 7/27/44. Bass solos, with Clyde Hart, pf.
Dedicated to J. B./Don't Blame Me.

PHILLIPS, JOE "FLIP" and his Orchestra
Signature, May, 1944. Neil Hefti, trp; Flip Phillips, tnr; Bill Shine, clar; Ralph Burns, pf; Billy Bauer, gtr; Dave Tough, drs; Chubby Jackson, bass.
Sweet and Lovely/Popsy.

RHAPSODY, MISS
Savoy, 7/6/44. Rhapsody Underhill, voc; Emmett Berry, trp; Walter "Foots" Thomas, alto & tnr; June Cole, pf; Cozy Cole, drs; Billy Taylor, bass.
Groovin' the Blues/Hey Lawdy Mama. 5511. Bye Bye Baby/My Lucky Day.

ROCHÉ, BETTY & EARL HINES SEXTET
Apollo, 4/26/44. Ray Nance, trp & vio; Flip Phillips, tnr & clar; "J. Harjes," alto; Earl Hines, pf; Al Casey, gtr; Sid Catlett, drs; Oscar Pettiford, bass; Betty Roché, voc. (on first four sides).
I Love My Lovin' Lover/Trouble

Trouble/Blues on My Weary Mind /I'll Get By/Design for Jiving/ Early to Jump.

SESSION SIX
Session, 4/2/44. Eddie Johnson, tnr; Nat Jones, alto; Jessie Miller, trp; Jimmy Jones, pf; John Levy, bass; Alvin Burroughs, drs.
Big Oaks/I Wished on the Moon/ Yesterdays/We Want in the Act.

SHAVERS, CHARLIE and various combinations
Keynote, 4/15/44. Charlie Shavers, trp; Tab Smith, alto; Earl Hines, pf; Jo Jones, drs; Al Lucas, bass.
Star Dust/Curry in a Hurry. 1305. *Rosetta/Mountain Air.* 1304.
Keynote, 6/8/44. Charlie Shavers, Jonah Jones, trp; Bud Johnson, tnr; Johnny Guarnieri, pf; J. C. Heard, drs; Milton Hinton, bass.
I'm in the Market for You/You're Driving Me Crazy/Blue Lou/Legs Are Getting Brown.

SHELLEY'S TRIO
Signature, 5/26/44. Johnny Hodges; alto; Eddie Heywood, pf; Shelley Manne, drs.
Flamingo/Night and Day/Sunny Side of the Street/Time on My Hands.

SLACK, FREDDIE and his Orchestra
Capitol, 3/9/44. Karl Leaf, Lee Baxter, Neeley Plumb, Clyde Hylton, Ralph Lee, Barney Bigard, reeds; William Morris, Charlie Griffard, George Wendt, trp; Gerald Foster, Bill Lower, Jimmy

Skiles, trb; T-Bone Walker, gtr; Phil Stephens, bass; Henry Coleman, drs; Freddie Slack, pf.
Gee-Chee Love Song/Sit and Nip /Cuban Sugar Mill/Swinging on a Star.

SMITH, TAB and his Orchestra
Decca, May, 1944. Frank Humphries, trp; Tab Smith, alto; Mike Hedley, tnr; Raymond Tunia, pf; Walter Johnson, drs; Al McKibbins, bass; Trevor Bacon, voc.
You, Lovely You/All Night Long/I Live True to You/Brown Skin Gal.

SOUTH, EDDIE Trio
New York, 6/14/44. Eddie South, vio; Billy Taylor, pf; Eddie Brown, bass.
Black Gypsy/Movin' the Groove /Peg O' My Heart/Among My Souvenirs/Someday Sweetheart/Paganini in Rhythm.

SPANIER, MUGGSY & various combos
Commodore, 4/15/44. Muggsy Spanier, cor; Miff Mole, trb; Pee Wee Russell, clar; Dick Cary, pf; Eddie Condon, pf; Tony Spargo, drs; Bob Casey, bass.
Angry/Weary Blues/Snag It/ Alice Blue Gown.
Commodore, April, 1944. Muggsy Spanier, cor; Pee Wee Russell, clar; Ernie Caceres, bar; Dick Cary, pf; Eddie Condon, gtr; Joe Grauso, drs; Sid Weiss, bass.
Sweet Lorraine/September in the Rain. 1517.

STEWART, REX and his Orchestra
Keynote, 6/5/44. Rex Stewart, cor; Tab Smith, alto; Harry Carney, bar; Lawrence Brown, trb; Johnny Guarnieri, pf; Brick Fleagle, gtr; Cozy Cole, drs; Sid Weiss, bass.
Swamp Mist/Zaza/True to You/ Little Goose.

TATUM, ART Trio
Comet, April, 1944. Art Tatum, pf; Tiny Grimes, gtr; Slam Stewart, bass.
I Know That You Know/Body and Soul. T-2. *Dark Eyes/The Man I Love.* T-1. *On the Sunny Side of the Street/Flying Home.* T-3.

TAYLOR, BILLY and his Orchestra
Keynote, 8/1/44. Emmett Berry, trp; Vernon Brown, trb; Johnny Hodges, alto; Harry Carney, bar; Johnny Guarnieri, pf; Brick Fleagle, gtr; Cozy Cole, drs; Billy Taylor, bass.
Carney-val in Rhythm/Sam-pan/ two originals.

TEAGARDEN, JACK Teetotalers
Capitol, 11/16/43. Jack Teagarden, trb; Joe Sullivan, pf; Heinie Beau, clar; Billy May, trp; Dave Barbour, gtr; Art Shapiro, bass; Dave Matthews, tnr; Zutty Singleton, drs.
Mighty Lak a Rose/Stars Fell on Alabama/'Deed I Do.

THOMAS, WALTER and his Jump Cats
Celebrity, May, 1944. Emmett Berry, trp; Walter Thomas, tnr &

alto; Ben Webster, Bud Johnson, tnr; Clyde Hart, pf; Cozy Cole, drs; Oscar Pettiford, bass.
Blues on the Delta/Broke but Happy. 8125.

WARREN, EARL and his Orchestra
Savoy, 4/18/44. Ed Lewis, Harry Edison, Joe Newman, Al Killian, trp; Dickie Wells, Eli Robinson, Lewis Taylor, Ted Donnelly, trb; Earl Warren, Jimmy Powell, alto; Lester Young, Buddy Tate, tnr; Rudy Rutherford, bar; Clyde Hart, pf; Freddie Greene, gtr; Jo Jones, drs; Rodney Richardson, bass.
Empty Hearted/Tush. 507. *Circus in Rhythm/Poor Little Plaything.*

WASHINGTON, DINAH Sextet
Keynote, 12/29/43. Joe Morris, trp; Arnette Cobbs, tnr; Rudy Rutherford, clar; Milton Buckner, pf; Fred Radcliffe, drs; Vernon King, bass; Dinah Washington, voc; Lionel Hampton, pf. (1); and drs (2).
Evil Gal Blues / Homeward Bound (1). 605. *I Know How to Do It/Salty Papa Blues* (2). 606.

WEBSTER, BEN and various combinations
Savoy, April, 1944. Ben Webster, tnr; Johnny Guarnieri, pf; David Booth, drs; Oscar Pettiford, bass.
Kat's Fur (comp. Webster)/ *Honeysuckle Rose/Blue Skies/I Surrender Dear.*
Session. Ben Webster, tnr; Mar-

lowe Morris, pf; Sid Catlett, drs; John Simmons, bass.
Perdido/I Surrender Dear.

WELLS, DICKIE Orchestra
Signature, 12/21/43. Bill Coleman, trp; Wells, trb; Lester Young, tnr; Ellis Larkin, pf; Freddy Greene, gtr; Jo Jones, drs; Al Hall, bass.
I Got Rhythm/I'm Fer It Too. 90002. *Linger Awhile/Hello Babe.*

WETTLING, GEORGE and various combinations
Commodore, 7/2/44. Billy Butterfield, trp; Wilbur de Paris, trb; Edmond Hall, clar; Dave Bowman, pf; George Wettling, drs; Bob Haggart, bass.
Struttin' with Some Barbecue/ Heebie Jeebies/Pitchin' the Witch/ How Come You Do Me Like You Do?
Black & White, 7/1/44. Mezz Mezzrow, clar; Gene Schroeder, pf; George Wettling, drs.
That's a Plenty/I Found a New Baby/Some of These Days.

WILLIAMS, MARY LOU and various combinations
Asch, 6/5/44. Dick Vance, trp; Vic Dickenson, trb; Don Byas, tnr; Fats Greet, clar; Mary Lou Williams, pf; Jack Parker, drs; Al Lucas, bass.
Stardust (Parts I & II)/*Sweet Juice/Gjon Mili's Jam Session.*
Asch. Frankie Newton, trp; Ed Hall, clar; Vic Dickenson, trb; Mary Lou Williams, pf & arr; Jack Parker, drs; Al Lucas, bass.

Little Joe. 1002. *Lullaby of the Leaves.* 1004. *Roll 'Em.* 1003. (All in Album A-450)/*Satchel Mouth Baby.*
Asch. Mary Lou Williams, piano solos.
Mary Lou's Boogie. 1003. *St. Louis Blues.* 1004. *Drag 'Em.* 1002. (All in Album A-450).
Asch, 6/29/44. Bill Coleman, trp; Mary Lou Williams, pf; Al Hall, bass.
Signs of the Zodiac, Album 451: *Aries, Taurus, Gemini, Cancer, Leo, Virgo, Libra, Scorpio, Saggitarius, Capricornus, Aquarius, Pisces.*

WILLIAMS, COOTIE and various combinations
Hit, 1/4 & 1/6/44. Ernest V. Perry, George Treadwell, Harold Johnson, Cootie Williams, trp; Ed Burke, George Stevenson, R. H. Horton, trb; Eddie Vinson, Charlie Holmes, alto; Ed Davis, Lee Pope, tnr; Ed di Verneuil, bar; Earl Powell, pf; Sylvester Payne, drs; Norman Keenan, bass.
Things Ain't What They Used to Be (voc. & alto, Eddie Vinson)/ *Cherry Red Blues* (same). 7084. *Tess's Torch Song* (voc. Pearl Bailey)/*Now I Know* (same). 7075.
Hit, 1/4 & 1/6/44. Cootie Williams, Ed Vinson, Ed Davis, rhythm as above.
Got to Do Some War Work (voc. Cootie)/*Honeysuckle Rose/ Sweet Lorraine/My Old Flame/I Don't Know/Floogie Boo/You*

Talk a Little Trash and I'll Spend a Little Cash/Echoes of Harlem. Album H-122.

YANCEY, ALONZO piano solos
Session, 1943. Hobo Rag/Ecstatic Rag. 10003.

YANCEY, JIMMY piano solos
Session, Dec., 1943. Jimmy's Rocks/Boodlin'. 10001. *Shave 'Em Dry/At the Window.* 10005. *Eternal Blues/Yancey Special.* 12001. *'Midnight Stomp/Roll It on the Floor.* As piano, 12003; as organ, 12002. *Rough and Ready/Mama's Blues,* 12004.

YOUNG, JESSE piano solos
Session, 1943. Flyin' Santa Fe/Skipper. 10004.

YOUNG, TRUMMY and his Orchestra
Session, 2/7/44. Trummy Young, trb; John Malchi, pf; Leo Williams, tnr; Harry Curtis, alto; Tommy Potter, bass; Eddie Byrd, drs.
Talk of the Town/Hollywood/Man I Love (Parts I & II).

YOUNG, LESTER Quartet
Keynote, 12/28/43. Young, tnr; Johnny Guarnieri, pf; Sidney Catlett, drs; Slam Stewart, bass.
I Never Knew/Just You, Just Me. 603. *Sometimes I'm Happy/Afternoon of a Basie-ite.* 604.

ZUTTY'S CREOLE TRIO
Capitol, 6/30/44. Barney Bigard, clar; Fred Washington, pf; Zutty Singleton, drs.
Barney's Bounce/Lulu's Mood.

ZUTTY'S CREOLE BAND
Capitol, 6/30/44. Barney Bigard, clar; Norman Bowden, trp; Shorty Haughton, trb; Fred Washington, pf; Bud Scott, gtr; Ed Garland, bass; Zutty Singleton, drs.
Didn't He Ramble / Crawfish Blues.

THE RECORD LABELS

Apollo
H. Siegal, Rainbow Music Shop, 102 W. 125th St., New York 27. UN 4-8576.

Asch
Moe Asch, 117 W. 46th St., New York 19. BR. 9-3137.

Beacon
Joe Davis, Beacon Record Co., 331 W. 51st., New York 19. CI 5-7658.

Black & White
Black & White Record Co., 2117 Foster Ave., Brooklyn 10, N. Y.

Bluebird
RCA-Victor Mfg. Co., Camden, N. J. Camden 8000.

Blue Note
Alfred Lion, Blue Note Records, 767 Lexington Ave. New York 22. RE 4-4167.

Brunswick
See Decca.

Capitol
Glenn Wallichs, Capitol Records Inc., 1483 N. Vine, Hollywood 28, Calif., and 225 W. 57th St., New York 19. CO 5-8054.

Celebrity
See Beacon.

Columbia
Columbia Records, Inc. 799 Seventh Av., New York 19. CI 5-7300.

Comet
Paul Reiner, Music Distributing Co., 1408 W. 9th St., Cleveland 13, Ohio. Cherry 3124. Comet, Inc., 420 Lexington Ave., New York 17.

Commodore
Milt Gabler, Commodore Music Shop, 136 E. 42nd St., New York 17. MU 2-7967.

Criterion
See Capitol.

Decca
Decca Records, Inc., 50 W. 57th St., New York 19. CO 5-2300.

Delta
Robert Shad, Delta Records, 119 W. 57th St., New York 19.

De Luxe
Joseph Leibowitz, De Luxe Records Distributing Co., Linden, N. J. Linden 2-4631.

Excelsior
Excelsior Record Co., 3661 Gramercy Place, Los Angeles 7, Calif.

Feature
Feature Records, 1440 Broadway, New York 18. PE 6-8600.

Gennett
See Beacon

Grand
George Wiener, Grand Records, 1619 Broadway, New York 19. CO 5-4753.

Hit
Eli Oberstein, Classic Records, 7 W. 46th St., New York 19. BR 9-5053.

Jazz
Art Hodes, 236 W. 10th St., New York 14. CH 2-0836.

Jazz Information
See Commodore.

Jazz Man
Dave Stuart, 6331 Santa Monica Blvd., Hollywood, Calif.

Jump
Clive Acker, The Turntable, 1132 Tamarind Ave., Hollywood 28, Calif. Granite 9309.

Keynote
Eric Bernay, Keynote Recordings, Inc., 522 Fifth Ave., New York 18. MU 2-5338.

King Solomon
See Savoy.

Liberty
Liberty Music Shops, 450 Madison Av., New York 22.

Musicraft
Musicraft Corp., 40 W. 46th St., New York 19. BR 9-0320.

National
National Records Co., 1841 Broadway, New York 23. CO 5-7280.

Okeh
See Columbia.

Savoy
Herman Lubinsky, Savoy Records, 58 Market St., Newark, N. J. Mitchell 2-6090.

S-D
John Steiner, S-D Records, 104 E. Bellevue Pl., Chicago 11. DEL 9779.

Session
Phil Featheringill, Session Record Shop, 125 N. Wells St., Chicago 2. AND 1877.

Signature
Bob Thiele, Signature Records, 601 W. 26th St., New York 1. LA 4-5159.

Victor
RCA-Victor Mfg. Inc., Camden, N. J. Camden 8000.

Chapter VII

Musicians' Bio-Discographies

Since the individual musicians named by *Esquire's* Board of Experts totaled over 300, space limitations necessitated the ruling that only the biographies of those musicians receiving seven points or more be included in this chapter (see Point Tabulation, pages 93-108). Exceptions were made, however, for the winners of the All-American New Stars, some of whom won that position with less than seven points. But in addition, because we are featuring New Orleans jazz and jazzmen in this edition of the JAZZ BOOK, the biographies of some three score New Orleans men are here published, many of them for the first time anywhere. Information about some of the performers named in the personnels in Chapter I and included in the picture sections will be found in this chapter.

Gold Award winners have been honored with a discography, except in those instances where the winner was given a complete discography in the 1944 ESQUIRE JAZZ BOOK—in which case reference is made to the earlier edition. Also granted discographies are some of the important New Orleans musicians—again in keeping with the feature material; points received by these musicians is noted, even if less than seven. Waller, Noone and O'Neill Spencer—all of whom died the past year—likewise are given discographies. Current recordings with personnels are listed in Chapter VI.

As in 1944, the discographies include the following information: (1) the name of the band with whom the instrumentalist made the records; (2) the approximate collectors' market value of the records when *in new condition;* (3) the name of the record label; (4) the number of the record on its original issuance; (5) the label and number of the same recording which, as in some cases only, has been reissued at a date subsequent to its original issue. I have drawn heavily from my *Yearbook of Popular Music* not only for collector-valuations, but also for biographies and discographies. As for the valuations, let me warn, as I did in the *Yearbook*, that the figures represent a *scale of values* based on records in *new condition.* Records in any condition other than mint must be scaled down in value according to their actual playing condition. The collectors' market value of records, then, on a scale of from retail to 50, is listed immediately after the name of the band, and in a few cases immediately after the name of the record label.—P.E.M.

ALLEN, Henry Jr. (Red). *Trumpet, leader, vocal.* Received 2 points as trumpeter: *Miller;* 3 points as leader: *Miller.* Born Jan. 7, 1908, Algiers, La. Began study of instrument early in life—his father was instructor and leader of a brass band in which Henry Jr. played, side by side with the best New Orleans hornmen, such as King Oliver, Bunk Johnson, Louis Armstrong, Mutt and Jack Carey, Sidney Bechet, Papa Celestin, Punch Miller, Jimmie Noone, Manual Perez. Young Allen started his real professional career with the Excelsior Band (1924), then shifted to a group whose leadership he shared with clarinetist John Casimir (Allen & Casimir Band, 1925). He then played the riverboats with Fate Marable (1926), after which he joined King Oliver in Chicago (1927) only to return to his native city to work with the Pelican Band (1927) and again with Marable (1928-29) on the Steamer Capitol. He then rejoined some of the men with whom he had worked in Oliver's group: this took him to New York and the Luis Russell band (1929-33), which remained constant in personnel for almost four years. But in 1933 he left to join Fletcher Henderson (1933-34), after which he was featured with the

Blue Rhythm Band (1934-36) and then with Armstrong (1937-40). After this he became leader of his own small band (1940-44) and has been playing the swing spots in New York and Chicago since. Recorded with Russell, Armstrong, Coleman Hawkins, Allen-Hawkins Orchestra, own band, Blue Rhythm, Rhythmakers, Jay C. Higginbotham, Wilton Crawley, Spike Hughes, Henderson. Solos: *Queer Notions* and *Nagasaki* (Henderson); *Heartbreak Blues* (Hawkins); *Biffly Blues,. Feeling Drowsy, Patrol Wagon Blues, Rug Cutter's Swing* (own band); *Ride, Red, Ride* (Blue Rhythm); *Who Stole the Lock* (Rhythmakers); *Mugging Lightly, Panama, Freakish Blues, High Tension* (Russell).

RED ALLEN DISCOGRAPHY

With Louis Armstrong (retail-2):

Decca

1347 Red Cap/Public Melody Number One
1353 Cuban Pete/She's a Daughter of a Planter
1369 Sun Showers/Yours and Mine
1408 Alexander's Ragtime Band/ Heart Full of Rhythm
1635 Jubilee/True Confession
1636 Satchel Mouth Swing/I Double Dare You
1653 Trumpet Player's Lament/ Sweet as a Song
1660 Once in a While/Sunny Side of the Street
1661 Struttin' With Some Barbecue/Let That Be a Lesson to You

Okeh

8756 I Ain't Got Nobody/Rockin' Chair
8774 Dallas Blues/Bessie Couldn't Help It

With Louis Armstrong (retail-2) —continued

41350 St. Louis Blues
41375 Song of the Islands/Blue Turning Grey Over You

With Luis Russell (5-15):

Okeh

8734 Jersey Lightning/New Call of the Freaks
8760 Savoy Shout
8766 Feelin' the Spirit/Doctor Blues
8780 Saratoga Shout/Song of the Swanee
8811 Louisiana Swing/On Revival Day
8830 Poor Li'l Me/Muggin' Lightly
8849 Panama/High Tension

Victor

22789 Goin' to Town/Say the Word
22793 You Rascal You
22815 Freakish Blues

With Luis Russell (5-15)—continued

Vocalion

1579 Ease on Down/Saratoga Drag

Melotone

12000 I Got Rhythm

With Blue Rhythm Band (2-4):

Columbia

2963 Out of a Dream/Let's Have a Jubilee

2994 Solitude/Keep Rhythm Going

3020 Back Beats/Spitfire

3038 African Lullaby/Swingin' in E Flat

3044 Brown Sugar Mine/Dancing Dogs

3071 Harlem Heat/There's Rhythm in Harlem

3078 Cotton/Truckin'

3083 Dinah Lou/Waiting in the Garden

3087 Ride, Red, Ride/Congo Caravan

3111 Yes, Yes/Broken Dreams of You

3134 Jes' Naturally Lazy/Everything Still Okay

3135 St. Louis Wiggle Rhythm/Red Rhythm

3147 Merry Go Round/Until the Real Thing Comes Along

3156 Balloonacy/Barrelhouse

3157 Showboat Shuffle/The Moon is Grinning

With Blue Rhythm Band (2-4)—continued

3158 Ghost Goes to Town/Algiers Stomp

3162 Callin' Your Bluff/Big John Special

With the Rhythmakers (10-20):

Melotone

12457 Anything for You/Mean Old Bedbug Blues

12481 Yellow Dog Blues/Yes Suh

12510 It's Gonna Be You/Shine on Your Shoes

12513 Who Stole the Lock/Someone Stole Gabriel's Horn

With Fletcher Henderson (2-5):

Vocalion

2527 Yeah Man/King Porter Stomp

2583 Can You Take It/Queer Notions

Columbia

2825 It's the Talk of the Town/Nagasaki

Decca

157 Limehouse Blues/Wrappin' It Up

158 Shanghai Shuffle/Memphis Blues

213 Tidal Wave/Down South Camp Meeting

214 Big John's Special/Happy as the Day Is Long

With Fletcher Henderson (2-5)—continued

342 Rug Cutter Swing/Wild Party
555 Liza/Hotter than Hell

With Spike Hughes (2):

English Decca

3717 Donegal Cradle Song/Firebird
3836 Music at Sunrise
3972 Sweet Sue/How Come You Do Me Like You Do
5101 Air in D Flat

With Coleman Hawkins (20):

Okeh

41566 Jamaica Shout/Heartbreak Blues

With Allen-Hawkins (1-2):

Melotone

12759 Shadows on the Swanee/Swingin' Along on a Shoe String
12769 The River's Takin' Care of Me/Aintcha Got Music
12842 You're Gonna Lose Your Gal/My Galveston Gal
12858 Dark Clouds/Hush My Mouth

Perfect

15802 Shadows on the Swanee/Swingin' Along on a Shoe String

With Allen-Hawkins (1-2)—continued

15808 The River's Takin' Care of Me/Aintcha Got Music

With Own Band (1-5):

Victor

23006 Roamin'/Patrol Wagon Blues
23338 Singing Pretty Songs/I Fell in Love with You
38017 Pleasin' Paul/Make a Country Bird Fly Wild
38073 Biffly Blues/It Should Be You
38080 Feeling Drowsy/Swing Out
38088 Funny Feathers Blues/How Do They Do It
38121 Dancing Dave/Everybody Shout
38140 Sugar Hill Function/You Might Get Better

Melotone

11345 Rug Cutter's Ball
13016 Don't Let Your Love Go Wrong/Why Don't You Practice
13045 I Never Slept a Wink/I Wish I Were Twins
13096 Pardon My Southern Accent/How's About Tomorrow Night
13145 Rug Cutter's Swing/There's a House in Harlem
13304 Believe It Beloved/It's Written All Over Your Face
13322 Whose Honey Are You/Smooth Sailing

ARMSTRONG, Daniel Louis (Satchmo'). *Trumpet, vocal, leader.* Received 12 points as trumpet: *Cavanaugh, Goffin, Mize, Smith;* 31 points as male vocal: *Avakian, Braveman, Cavanaugh, Goffin, Hoefer, Lim, Mize, Russell, Smith, Thiele, Williams.* Born July 4, 1900, New Orleans, Louisiana. Picked up knowledge of his instrument principally at the Waif's Home for Boys in New Orleans, where he was placed at age 13 for firing a gun during a New Year's Eve Celebration. He began playing in bands just a few years later and was soon accepted as a desirable sideman by King Oliver, Kid Ory, Fate Marable and other miscellaneous New Orleans bands. After several years on the riverboats with Marable, he was called to Chicago in July, 1922, by King Oliver, with whose band he remained for two years. In 1924 New York made a bid for him in the person of Fletcher Henderson; he stayed a year, returned to Chicago to play with Ollie Powers and Erskine Tate's Vendome Theatre Orchestra (he doubled the two jobs for almost a year); with Carroll Dickerson at the Sunset Café and Savoy Ballroom; with Clarence Jones at the Metropolitan Theatre. In the fall of 1927 he headed his own band for a few months, but not until the spring of 1929 when he was featured in the *Hot Chocolates* revue in New York did he finally organize and head his own group. It subsequently played New York's Coconut Grove, Chicago's Show Boat Café and Culver City's Cotton Club. Twice he made trips to London and the Continent; once for the last six months of 1932 and the second time from July, 1933, to January, 1935. While there he appeared as soloist in reviews, in addition to fronting bands. Upon his return to U. S., he took over Luis Russell's already organized band and with frequent changes of personnel, has fronted his own band ever since. He has made numerous appearances in movies, several in Broadway revues. Recorded with Oliver, Henderson, Tate, Johnny Dodds, his own recording groups (Hot Five and Hot Seven), Clarence Williams and numerous accompaniments. Solos: *West End Blues, Skip the Gutter, Once in a While, Savoy Blues, Potato Head Blues, Knee Drops, Cornet Chop Suey*—all by his own band; *Stomp Off Let's Go* (Tate); *Wild Man Blues* (both his own band and Dodds); *Drop that Sack* (Lil's Hot Shots); *TNT, Sugar Foot Stomp, Carolina Stomp* (Henderson); *Mandy* (Williams). For a complete Armstrong Discography, refer to pages 134-142 of the 1944 Esquire Jazz Book.

AULD, George (Georgie). *Tenor* and *alto saxophone, leader.* Received 7 points as tenor: *Burley, Feather, Jovien;* 1 point as New Star leader: *Simon;* 1 point as New Star alto: *Ulanov.* Born May 19, 1919, Toronto Canada. Studied and played the alto saxophone during school days and at the age of 12 won a Rudy Wiedoeft scholarship from the then-popular altoman—with whom George studied for nine months. (He had moved to New York in 1929 and became an American citizen.) On the day he heard tenor saxophonist Coleman Hawkins' record of *Meditation,* he found his true ability. He borrowed a tenor from a fellow musician, sat in on a jam session, and from that point forward became a hot tenorman. That was 1935, when he fronted his own small combination for four months at Nick's in New York. Later that year he joined Bunny Berigan (1935-37); then he moved to Artie Shaw for a year (1938), after which he tried his luck with his own band for five unsuccessful months. He began jobbing around New York, playing record dates with Roy Eldridge, Benny Carter, Teddy Wilson and others. In 1940 he joined Benny Goodman and stayed a year; in August, 1941, he connected with the 31-piece Artie Shaw organization until its break-up in January, 1942, at which time he again launched his own band (1942-44). Tenor solos: *Solid Sam* (Shaw); *Joe Turner Blues* (Carter); *It's a Smooth One, Good Enough to Keep, Scarecrow* (Goodman).

BAILEY, Mildred. *Vocal.* Received 38 points: *Burley, Braveman, Cavanaugh, Dexter, Hammond, Hoefer, Jax, Jovien Levin, Lim, Miller, Smith, Stacy, Thiele, Ulanov.* Born about 1907, Tekoa, Washington, but attended school in Spokane. When her brother, Al Rinker, teamed up with Bing Crosby (The Rhythm Boys), she became definitely interested in music and since she could play no instrument, took to singing. She worked as a song plugger in a Seattle music shop, and this gave her an opportunity to "practice" her vocalisms. Paul Whiteman heard her in 1929 and she became his vocalist, one of the first to sing regularly with a band. Remained with Whiteman till about 1934, when she became a solo act. Sang with Red Norvo's band (1936-39), and then went back to solo work. Recorded with Norvo, Dorsey Brothers and numerous studio combinations under her own name. Solos: *Smoke Dreams* (Norvo); *Is That Religion* (Dorseys); *Washboard Blues, Someday Sweetheart* (own band).

One of the really great jazz pianists, the first and thus far the only expert jazz organist, Thomas (Fats) Waller died enroute from California to New York in December of 1943 – unexpectedly, much in the same manner as he had lived out his life. From boyhood days, he never accepted conventional patterns of living: he chose to be himself, to find his inner expression in his music, and he never lost sight of this driving spontaneity which enabled him to play supremely well, to write melodic and happy tunes by the score. Down Beat photo by Otto F. Hess.

Jimmie Noone   O'Neill Spencer   Bob Zurke

These three prominent musicians died during 1944. Noone reached the zenith of his artistry when he worked in the company of Earl Hines at the Apex Club. Spencer hit his peak with John Kirby, Zurke with Bob Crosby. Noone photo by Baby Dodds; Spencer, Ray Rising—Down Beat.

| Oscar Moore | Lawrence Brown | Roy Eldridge | Willie Smith |

All-American Silver Award winners: fast-plucking guitarist Moore; lush-toned trombonist Brown; driving trumpeter Eldridge; easy-blowing altoman Smith, recently discharged from the Navy. Moore photo by Capitol—Charlie Mihn; Eldridge, Down Beat photo by Ray Rising.

| Joe Turner | Billie Holiday | Benny Carter | Lester Young |

All-American Silver Award Winners: blues-shouting vocalist Turner; individually-phrasing vocalist Holiday; veteran altoman Carter; stylized tenorman Young, who recently was inducted by the Army. Turner photo by Down Beat—Myron Ehrenberg; Carter photo by Murray Korman.

| Billy Strayhorn | Art Tatum | Slam Stewart | Count Basie |

All-American Silver Award Winners: arranger-composer Strayhorn, who proved to be almost as popular as his mentor, Ellington; rapid-fire pianist Tatum, with his Trio bassist, fancy-bowing Stewart; leader-pianist Basie, with a popular band. Basie photo by James J. Kriegsmann.

MILDRED BAILEY DISCOGRAPHY

With Delta Rhythm Boys (retail):

Decca

3691 I'm Afraid of Myself/Georgia on My Mind
3755 Sometime's I'm Happy/Rockin' Chair
3953 It's So Peaceful in the Country/Lover, Come Back to Me

With Benny Goodman (5):

Columbia

2892 Junk Man/Ol' Pappy
2907 Georgia Jubilee/Emmaline

With Dorsey Brothers (2-5):

Brunswick

6558 Is That Religion/Harlem Lullaby
6587 Lazy Bones/Cabin in the Pines
6655 Shoutin' In That Amen Corner/Snowball
6680 Doin' Uptown Lowdown/Liberty or Love

With Own Band (1-3):

Vocalion

3056 I'd Rather Listen to Your Eyes/I'd Love to Take Orders from You
3057 When Day Is Done/Someday Sweetheart
3367 For Sentimental Reasons/Love I'm After

With Own Band (1-3)—continued

3378 Long About Midnight/More Than You Know
3449 My Last Affair/Trust in Me
3456 Where Are You/You're Laughing at Me
3508 There's A Lull in My Life/Never in a Million Years
3553 Little Joe/Rockin' Chair
3615 Heaven Help This Heart of Mine/If You Ever Should Leave
3626 The Natural Thing to Do/The Moon Got in My Eyes
3712 Bob White/Stone's Throw from Heaven
3758 Loving You/Right or Wrong
3931 I See Your Face Before Me/Thanks for the Memory
3982 From Land of Sky Blue Water/Lover Come Back to Me
4016 Don't Be That Way/I Can't Face Music
4036 At Your Beck & Call/Bewildered
4083 I Let a Song Go out of My Heart/Rock It for Me
4109 If You Were in My Place/Moonshine Over Kentucky
4139 Washboard Blues/Round the Old Deserted Farm
4224 Born to Swing/Small Fry
4253 As Long as You Live/So Help Me
4282 Now It Can Be Told/I Haven't Changed a Thing

With Own Band (1-3)—continued

4345 Love Is Where You Find It/
I Used to Be Color Blind

4406 My Reverie/What Have You
Got That Gets Me

4432 Old Folks/Have You Forgotten So Soon

4474 Lonesome Road/My Melancholy Baby

4548 I Go for That/They Say

4619 I Cried for You/Begin the
Beguine

4632 What Shall I Say/Blame It
on My Last Affair

Okeh

3378 Long About Midnight/More
Than You Know

3982 From the Land of the Sky
Blue Water/Lover, Come
Back to Me

4474 Lonesome Road

4619 Begin the Beguine/I Cried
for You

Columbia

35348 Hold On/Nobody Knows
the Way I Feel This Mornin'

35370 Little High Chairman/
Wham

35409 A Bee Gezindt/After All

35463 Fools Rush In/From Another
World

35532 Tennessee Fish Fry/How
Can I?

35589 I'll Pray for You/Blue

35626 I'm Nobody's Baby/Give Me
Time

With Own Band (1-3)—continued

Bluebird

6945 Rockin' Chair/Georgia on
My Mind

7763 Stop the Sun, Stop the Moon
/Home

7773 Dear Old Mother Dixie/Too
Late

Decca

4252 Sometime/Wherever You
Are

4267 I Think of You/More Than
You Know

With Her Alley Cats (retail):

Decca

18108 Honeysuckle Rose/Willow
Tree

18109 Squeeze Me/Downhearted
Blues

With Gene Austin (1):

Victor

22891 Georgia on My Mind

With Red Norvo (1-2):

Brunswick

7732 Picture Me Without You/
Begins & Ends with You

7744 I Know that You Know/
Porter's Love Song

7761 Can Happen to You/When
Kiss Not Kiss

7767 Now that Summer Is Gone/
Peter Piper

With *Red Norvo* (*1-2*)—*continued*

7813 Slummin' on Park Avenue/ Got My Love
7815 Smoke Dreams/Thousand Dreams of You
7868 Liza/Anything for You
7896 Jivin' the Jeep/Remember
7928 Everyone's Wrong But Me/ Posin'
7932 The Morning After/Do You Ever Think of Me
7970 Tears in My Heart/Worried Over You
7975 Russian Lullaby/Clap Hands Here Comes Charlie
8068 Love Is Here to Stay/Doing All Right
8069 It's Wonderful/Always & Always
8085 Serenade to Stars/More Than Ever
8088 Please Be Kind/Week End of Private Secretary

With *Red Norvo* (*1-2*)—*continued*

8089 There's Boy in Harlem/How Can You Forget
8103 Tea Time/Jeannine
8135 Says My Heart/Leave Me Breathless
8145 Savin' Myself for You
8175 After Dinner Speech/Cigaret & Silhouette
8182 Sunny Side of Things/Put Heart in Song
8194 Wigwammin'/How Can I Thank You
8202 Jump, Jump, Here/Garden of the Moon

With Casa Loma Orchestra (*2*):

Brunswick

6184 You Call It Madness/Wrap Your Troubles in Dreams
6190 Blues in My Heart/When It's Sleepy Time Down South

BAQUET, George. *Clarinet.* Born 1883, New Orleans, La., where he began playing in bands about 1900—The Onward Brass Band and The Imperial Orchestra. Toured with P. T. Wright's Georgia Minstrels (1902-03), returned to his native city (1904) to join John Robichaux, then to The Superior Band (1906), The Magnolia Band and The Olympia Band (alternating, 1908-14). He first heard Bolden in 1904, after which he frequently went Uptown in New Orleans to sit in with Buddy. In May 1914 Baquet joined Bill Johnson's Original Creole Band in Los Angeles (1914-18). Upon the break-up of the Creoles he migrated to Philadelphia, where he has remained ever since. Currently, and for some years past, he has led his own small group at Wilson's Café in that city.

BARBARIN, Paul. *Drums.* Born May 5, 1901, New Orleans, La., where early in life he engaged in playing with local dance bands. In

1918 he came to Chicago to play with King Oliver; when Luis Russell took the band over in New York in 1928, Barbarin remained with it steadily, including also several years of its existence under the leadership of Louis Armstrong. About 1939 he returned to New Orleans to form his own organization for about a year; joined Red Allen (1942), Sidney Bechet (1943), since which he has again been playing with local New Orleans bands. Recorded with Oliver, Russell, Armstrong, Wilton Crawley, Henry Allen—and his drum work may be heard on all these records.

BASIE, William (Count). *Leader, piano.* Received 5 points as pianist: *Burley, Hammond;* 15 points as leader: *Burley, Braveman, Hammond, Hoefer, Lim, Stacy.* Born August 21, 1906, Red Bank, N. J., where he attended high school and began study of piano under his mother's tutelage. For about seven years after being graduated from high school he jobbed with numerous local outfits in the New York area. About 1930 he joined a traveling show which went broke in Kansas City, Mo., and he was stranded there, so decided to "look around." He found work quickly with Walter Page and Bennie Moten. In 1935 Basie organized his own band and through broadcasts over W9XBY came to the attention of John Henry Hammond, who took a personal interest in the band, arranged to have it booked by MCA. After an engagement at Chicago's Grand Terrace in the fall of 1936, Basie became increasingly successful and soon reached big-name status. Recorded with Moten, Page, own band. Solos: several albums by Decca; *Topsy, Swinging at the Daisy Chain* and many others by his own band, which listed in the Buck Clayton Discography.

BAUDUC, Ray. *Drums.* Born July 18, 1908, New Orleans, La. Evinced an early interest in drums and at age 14 was working with a small local band. Post-high school days found him in New York working for Joe Venuti (1926); there followed engagements with the Scranton Sirens, Ben Pollack, Red Nichols, Freddie Rich and then with Bob Crosby (1935-43). He is now in the Armed Forces. Publicly reputed to be a "two-beat" drummer, Bauduc himself says: "This two-beat talk is overrated stuff." Solos: *The Big Noise from Winnetka* (duo with bassist Bob Haggart); *South Rampart St. Parade* and *March of the Bob Cats* (Crosby).

BECHET, Sidney. *Soprano saxophone, clarinet, leader.* Received
13 points as saxophonist: *Avakian, Goffin, Hoefer, Miller, Smith.* Born
May 14, 1897, New Orleans, Louisiana. Took a lively teen-age interest in music; when six began his self-taught lessons on clarinet, which
he continued throughout his boyhood days. At age eight he "sat in"
with Freddie Keppard's New Orleans band and at nine gained the
admiration and friendship of clarinetist George Baquet, who took
great pains to teach the lad, but even then Bechet depended almost
entirely on his memory rather than on written notes. He played in
his brother's band at 13; professionally joined the famous Eagle Band
of New Orleans in 1914. The following year he toured Texas with
Clarence Williams and upon his return to New Orleans played with
the Olympia band under King Oliver (1917). In the summer of that
year he migrated to Chicago with the Bruce & Bruce stock company,
playing through the South on its way to the northern metropolis.
Upon arrival there, he immediately grabbed a job at the De Luxe
Cabaret with Freddie Keppard; he alternated between that spot and
the Pekin Cabaret (with pianist Tony Jackson) until late 1919, when
he joined Will Marion Cook's concert orchestra and went to Europe
with it, not returning to the U. S. until 1922. He then jobbed around
New York, making the famous Clarence Williams Blue Five dates
with trumpeter Louis Armstrong. In 1925 Bechet returned to Europe
with *The Black Revue;* left the show after a year and joined a band
which toured Russia (where he met trumpeter Tommy Ladnier for
the first time). Back in Paris in 1927, *The Black Revue* was reorgan-
ized and Bechet led the show's 14-piece orchestra; it toured all over
Europe. In mid-1928 he joined Noble Sissle in Paris, but the following
year he was again heading his own group at the Haus Vaterland in
Berlin. Early in 1930 Sissle wired him to come back to America to
rejoin, which he did, only to return to Europe again with Sissle for
another tour. *The Black Revue* was revived for the third time and
Bechet left Sissle (1930) to assume leadership of its orchestra. Again
Sissle wired for him and later in 1930 he returned to the U. S., where
he has remained ever since. He played with Sissle for eight months in
1931 and again from 1934 to the end of 1938. In the interim he led his
own groups, jobbed around New York and since leaving Sissle has
recorded with and led his own small combinations throughout the
country. During the season of 1932-33 his New Orleans Feetwarmers

played New York's Savoy Ballroom, and cut the now famous six sides for the Victor label. Compositions: *Voice of the Slaves, Polka Dot Rag, Chant in the Night.* Soprano solos: *Dear Old Southland, Summertime, Chant in the Night* (own band); *Characteristic Blues, I'm Just Wild About Harry* (Sissle); *Maple Leaf Rag* (Feetwarmers). Clarinet solos: *Polka Dot Rag*—issued as *Sweetie Dear* (Feetwarmers); *Lonesome Blues* (own band).

SIDNEY BETCHET DISCOGRAPHY

With Clarence Williams (5-10, except* 35-50):

Okeh

4925 *Wild Cat Blues/Kansas City Blues

4926 Lady Luck Blues/Kansas City Man Blues

4927 Oh Daddy Blues/I've Got the "Yes We Have No Bananas" Blues

4966 Tain't Nobody's Business If I Do/Achin' Hearted Blues

4975 *New Orleans Hop Scop Blues

4993 Old Fashioned Love/Oh Daddy Blues

8090 Blind Man Blues/Atlanta Blues

8096 Down on the Levee Blues/ Lonesome Woman Blues

8099 Graveyard Dream Blues/A Green Gal Can't Go Wrong

8107 If I Let You Get Away With It Once/E Flat Blues

8122 Jail House Blues

8154 He's Never Gonna Throw Me Down/Too Late Now, Get Your Money Back

8171 *Texas Moaner Blues/House Rent Blues

With Clarence Williams (5-10, except * 35-50)—continued

8173 You've Got the Right Key But the Wrong Keyhole

8193 Who'll Chop Your Suey/ Done Made a Fool Out of Me

8197 I'm So Glad I'm Brownskin/ Off and On Blues

8212 Baby I Can't Use You No More/Trouble Everywhere I Roam

8215 *Papa De Da Da

8245 *Coal Cart Blues/Santa Claus Blues

40006 *Mean Blues/Shreveport

40260 *Mandy Make Up Your Mind/I'm a Little Blackbird

40321 *Cake Walkin' Babies From Home

40330 *Pickin' On Your Baby/Cast Away

Gennett

5626 *Nobody Knows the Way I Feel This Mornin'/Early Every Morning

With Duke Ellington:

..... Unissued: Twelfth Street Rag

With Bennie Peyton's Jazz Kings:

..... Unissued: High Society/
Tiger Rag

With Red Onion Jazz Babies (25):

Gennett

5627 Cake Walkin' Babies From
Home

*With New Orleans Feetwarmers
(10-25):*

Victor

23358 Lay Your Racket/I Want
You Tonight (Blu 10472)
23360 Maple Leaf Rag/Sweetie
Dear (Blu 7614)
24150 I've Found New Baby/Shag
(Blu 10022)

With Noble Sissle (1-5):

Brunswick

6073 Loveless Love/Got the
Bench Got the Park
6129 Basement Blues

Variety

552 I'm Just Wild about Harry/
Bandanna Days
648 Characteristic Blues/Okey
Doke
..... Unissued: St. Louis Blues/
Dear Old Southland

Decca

153 Polka Dot Rag/Under the
Creole Moon
154 Loveless Love/Old Ark Is
Moverin'

With Noble Sissle (1-5)—continued

766 I Wonder Who Made
Rhythm

With Noble Sissle (1):

Decca

778 That's What Love Did to
Me/You Can't Live in Har-
lem
788 'Tain't a Fit Night Out for
Man
847 I Take to You/Rhythm of
the Broadway Moon

Acc. Trixie Smith (1):

Decca

7469 Trixie Blues/My Daddy
Rocks Me (7617)
7489 Freight Train Blues/My Un-
usual Man
7528 He May Be Your Man/Jack,
I'm Mellow

*Acc. Coot Grant and Kid Wilson
(1):*

Decca

7500 Uncle Joe/Blue Monday on
Sugar Hill
..... Unissued: Toot It Brother
Armstrong/I Am a Woman

With Haitian Orchestra (1):

Baldwin

1012 Meringue de Amour/Ti
Ralph
1013 Diane/Nana

With Haitian Orchestra (1)—continued

Varsity

8360 Baba/Tropical Mood
8405 Rose Rhumba/Sous Les Palmiers

With Tommy Ladnier (retail-1):

Bluebird

10086 Weary Blues/JaDa
10089 Really the Blues/When You & I Were Young Maggie

With Jelly Roll Morton (retail-1):

Bluebird

10429 Winin' Boy Blues/Oh Didn't He Ramble
10434 High Society/I Thought I Heard Buddy Bolden Say

With The Port of Harlem Seven (retail):

Blue Note

6 Pounding Heart Blues
7 Blues for Tommy

With Louis Armstrong (retail):

Decca

18090 Perdido St. Blues/2:19 Blues
18091 Down in Honky Tonk Town/Coal Cart Blues

With Bechet-Spanier Big Four (1-3):

Hot Record Society

2000 Lazy River/Sweet Lorraine
2001 China Boy/4 or 5 Times

With Bechet-Spanier Big Four (1-3)—continued

2002 That's a Plenty/If I Could Be with You
2003 Squeeze Me/Sweet Sue

With His Own Trio (1-2):

Victor

26746 Blues for You Johnny/Ain't Misbehavin'
27204 Blues in Thirds/One O'Clock Jump
27240 Save It Pretty Mama/Stompy Jones

With His Own Quartet (retail):

Blue Note

13 Lonesome Blues/Dear Old Southland
502 Bechet's Steady Rider/Saturday Night Blues

With His Own Quintet (retail):

Blue Note

6 Summertime

With His Own Band (retail-2):

Vocalion

4537 Jungle Drums/Hold Tight
4575 Chant in the Night/What a Dream

Bluebird

8509 Sidney's Blues/Make Me a Pallet on the Floor
10623 Preachin' Blues/Indian Summer

With His Own Band (retail-2)—
continued

Victor

26640 Wild Man Blues/Shake It &
 Break It
26663 Old Man Blues/Nobody
 Knows Way I Feel
27904 I'm Coming Virginia/Geor-
 gia Cabin

With His Own Band (retail-2)—
continued

20-1510 The Mooche/Blues in the
 Air

Decca

2129 Blackstick/When the Sun
 Sets Down South
7429 Viper Mad/Sweet Patootie

BIGARD, Barney. *Clarinet.* Received 11 points: *Cavanaugh, Dexter, Hoefer, Jovien, Thiele.* Born 1906, New Orleans, Louisiana. He began his study of the clarinet early in life with Lorenzo and Louis Tio. Launched big-time career with Octave Gaspard in New Orleans (1923) then played with King Oliver (1925-26), Charlie Elgar (1926-27), Luis Russell (1927-28), Duke Ellington (1928-42). After 12 years as Ellington's featured clarinetist, he left the band in the summer of 1942, staying in California, where he heads his own small combination (1942-44); joined Freddie Slack (1943). Recorded with Oliver, Jelly Roll Morton, Ellington and his own studio combination. Solos: *The Mooche, Clarinet Lament, Across the Track Blues, Blue Light, Old Man Blues, Subtle Lament, Saratoga Swing* (all Ellington); *Finesse* (Improvisations in *Ellingtonia* with Rex Stewart and Django Reinhardt); *Lament for Javanette* (own band). Many of the records on which he solos are listed in the Duke Ellington Discography. See also the 1944 ESQUIRE JAZZ BOOK for a selected Bigard Discography.

BONANO, Joseph (Sharkey). *Trumpet.* Born April 9, 1904, New Orleans, La., where he attended school. At 16 he began studying his instrument and soon afterwards was heading his own band at Milenburg Lake. Except for a period with Jean Goldkette (1927) he has fronted his own groups ever since. In the middle thirties he recorded a series of 12 sides for the Vocalion label: *Mudhole Blues/ Swing Out* (3353); *High Society/Satisfied* (3380); *Mister Brown/ Smiling* (3400); *Wash It/Blowing Steam* (3410); *Old Fashioned Love/Big Boy* (3450); *Rusty Gate/Swanee Shore* (3470).

BRAUD, Wellman. *String Bass*. Born Jan. 25, 1891, St. James, La., but was raised in New Orleans where he attended high school. Initial instrument was violin, which he first studied at age 12, later playing fiddle in a string trio at the Terminal House and at Tom Anderson's Annex. Finally he arrived at the bass and in 1917, when he migrated to Chicago, he joined a band composed entirely of New Orleans men and led by Sugar Johnny, a cornetist whose real name no one seems to remember. In the early twenties he played with Elgar's Creole Band, after which he made a short trip to Europe. He then settled in New York, joined Wilbur Sweatman (1923), toured with a burlesque show (1923-26), finally joining Duke Ellington (1926-35). Now retired from music except for a few occasional gig dates, he operates a poolroom in Harlem.

BROWN, Lawrence. *Trombone*. Received 21 points: *Braveman, Cavanaugh, Dexter, Feather, Levin, Simon, Stacy, Ulanov.* Born Aug. 3, 1905, Lawrence, Kansas, where he studied instrument in school. Began career with Curtis Mosby, played with Paul Howard (1927-30), Les Hite and Louis Armstrong (1931), Duke Ellington (1932-44). Solos: *The Sheik, Rose of the Rio Grande* (Ellington); *Lazy Man's Shuffle* (Rex Stewart). See the Duke Ellington Discography for a comprehensive list of Brown's recordings, which include most of the Brunswicks, Masters, late Victors.

BRUNIS, Georg Clarence (real name, Brunies). *Trombone*. Received 8 points: *Goffin, Jax, Smith.* Born Feb. 6, 1900, New Orleans, La., of musical parents, his father having been a violinist and his mother a guitarist. He was a member of Jack (Papa) Laine's "Kid" Band in New Orleans as early as 1908. In 1919 he played his first professional engagement with the New Orleans Rhythm Kings. From 1923 to 1935 he was a member of Ted Lewis' band. Subsequently played with Bobby Hackett, Louis Prima, Wingy Manone, Eddie Condon, Sharkey Bonano and Muggsy Spanier. Recorded with Lewis, Chauncey Morehouse, Manone, Prima, Bonano, Condon, Hackett, Bill Davison, Rhythm Kings, Spanier, own band on the Commodore label.

BURBANK, Albert. *Clarinet.* Born March 25, 1902, New Orleans, La. While a young boy his parents took him to picnics at Milenburg, where he watched the clarinet players in bands with intense interest. Comments Burbank: "Their rendition of jazz intrigued me. That's what I wanted to play—a clarinet, and the players I idolized were Lorenzo Tio, Picou and Big Eye Louie Nelson." At 18 when he started working he was at last able to buy a clarinet, took lessons and soon began jobbing with local bands. "I aimed," reflects Burbank, "to play as good as the best so I could be at least half as good. I didn't go from one instrument to another; I started with a clarinet— I knew what I wanted." During the course of years he has played with Picou in the Olympia Band, Sam Morgan, Buddy Petit and many others in spots such as Spanish Fort, Milenburg, Economy Hall, San Jacinto, etc. Most recently he has been playing with the Eureka Brass Band and a small dance group at a Lake Ponchartrain resort. In the opinion of William Russell, Burbank ranks among the greatest of New Orleans clarinetists.

CAREY, Thomas (Mutt), *Cornet.* Received 4 points: *Avakian, Williams.* Born 1892, New Orleans. Began musical career on drums, but gave them up when they proved cumbersome to carry home. Acquired his knowledge of the cornet from his brothers, one of whom, trombonist Jack Carey, was a famous leader of early New Orleans jazz. About 1914 Mutt became a regular member of Kid Ory's Brown-Skinned Babies. Joined a road show (Mack & Mack), which boasted a four-piece band including Johnny Dodds. This was 1917 and when the show reached Chicago, Mutt stayed to play at the Dreamland, following Oliver. Upon his return to New Orleans not long after he joined Wade Whaley (1918), then migrated to California to work with Kid Ory in Oakland and San Francisco (1919-21). He settled in that state, and although he has taken odd jobs such as delivering mail and working as a Pullman porter, he has never given up music, continuing to play whenever the opportunity comes. Recently (1943-44), he has been performing with Kid Ory's Creole Band in San Francisco, from which city the Standard Oil broadcasts on jazz originated. Recorded with Ory on the Sunshine label (1921).

CARNEY, Harry. *Baritone saxophone.* Received 19 points: *Avakian, Cavanaugh, Dexter, Hammond, Levin, Lim, Miller, Thiele.* Born April 1, 1910, Boston, Mass., where he attended school. Studied at school and under private teachers. Professionally launched his career in 1925, with Bobby Sawyer; after a short engagement with Henry Sapro, he joined Duke Ellington in 1927 and has been with that band ever since. Baritone solos: *Harlem Speaks, Stompy Jones, Jive Stomp, Cocktails for Two, Caravan, Exposition Swing, Buffet Flat* (all Ellington). Refer to the Duke Ellington Discography for a comprehensive list of Carney's recordings—all the Victors, Brunswicks, Masters.

CARTER, Bennett Lester (Benny). *Alto saxophone, trumpet, clarinet, leader.* Received 33 points as altoman: *Braveman, Cavanaugh, Dexter, Feather, Goffin, Hoefer, Levin, Lim, Miller, Stacy, Thiele, Ulanov;* 4 points as leader: *Dexter, Thiele.* Born Aug. 8, 1907, New York City, where he attended grammar and high school; later went to Wilberforce University. Took a few piano lessons from his mother in 1924 and studied briefly under private teachers, but is mostly self-taught. Started playing professionally in 1924 with June Clark, after which, in succession, he played with Billy Page, Horace Henderson (at college), Duke Ellington, Billy Fowler, Fletcher Henderson, Charles Johnson, Chick Webb, McKinney's Cotton Pickers (1931-32), own band (1933), Willie Bryant (1934). In 1935 he went to Europe and spent three years as a staff arranger at the British Broadcasting Corp., in addition to leading his own band. When he returned to the U. S. in May, 1938, he again organized his own band and has since alternated in that capacity between large and small combinations. Recorded with F. Henderson, McKinney, own band, Chocolate Dandies, Teddy Wilson, Lionel Hampton, Spike Hughes, Mezz Mesirow. Alto solos: *I'm in the Mood for Swing* (Hampton), *Pastoral* (Hughes), *I'd Love It* (McKinney), *Shuffle Bug Shuffle* (own band). Clarinet solos: *Miss Hannah* (McKinney), *Dee Blues* (Dandies).

CASEY, Albert (Al). *Guitar.* Received 31 points: *Braveman, Cavanaugh, Goffin, Hammond, Jax, Levin, Mize, Simon, Smith, Stacy, Thiele, Ulanov.* Born Sept. 15, 1915, Louisville, Kentucky. His first musical interest was evinced on the violin at age 8. Finished his schooling in New York, where he met Fats Waller, whom he joined in the mid-1930's. He remained with the Waller band until its demise in 1943, except for a period (1939-40), when he played with Teddy Wilson. He now heads his own Trio (1943-44). Recorded with Teddy Wilson, Mezz Mesirow, Chu Berry, Frankie Newton, Pete Brown and extensively with Waller. Solos: *Buck Jumpin'*, *Honeysuckle Rose* (Waller). For a complete Casey Discography refer to pages 156-58 of the 1944 ESQUIRE JAZZ BOOK.

CATLETT, Sidney (Big Sid). *Drums*. Received 24 points: *Braveman, Goffin, Hoefer, Jax, Levin, Lim, Miller, Mize, Stacy, Ulanov*. Born Jan. 17, 1910, Evansville, Ind. Began musical activities in school (in Chicago) and studied under private teachers. He played in local bands in Chicago for four years and then hit his stride playing engagements with Sammy Stewart, Chicago's Michigan Theatre (1930-33), McKinney's Cotton Pickers (1933-34), Jeter-Pilar (1934-35), Don Redman (1934-38), Louis Armstrong (1938-42), except for short stands with Roy Eldridge and Benny Goodman (1941), free-lance (1942), Teddy Wilson (1943). Now heads his own small combination (1943-44). Recorded with Redman, Armstrong, Goodman, Eddie Condon, F. Henderson, Benny Carter, Spike Hughes. For complete Catlett Discography refer to pages 68-69 of the 1944 ESQUIRE JAZZ BOOK.

CLAYTON, Wilbur D. (Buck). *Trumpet*. Received 20 points: *Burley, Braveman, Cavanaugh, Dexter, Hammond, Jax, Thiele*. Born Nov. 12, 1911, Parsons, Kansas, where he attended high school. Studied some music in school, but mostly self-taught: piano (1925-27), trumpet (1929-31). Migrated to California where he joined La Vern Floyd's orchestra (1932); then to Earl Dancer (1932-34), after which he fronted his own band (1934-36), with which he spent most of this time furthering the cause of jazz by playing in China. He then entered the Count Basie band (1936-44), which he left upon his induction into the Armed Services. Currently he is a member of the U. S. Army Band at Camp Shanks, N. Y. Recorded with Basie, Teddy Wilson, Kansas City Six, The Quintones, Mildred Bailey, Kansas City Seven. Solos: *Fiesta in Blue, Swingin' the Blues, Good Morning Blues* (Basie); *Why Was I Born* (Wilson).

BUCK CLAYTON DISCOGRAPHY

With Count Basie (retail-2):

Okeh

5085 Here Comes Charlie/Pound Cake
5169 Nobody Knows/Song of the Island
5816 The World Is Mad
5963 It's the Same Old South
5987 Who Am I/Stampede in G
6010 Rocking the Blues
6157 Wiggle Woogie
6180 Feedin' the Bean
6244 Goin' to Chicago/9:20 Special
6330 Basie Boogie/Let Me See
6475 King Joe
6527 Tom Thumb/My Old Flame
6634 One O'Clock Jump

Vocalion

5118 Lester Leaps In

Columbia

35321 I Left My Baby/Riff Interlude
35338 Hollywood Jump/Someday Sweetheart
35348 Easy Does It/Louisiana
35357 Ham 'n Eggs/Between the Devil and the Deep Blue Sea
35500 Somebody Stole My Gal/ Let's
35521 I Never Knew/Tickle-Toe

Decca

1121 Pennies from Heaven/Swinging at the Daisy Chain

With Count Basie (retail-2)—continued

1141 Roseland Shuffle/Honeysuckle Rose
1228 Boo-Hoo/Glory of Love
1252 Boogie Woogie/Exactly Like You
1363 One O'Clock Jump/John's Idea
1379 Listen My Children/Smarty
1446 Our Love Was Meant to Be/ Good Morning Blues
1538 Time Out/Let Me Dream
1581 I Keep Remembering/Out of the Window
1682 Blues in the Dark/Georgianna
1728 Every Tub/Now Will You Be Good
1770 Topsy/Don't You Miss Your Baby
1880 Swingin' the Blues/Sent for You Yesterday and Here You Come Today
1965 Blue and Sentimental/Doggin' Around
2004 London Bridge Is Falling Down/Stop Beating 'Round the Mulberry Bush
2030 Texas Shuffle/Mama Don't Want No Peas and Rice and Cocoanut Oil
2212 Dark Rapture/Jumpin' at the Woodside
2224 Panassie Stomp/Do You Wanna Jump, Children
2249 Sing for Your Supper/My Heart Belongs to Daddy

With Count Basie (retail-2)—continued

2284 Blame It on My Last Affair/ Blues I Like to Hear
2325 Shorty George/Thursday
2355 Boogie Woogie/How Long
2406 Cherokee (2 pts.)
2498 Dirty Dozens/When the Sun
2631 Lady Be Good/You Can Depend on Me
2722 The Fives/Hey Lawdy Mama
2780 Oh Red/Donkey Serenade
2922 Evil Blues/Jive at Five
3071 Red Wagon/Dupree Blues
3708 One O'Clock Jump/Swingin' at Daisy Chain
3709 Shorty George/Jumpin' at the Woodside
3882 Blue and Sentimental/You Can Depend on Me
18125 Doggin' Around/Good Morning Blues

With Teddy Wilson (1-3):

Brunswick

7824 This Year's Kisses/He Ain't Got Rhythm
7859 Why Was I Born/I Must Have That Man
7903 Mean to Me/I'll Get By
7911 Foolin' Myself/Easy Living
7917 Sun Showers/Yours and Mine
7926 I'll Never Be the Same/I Found a New Baby
8008 My Man/I Can't Help Loving That Man

With Teddy Wilson (1-3)—continued

8015 Things Are Looking Up/ Nice Work if You Can Get It

With Billie Holiday (1-2):

Vocalion

3593 Me, Myself and I/Without Your Love
3605 Born to Love/Sailboat in the Moonlight

With Harry James (1-2):

Brunswick

8035 Life Goes to a Party/When We're Alone
8038 Jubilee/Can't I
8055 One O'Clock Jump/It's the Dreamer in Me
8067 Texas Chatter/Song of the Wanderer
8136 Lullaby in Rhythm/Out of Nowhere

With Kansas City Five (retail):

Commodore

510 I Know That You Know/ Laughing at Life
511 Good Morning Blues

With Kansas City Six (retail):

509 Countless Blues/I Want a Little Girl
511 Them There Eyes
512 Pagin' the Devil/Way Down Yonder in New Orleans

COLE, Nathaniel ("King" Nat). *Piano, leader.* Received 6 points as pianist: *Feather, Jovien, Ulanov*; 8 points as vocalist with 4 as New Star vocal: *Cavanaugh, Feather, Stacy, Ulanov.* Born March 17, 1917, Montgomery, Ala. Attended school in Chicago. Began his study of piano under the encouragement of his family and with private teachers. Organized his own band which played local dates in Chicago; and during his post-high school days, the band toured vaudeville with the *Shuffle Along* revue, which broke up in Los Angeles. Cole stayed, became a solo pianist at night spots there, finally organizing a trio (guitar, bass, piano). This trio migrated to New York and has been playing in night spots ever since. Solo: *Early Morning Blues, Sweet Lorraine* (Cole Trio).

COLEMAN, William (Bill). *Trumpet.* Received 7 points: *Cavanaugh, Hammond, Stacy.* Born Aug. 4, 1904, Paris, Kentucky. Attended high school in Cincinnati, O. Played in a youngsters' band during high school days, mostly self-taught. Beginning in 1925 jobbed around New York with trombonist J. C. Higginbotham and other local groups. Then played with Lloyd and Cecil Scott (1926-29 and again 1930), Luis Russell (1929 and again 1932-33), Charlie Johnson (1931), Ralph Cooper (1931-32), Lucky Millinder (1933), Benny Carter (1933-34), Teddy Hill (1934-35). In the fall of 1935 he went to Europe, touring the entire Continent, as well as India and Egypt. Upon his return to the United States late in 1939, he played with Benny Carter and Teddy Wilson (1940-43). Solo: *Bill Coleman Blues* (own recording combination).

COLLINS, Lee. *Trumpeter.* Born Oct. 17, 1901. New Orleans, La. Self-taught on the cornet, he early began playing with the New Orleans bands of the Storyville district (1916-29), except for a few months in 1924 when he played with King Oliver in Chicago; subsequently worked with Luis Russell (1930); Zutty Singleton (1931), since which time he has been playing with his own and local bands in the Chicago area. Recorded with the Jones-Astoria Eight—four sides for the Victor label; and with Jelly Roll Morton on the Autograph label.

CROSBY, Israel. *String bass.* Received 8 points: *Hammond, Jax, Stacy.* Born Jan. 19, 1919, Chicago, Ill. Began on trumpet, changing to string bass in 1934. First professional engagement was with Johnny Long (Chicago); also worked with Anthony Fambro and Albert Ammons in Chicago (1935), Fletcher Henderson (1936-38), Three Sharps and a Flat (1939), Horace Henderson (1940-42), Teddy Wilson (1941-42). Recorded with Jimmie Noone, Benny Goodman, Roy Eldridge, Albert Ammons, Teddy Wilson, Gene Krupa, Dane Paton, Bumble Bee Slim (blues singer), Art Tatum, Fletcher Henderson. Solos: *Blues in C Sharp Minor* (Wilson); *Blues of Israel* (Krupa); *Barrelhouse* (accompaniment for pianist Jess Stacy).

DICKENSON, Victor (Vic). *Trombone.* Received 8 points: *Hammond, Jax, Stacy.* Born Aug. 6, 1906, Xenia, Ohio, where he began his formal education; but upon moving to Columbus, Ohio, his interest in the trombone had grown to such proportions that he taught himself most of what he learned, improving with experience and finally learning to read. He jobbed with local bands in Columbus as early as 1922; joined Don Phillips at the Broadway Gardens and Leonard Gay (both in Madison, Wis.) during the middle twenties. Speed Webb picked him up in Madison (1927-29), after which Vic worked with Zach Whyte (1929-30), Blanche Calloway and miscellaneous gigging jobs (1931-35), Claude Hopkins (1936-39), Benny Carter (1939 and again 1940-41), Count Basie (1940), Sidney Bechet (1941), Lips Page (1941-42), Frankie Newton (1942), Eddie Heywood (1943-44). Recorded with Basie, Bechet, Hopkins, Albert Ammons, Edmond Hall, James P. Johnson, Mary Lou Williams. Solos: *Blues in the Air, The Mooche* (Bechet); *Joymentin', Victory Stride* (Johnson); *The World Is Mad, Louisiana* (Basie); *Church St. Sobbin' Blues* (Hopkins).

DODDS, Johnny. *Clarinet.* Born New Orleans, La., April 12, 1892; died Aug. 8, 1940, in Chicago. Began his study of the clarinet at age 16. By 1912 he was working with numerous New Orleans bands, among them Kid Ory, Eagle Band and many others. A pioneer in the jazzmen's New Orleans-to-Chicago movement, Dodds left his native city in 1918 with Billy Mack's vaudeville troupe which eventually took him to Chicago. But he returned to his native city again before joining King Oliver's history-making organization (1920-24), after which he took his own band into Kelly's Stables, for a six-year run. From that time until his death, he continued to lead his own band at various small Chicago night spots. Recorded with King Oliver, Jimmy Blythe, Jimmy Bertrand, Louis Armstrong, New Orleans Wanderers and his own band. Solos: *Drop That Sack* (Lil's Hot Shots); *Wild Man Blues, Once in a While* (Armstrong); *Perdido St. Blues; Too Tight* (Wanderers); *Canal St. Blues, Dipper Mouth* (Oliver).

JOHNNY DODDS DISCOGRAPHY

With King Oliver (30-50):

Gennett

5132 Dippermouth Blues/Weatherbird Rag
5133 Just Gone/Canal St. Blues
5134 Mandy Lee Blues/I'm Going Away to Wear You Off My Mind
5135 Chimes Blues/Froggie Moore
5184 Snake Rag

Paramount

12088 Southern Stomps
20292 Riverside Blues/Mabel's Dream

Okeh

4906 Sweet Lovin' Man/Sobbin' Blues
4918 Dippermouth Blues/Where Did You Stay Last Night
4933 Snake Rag
4975 Jazzin' Babies Blues
8148 I Aint Gonna Tell Nobody/Room Rent Blues
8235 Sweet Baby Doll/Mabel's Dream
40000 Tears/Buddy's Habit
40034 Riverside Blues/Workingman Blues

With King Oliver (30-50)—continued

Columbia

13003 Chattanooga Stomp/New Orleans Stomp
14003 London Café Blues/Camp Meeting Blues

With Lil's Hot Shots (40):

Vocalion

1037 Drop That Sack/Georgia Bo Bo

Acc. Hociel Thomas (5-15):

8258 Put It Where I Can Get It/Adam and Eve Had the Blues
8289 Washwoman's Blues/Gambler's Dream
8326 I've Stopped My Man/Sunshine Baby

Acc. Butterbeans and Susie (15):

Okeh

8355 He Likes It Slow

With Louis Armstrong

Okeh (35-50):

8261 Gut Bucket Blues/Yes I'm in a Barrel (Co 36152)

8299 Oriental Strut/You're Next (HRS 10; Co 36155)

8300 Heebie Jeebies (Co 36155)/ Muskrat Ramble (Co 36153)

8318 Come Back Sweet Papa/ Georgia Grind

8320 Cornet Chop Suey (HRS 2; Co 36154)/My Heart (Co 36154)

8343 I'm Gonna Gitcha/Don't Forget to Mess Around

8357 Droppin' Shucks/Whosit

8379 Big Fat Ma & Skinny Pa/ Sweet Little Papa

8396 King of Zulus/Lonesome Blues

8423 Sunset Cafe Stomp/Big Butter & Egg Man

8436 Jazz Lips/Skid Da De Da (Co 36153)

8447 Irish Black Bottom/You Made Me Love You

8474 Gully Low Blues/Wild Man Blues

8482 Willie the Weeper/Alligator Crawl

8496 Melancholy Blues/Keyhole Blues

8503 Potato Head Blues (Co 35660)/Put 'Em Down Blues

8519 Weary Blues/I'll Come Back

8535 Hotter Than That/Savoy Blues

8551 Got No Blues/I'm Not Rough

With Louis Armstrong Okeh (30-50)—continued

8566 Struttin' with Some Barbecue/Once in a While

With Own Band

Brunswick (10-30):

3567 Wild Man Blues/Melancholy

3568 Come On and Stomp, Stomp, Stomp/After You've Gone

3574 Clarinet Wabble/San

3585 Oh Lizzie/New St. Louis Blues

3997 When Erastus Plays His Old Kazoo/Joe Turner Blues

7124 Come On and Stomp, Stomp, Stomp/After You've Gone

Vocalion (30-50):

1108 Melancholy

1148 After You've Gone/Come On and Stomp, Stomp, Stomp

15632 Weary Blues/New Orleans Stomp

Paramount (6-10):

12471 Oh Daddy

12483 Loveless Love/19th Street Blues

Victor (2-4):

21552 Blue Washboard Stomp/Bull Fiddle Blues

21554 Blue Clarinet Stomp/Blue Piano Stomp

23396 Goober Dance/Indigo Stomp

38004 Bucktown Stomp/Weary City

38038 Pencil Papa/Sweet Lorraine

Bluebird Reissues (retail):

8549 Bucktown Stomp

10239 Weary City/Bull Fiddle Blues

10238 Indigo Stomp

10240 Too Tight/Goober Dance

10241 Heah Me Talkin'/My Little Isabel

Decca (retail):

1676 Melancholy/Stack O'Lee Blues

2111 Wild Man Blues/29th and Dearborn

3519 Wild Man Blues

3864 Melancholy

7413 Shake Your Can/Blues Galore

18094 Red Onion Blues/Gravier St. Blues

With Jelly Roll Morton (4-8):

Victor

20772 Billy Goat Stomp/Hyena Stomp

20948 The Pearls/Beale St. Blues

21064 Mr. Jelly Lord/Wolverine Blues

21345 Jungle Blues

With Chicago Footwarmers (2-3):

Okeh

8533 Grandma's Ball/Ballin' the Jack

8548 Oriental Man/My Baby

8599 Brush Stomp (Co 35681)/ Get 'Em Again Blues (Co 35681)

With Chicago Footwarmers (2-3)— continued

8613 Brown Bottom Bess/Lady Love

8792 Sweep 'Em Clean/My Girl

With New Orleans Wanderers (15):

Columbia

698 Perdido St. Blues/Gatemouth

735 Too Tight/Papa Dip

With New Orleans Bootblacks (10):

Columbia

14337 Mad Dog/Flat Foot

14465 I Can't Say/Mixed Salad

With Lovie Austin (3-6):

Paramount

12361 Frog Tongue Stomp/Jackass Blues

12369 Sunday Morning Blues/Walk Easy 'Cause My Papa's Here

12380 Galion Stomp/Chicago Mess Around

12391 Merry Maker's Twine/In the Alley Blues

With Jimmy Blythe (5-10):

Paramount

12368 Bohunkus Blues/Buddy Burton's Jazz

12376 Messin' Around/Adam's Apple

With Jimmy Blythe (5-10)—continued

Champion

15344 There'll Come a Day/Weary Way Blues

Vocalion

1135 Weary Way Blues/Poutin' Papa
1136 Have Mercy/Hot Stuff

Acc. Wilmer Davis (2):

Vocalin

1034 Gut Struggle/Rest Your Hips

With Chicago Hottentots (3):

Vocalion

1008 All Night Shags/Put Me in the Alley

With Freddie Keppard (50):

Paramount

12399 Stock Yards Strut/Salty Dog

With Dixieland Thumpers (4-6):

Paramount

12525 Weary Way Blues/There'll Come a Day
12594 Oriental Man/Sock That Thing

With Paramount Pickers (5):

Paramount

12779 Salty Dog/Steal Away

With State St. Ramblers (5):

Gennett

6232 Cootie Stomp/Weary Way Blues

With Dixieland Jug Blowers (3):

Victor

20415 Memphis Shake
20420 House Rent Rag
20469 Hen Party Blues

Acc. Sippie Thomas (2):

Victor

38502 I'm a Mighty Tight Woman

With Jimmie Bertrand (1-3):

Vocalion

1035 Struggling/Little Bits
1060 47th St. Stomp/Idle Hour Social
1099 If You Want to Be My Sugar Papa/I'm Goin' Huntin'
1100 Easy Come, Easy Go/Blues Stampede
1180 Oriental Man/My Baby

With Beale St. Washboard Band (2):

Vocalion

1403 Forty and Tight (Perfect 196, Oriole 8120, Romeo 5120, Conqueror 7980)

DODDS, Warren (Baby). *Drums*. Received 9 points: *Avakian, Russell, Williams*. Born Dec. 24, 1896, New Orleans, La., but attended high school in Bay St. Louis, Miss., having completed grammar school in New Orleans. Started playing drums in 1910, studying on his own and with private teachers, among them Dave Perkins, Walter Grundy and Manuel Manetta. He joined Willie Hightower in New Orleans (1913-16), at the same time doubling with Manuel Manetta at the Villa, Papa Celestin at the 101 Ranch, and with a quartet at George Fewclothes—the band there being comprised of Dodds, trombonist Roy Palmer, trumpeter Sidney Desvigne and pianist Sidney Decou. Subsequently Dodds worked with Jack Carey, The Eagle Band (1916-17), with Celestin at Jack Sheen's (1918); Fate Marable on the riverboats (1919-21); King Oliver (1921-24—he joined Oliver in San Francisco); with his brother Johnny's band (1924 and again 1928-39); with Lil Armstrong at Dreamland when the band boasted Kid Ory, Armstrong and Bud Scott (1925); with Hugh Swift at the Beverly Gardens and Jeffrey Tavern in Chicago (1926-27); with Elgar's Creole Band at Chicago's Savoy (1927). Finally in 1940 he fronted his won band, worked for a stretch with Jimmie Noone (1941) and has since been jobbing local dates with various combinations. Recorded with Louis Armstrong, Oliver, Johnny Dodds, Chicago Footwarmers, Sidney Bechet, Washboard Stompers, Jelly Roll Morton, Jimmy Blythe, Richard M. Jones, Lil Armstrong, New Orleans Wanderers, Lil's Hot Shots and numerous accompaniments for blues singers.

DOMINIQUE, Anatie (Natty). *Trumpet*. Born Aug. 2, 1896, New Orleans, La., where he attended high school. First musical interest was drums; studied privately on trumpet beginning in 1911 and by 1912 or thereabouts he was performing with Manuel Perez and The Imperial Band, continuing with other famous New Orleans parade bands and dance combinations until he migrated to Chicago, just after World War I. His activities include 14 years, not consecutive, with Johnny Dodds, a year-and-a-half with Jimmie Noone, three-and-a-half years with Carroll Dickerson, one year with Louis Armstrong, three years with Jimmie Blythe and shorter stays with Earl Hines, Jelly Roll Morton and Richard M. Jones. Recorded with Morton,

Dodds, Hines, Jones, Blythe, Armstrong. Composer of *Brush Stomp, Sweep 'Em Clean, Too Tight Blues, Little Isabel, Lady Love.*

ELDRIDGE, Roy ("Little Jazz"). *Trumpet, leader.* Received 14 points: *Braveman, Feather, Jovien, Lim, Simon, Ulanov.* Born 1911, Pittsburgh, Pennsylvania, where he attended high school. Joining a carnival show, he took to the road for two years, playing both trumpet and drums in the brass band. In 1928 he joined Horace Henderson's band, remaining for eight months. There followed engagements with the Chocolate Dandies (six months), Speed Webb (one year), Cecil Scott, Elmer Snowden, Charlie Johnson, Teddy Hill, McKinney's Cotton Pickers, Fletcher Henderson. From 1936 to 1940 he fronted his own band, which he disbanded to become feature soloist with Gene Krupa, 1941-43, again heading own outfit (1943-44). Recorded with Henderson, own band, Teddy Wilson, Benny Carter, Krupa, Mildred Bailey, Chu Berry. Solos: *Body and Soul, Stardust, 46 West 52, Sittin' in* (Berry); *Rockin' Chair* (Krupa); *Blues in C Sharp Minor* (Wilson); *Jangled Nerves* (Henderson); *That Thing* (own band).

ELGAR, A. Charles (Charlie). *Leader, violin, tenor saxophone, clarinet, teacher.* Born June 13, 1885, New Orleans, La. Began study of violin at age 12, continued under several private teachers; later attended Medard Academy, Southern University, Marquette University, studying numerous instruments, harmony, theory, etc., in addition to the French language. Migrated to Chicago, became associated with the Coleridge Taylor School of Music (1902-12), during which time he occasionally played with local groups. Organized his own band (1912-30); it comprised only five pieces when it played the Fountain Inn in Chicago (1912-13); augmented to 15 pieces for Dreamland Ballroom and Municipal (Now Navy) Pier (1916-22); Green Mill Gardens (1922-23); Wisconsin Roof Garden, Milwaukee (1925-27); Arcadia Ballroom, Chicago (1927-28); Eagles Ballroom, Milwaukee (1928); Savoy Ballroom, Chicago (1928-29); Sunset Café (1929-30). Part of the period between 1923-25 was devoted to an engagement with Will Marion Cook's Syncopators, and with this

group he played in London's Empire Theatre. Since 1930, Elgar
has devoted most of his time to teaching, supervising Federal Music
Projects and acting in his capacity as a member of the Board of
Directors of Local 208, Chicago. The 1927 Elgar band recorded four
sides for Vocalion: *Café Capers/Walk, Jenny, Walk* (15477); *Night-
mare/Brotherly Love* (15478). In 1918 the band gave a "swing"
concert at Orchestra Hall, Chicago.

ELLINGTON, Edward Kennedy (Duke). *Composer, arranger,
leader, piano.* Received 30 points as arranger: *Burley, Braveman,
Cavanaugh, Dexter, Feather, Goffin, Lim, Mize, Smith, Thiele, Simon;*
43 points as leader: *Braveman, Cavanaugh, Dexter, Feather, Hoefer,
Jax, Jovien, Levin, Lim, Mize, Simon, Smith, Stacy, Thiele, Ulanov.*
Born Apr. 29, 1899, Washington, D. C. Began his study of the piano
under his mother's instruction at 7, but evinced little interest until high
school days in his native city, when he was befriended by Oliver
(Doc) Perry who taught him fundamentals. He soon began working
with obscure local bands and secured a solo spot at the Poodle Dog
(Washington). His first effort at composition was called *The Poodle
Dog Rag.* Post-high school days found him organizing his own band,
The Washingtonians, which played for many local functions over a
period of several years. In 1923 bandleader Wilbur Sweatman enticed
the young pianist to join that organization, from which he was un-
ceremoniously expelled a few months later for inserting an ad lib
break in a conventionally arranged passage. This experience had
brought him to New York, however, and his next move was to sum-
mon his Washington associates and friends to his side. They found
work at Barrons', in Harlem, but not being too successful, returned to
Washington. They were back in New York the following year
(1924), Ellington having obtained a job at New York's Kentucky
Club (49th and Broadway), where he and his fellow-musicians remained for more than three years. Then in December, 1927, with
an augmented band, he moved into the Cotton Club, playing there
for five consecutive seasons. During this period he established a
national reputation. Frequent radio broadcasts from the Cotton Club
were announced by the now famous sportscaster, Ted Husing. Since
1932, the orchestra has toured almost continually, appearing in theatres, concert halls, ballrooms and night spots in 45 of the 48 states,

England and the Continent, a total of about a million-and-a-half miles
of travel. The band has appeared in five movies, the first being the
1930 Amos and Andy vehicle, *Check and Double Check*. In 1942
he appeared in two sequences of *Cabin in the Sky*. During the more
than 20 years of his leadership of this unique orchestra, Ellington
has been a tireless and prolific writer of music, using the extraordinarily fine artists who worked in the band to project effectively his
musical ideas—and often the contributions of these sidemen helped
bring the tunes to a high artistic level. For a variety of labels and under
various pseudonyms, the Ellington orchestra has recorded in greater
number than any other now extant name-band in America. Labels:
Gennett, Romeo, Brunswick, Vocalion, Victor, Harmony, Regal,
Cameo, Velvetone, Melotone, Oriole, Clarion, Hit of the Week,
Master, Variety, Perfect, Pathe, Columbia, Bluebird and Okeh.
Pseudonyms: The Washingtonians, The Jungle Band, The Ten Black
Berries, The Whoopee Makers, The Harlem Hot Chocolates, The
Harlem Footwarmers, The Georgia Syncopators, The Lumberjacks,
Earl Jackson's Musical Champions, The Six Jolly Jesters, Warren
Mills Blue Serenaders, Sonny Greer's Memphis Men, Joe Turner's
Memphis Men, in addition to several small contingents of the band
released under the name of Ellington sidemen Rex Stewart, Cootie
Williams, Barney Bigard and Johnny Hodges. Compositions: *Black,
Brown and Beige, New World a Comin', Reminiscing in Tempo,
Crescendo and Diminuendo in Blue, Blue Light, Ko-Ko, Azure,
Black and Tan Fantasy, East St. Louis Toodle-oo, Birmingham Break-
down, Misty Mornin'*, numerous others, including many of those
listed in the Discography below. Piano solos: *Reminiscing in Tempo,
Birmingham Breakdown, Swampy River, Black Beauty, Lot o'
Fingers, Sophisticated Lady, Misty Mornin'*.

DUKE ELLINGTON DISCOGRAPHY

With Own Band (10-20):

Gennett

3291 If You Can't Hold That
     Man/You've Got Those
     Wanna Go Back Again Blues
3342 Animal Crackers/Lil' Farina

*With Own Band (10-20)—con-
tinued*

Vocalion

1064 East St. Louis Toodle-oo/
     Birmingham Breakdown
1077 The Creeper/Imagination

With Own Band (10-20)—continued

1086 Song of the Cotton Field/ New Orleans Low Down
1153 Red Hot Band/Doin' the Frog
15556 Black and Tan Fantasy

Perfect

104 Parlor Social Stomp/Georgia Grind
14514 Trombone Blues/I'm Gonna Hang Around My Sugar
14968 Take It Easy/Jubilee

Pathe

7504 Parlor Social Stomp/Georgia Grind

Okeh

40955 Black and Tan Fantasy/ What Can a Poor Fellow Do
41013 Take It Easy/Jubilee Stomp

With the Washingtonians (5-10):

Harmony

505 Birmingham Breakdown
577 Bugle Call Rag/Sweet Mama
601 Stack O'Lee Blues

Romeo

618 Take It Easy
827 Hot and Bothered
829 The Mooche/Move Over
977 Saratoga Swing/Tight Like That
1101 Doin' the Voom Voom/Saturday Night Function
1556 Them There Eyes

With the Washingtonians (5-10)—continued

Velvetone

7072 East St. Louis Toodle-oo/ The Mooche
7088 Sweet Mama/Double Check Stomp

Brunswick

3526 Soliloquy/Black and Tan Fantasy

Cameo

8182 East St. Louis Toodle-oo/ Jubilee Stomp
8183 Take It Easy
8352 Black Beauty
9023 Hot and Bothered
9025 The Mooche/Move Over
9036 Saturday Night Function/ Beggar's Blues
9094 Mississippi Here I Am/Tight Like That
9175 Tight Like That/Saratoga Swing

Columbia

953 East St. Louis Toodle-oo/ Hop Head
1076 Down in Your Alley Blues

With Own Band (1):

Columbia

35214 The Sergeant Was Shy/Serenade to Sweden
35240 Bouncing Buoyancy/Lonely Co-ed
35291 Little Posey/Lady in Blue

With Own Band (1)—continued

35310 Tootin' Through the Roof/
Grievin'
35353 I Never Felt This Way Be-
fore/Weely
35640 Your Love Has Faded/Killin'
Myself
35776 Country Gal

With Own Band (retail):

Columbia Reissues

35208 Doin' the Voom Voom/I'm
Checkin' Out
35427 Mood Indigo/Solitude
35556 Stormy   Weather/Sophisti-
cated Lady
35683 Ducky Wucky/Swing Low
35834 Lazy Rhapsody/Blue Ramble
35835 Lightnin'/Jazz Cocktail
35837 Drop Me Off at Harlem
35955 Misty Mornin'/Blues with a
Feelin'
36112 Showboat Shuffle/In a Sentimental Mood
36114 Reminiscing in Tempo I and
II
36115 Reminiscing in Tempo III
and IV
36157 That Rhythm Man
36195 In the Shade of the Old Apple Tree/Harlem Speaks
36317 Moonglow/Truckin'
36836 Bundle of Blues

*With Earl Jackson Musical Cham-
pions (5):*

Melotone

12093 Rockin'   Chair/Black   and
Tan Fantasy

With the Georgia Syncopators (3):

Melotone

12444 I'm So in Love With You

With the Whoopee Makers (3):

Oriole

2528 I'm So in Love with You

Pathe

36899 The Mooche/Move Over
36923 Misty Mornin'/Hottentot
37059 Doin'   the   Voom   Voom/
Flaming Youth

Cameo

9025 Move Over
9037 Misty Mornin'

Romeo

829 Move Over
840 Hottentot

Perfect

15104 Misty Mornin'/Hottentot

Regal

8874 Flaming Youth

With Own Band (1-10):

Master

101 East St. Louis Toodle/I've
Got to Be Rug Cutter
117 There's a Lull in My Life/
It's Swell of You
123 Birmingham Breakdown/
Scattin' at Kit Kat
124 Can't Run/Lady Kissed
131 Caravan/Azure

With Own Band (1-10)—continued

137 Alabamy Home/All God's Chillum Got Rhythm

With Own Band (retail-5):

Victor

16006 Mood Indigo/Hot & Bothered/Creole Love Call

16007 East St. Louis Toodle-oo/ Lot of Fingers/Black & Tan Fantasy

21137 Creole Love Call (24861)/ Black and Tan Fantasy (24861)

21284 Washington Wobble (Blu 6782)/Harlem River Quiver (22791)

21490 Blues I Love to Sing (22985, Blu 6531)/Blue Bubbles (22985, Blu 6451)

21580 Black Beauty/Jubilee Stomp

21703 East St. Louis Toodle-oo/ Got Everything But You (Blu 6531, 10244)

22525 Ring Dem Bells (25076)/ Three Little Words (25076)

22586 Nine Little Miles from Ten-Ten-Tennessee/What Good Am I Without You

22587 Mood Indigo/When a Black Man's Blue

22603 Blue Again

22614 The River and Me/Keep a Song in Your Soul

22743 Limehouse Blues/Echoes of the Jungle

22791 It's Glory/Brown Berries

With Own Band (retail-5)—continued

22800 Mystery song

22938 Dinah/Bugle Call Rag

23016 Hittin' the Bottle/Lindy Hop

23017 You're Lucky to Me/Memories of You

23022 Old Man Blues/Jungle Nights in Harlem

23036 Sam & Delilah

23041 Shout 'Em Aunt Tillie/I'm So in Love

24431 Rude Interlude/Dallas Doings

24501 Dear Old Southland/Daybreak Express

24521 Stompy Jones/Blue Feeling

24617 Cocktails for Two/Live and Love Tonight

24622 Ebony Rhapsody (24674)/I Met My Waterloo (24719)

24651 Troubled Waters/My Old Flame

24755 Delta Serenade/Solitude

26536 Jack the Bear/Morning Glory

26537 You You Darlin'/So Far, So Good

26577 Ko-Ko/Conga Brava

26598 Concerto for Cootie/Me and You

26610 Cotton Tail/Never No Lament

26644 Bonjangles/Portrait of Bert Williams

26677 Dusk/Blue Goose

26719 My Greatest Mistake/At a Dixie Roadside Diner

26731 Harlem Air-Shaft/Sepia Panorama

With Own Band (*retail-5*)—continued

26748 Five O'Clock Whistle/There Shall Be No Night
26788 Rumpus in Richmond/In a Mellotone
27326 Flamingo/Girl in My Dreams Tries to Look Like You
27356 Jumpin' Punkins/Blue Serge
27380 Sidewalks of New York/Take the "A" Train
27434 John Hardy's Wife/After All
27502 Bakiff/Giddybug Gallop
27531 I Got It Bad and That Ain't Good/Chocolate Shake
27587 Moon Over Cuba/Just A-Settin' and A-Rockin'
27639 Bli-Blip/Rocks in My Bed
27700 Clementine/Five o'Clock Drag
27740 Chelsea Bridge/What Good Would It Do
27804 Are You Stickin'/I Don't Know What Kind of Blues I Got
27856 Moon Mist/"C" Jam Blues
27880 Perdido/Raincheck
36049 Creole Rhapsody
38007 I Must Have That Man/Bandanna Babies
38008 Diga Diga Doo/I Can't Give You Anything But Love (Blu 6280)
38034 The Mooche (24468)
38035 Doin' the Voom Voom/Flaming Youth
38036 High Life/Saturday Night Function
38045 Japanese Dream

With Own Band (*retail-5*)—continued

38053 Stevedore Stomp/The Dicty Glide
38058 Saratoga Swing/Misty Mornin'
38065 Hot Feet/Sloppy Joe
38079 Cotton Club Stomp/Arabian Lover
38089 Mississippi Dry/Swanee Shuffles
38092 The Duke Steps Out/Haunted Nights
38115 Breakfast Dance/March of the Hoodlums
38129 Jazz Lips/Double Check Stomp
38130 I Was Made to Love You/My Gal Is Good for Nothin' But Love
38143 Sweet Dreams of Love/Sweet Jazz o' Mine
20-1505 Sherman Shuffle/Hayfoot, Strawfoot

Piano Solos (*retail-10*):

Okeh

8436 Black Beauty/Swampy River

Brunswick

6355 Fast-Furious/Swampy River
7990 Mood Indigo/Solitude/Sophisticated Lady/In a Sentimental Mood

Master

102 Mood Indigo/Solitude/Sophisticated Lady/In a Sentimental Mood

Piano Solos (retail-10)—continued

Victor

27564 Dear Old Southland/Solitude

With Own Band (3-10):

Brunswick

6003 Home Again Blues/Wang
Wang Blues

6038 Rockin' in Rhythm/Twelfth
Street Rag

6093 Creole Rhapsody I and II

6265 Rose Room/It Don't Mean a
Thing If It Ain't Got That
Swing

6288 Lazy Rhapsody/Blue Tune

6317 Baby When You Ain't
There/Moon Over Dixie
(Co. 35835)

6336 Blue Ramble/The Shiek

6374 Harlem Speaks/Best Wishes

6404 Jazz Cocktail/Lightnin'

6432 Ducky Wucky/Swing Low

6467 Eerie Moan/Anytime Any-
day Anywhere

6516 Blackbirds Medley

6517 Porgy/I Can't Give You
Anything But Love

6518 I Must Have That Man/
Baby

6519 Diga Diga Do

6527 Slippery Horn/Drop Me Off
at Harlem

6600 Sophisticated Lady/Stormy
Weather

6607 Bundle of Blues/Get Yourself New Broom

6638 Jive Stomp/I'm Satisfied

With Own Band (3-10)—continued

6646 Harlem Speaks/In Shade of
Old Apple Tree

6987 Moonglow/Solitude

7310 Saddest Tale/Sumpin'
About Rhythm

7440 Merry-Go-Round/Admira-
tion

7461 Showboat Shuffle/In a Sentimental Mood

7514 Accent on Youth/Truckin'

7526 Cotton/Margie

7546 Reminiscing in Tempo I & II

7547 Reminiscing in Tempo III &
IV

7625 No Greater Love/Isn't Love
the Strangest Thing

7627 Kissin' Baby Goodnight/
Love Is Like a Cigaret

7656 Echoes of Harlem/Clarinet
Lament

7667 Oh Babe Maybe Some Day

7710 Shoe Shine Boy/Sad Night
in Harlem

7734 In a Jam/Uptown Downbeat

7752 Trumpet in Spades/Yearning
for Love

8004 Crescendo & Diminuendo in
Blue

8029 Chatter Box/Dusk in the
Desert

8044 Black Butterfly/Harmony in
Harlem

8063 New Black & Tan Fantasy/
Steppin' into Swing Society

8083 Lost in Meditation/Ridin' on
a Blue Note

8093 Skrontch/If You Were in
My Place

With Own Band (3-10)—continued

8099 Braggin' in Brass/Carnival in Caroline

8108 The Gal from Joe's/I Let Song Go Out of My Heart

8131 Slappin' Seventh Av./Honolulu

8168 Pyramid/When My Sugar Walks Down Street

8169 Dinah's in a Jam/You Gave Me the Gate

8174 Stevedore's Serenade/La De Doody Doo

8186 Rose of Rio Grande/Gypsy without a Song

8200 Love in Swingtime/Watermelon Man

8204 Prelude to a Kiss/Lambeth Walk

8213 I Haven't Changed a Thing

8221 Blues Serenade/Hip Chic

8231 Buffet Flat/Mighty Like the Blues

8256 Prologue to Black & Tan Fantasy/Please Forgive Me

8293 Battle of Swing/Jazz Potpourri

8297 Blue Light/Slap Happy

8306 Boy Meets Horn/Old King Dooji

8344 Subtle Lament/Pussy Willow

8365 Portrait of Lion/Something to Live For

8380 Smorgasbord & Schnapps/Solid Old Man

8405 In a Mizz/Cotton Club Stomp

With Own Band (3-10)—continued

8411 Way Low/You Can Count on Me

21105 Creole Love Call/St. Louis Blues

With The Jungle Band (3-8):

Brunswick

3987 Yellow Dog Blues/Tishimingo Blues

4044 Jubilee Stomp

4110 Louisiana/Awful Sad

4122 The Mooche

4238 Tiger Rag (2 parts)

4309 Harlem Flat Blues/Paducah

4345 Rent Party Blues/Doin' the Voom Voom

4492 Jungle Jamboree/Black & Blue

4705 Jolly Wog/Jazz Convulsions

4760 Sweet Mama/When You're Smiling

4776 Admiration/Maori

4783 Double Check Stomp/Accordion Joe

4887 Wall St. Wail/Cotton Club Stomp

4952 Dreamy Blues/Runnin' Wild

6003 Wang Wang Blues/Home Again Blues

6038 Rockin' in Rhythm/12th St. Rag

With The Harlem Footwarmers (5-10):

Okeh

8602 Diga Diga Do/Doin' the New Lowdown

With the Harlem Footwarmers (5-10)—continued

8623 Hot & Bothered/The Mooche
8638 Harlem Twist/Move Over
8662 Misty Mornin'/Blues with a Feelin'
8675 Chicago Stomp Down
8720 Snake Hip Dance/Jungle Jamboree
8746 Syncopated Shuffle/Blues of the Vagabond
8760 Lazy Duke
8836 Rocky Mountain Blues/Big House Blues
8840 Sweet Chariot/Mood Indigo
8869 Old Man Blues
41468 Ring Dem Bells/Old Man Blues

Columbia

14670 Big House Blues/Sweet Chariot

With Barney Bigard (retail-5):

Variety

515 Caravan/Stompy Jones
525 Frolic Sam/Clouds in My Heart
564 Lament for Lost Love/Four & One-Half St.
596 If You're Ever in My Arms Again/Get It Southern Style
626 Sponge Cake & Spinach/Moonlight Fiesta
655 Jazz à la Carte/Demi-Tasse

Vocalion

3985 Drummer's Delight/If I Thought You Cared

With Barney Bigard (retail-5)—continued

5378 Minuet in Blues/Barney's Goin' Easy
5422 Lost in Two Flats/Early Mornin'
5595 Madri Gras Madness/Watch the Birdie

Okeh

5663 Honey Hush/Just Another Dream

Bluebird

10981 A Lull at Dawn/Charlie the Chulo
11098 Lament for Javanette/Ready Eddy
11581 C Blues/Brown Suede

With Rex Stewart (1-5):

Variety

517 Rexatious (Vo 3810)/Lazy Man's Shuffle (Vo 3810)
618 Tea and Trumpets (Vo 3831)/Back Room Romp (Vo 3831)
664 Love in My Heart (Vo 3844)/Sugar Hill Shim Sham (Vo 3844)

Vocalion

5448 "Fat Stuff" Serenade/I'll Come Back for More
5510 San Juan Hill

Bluebird

10946 Without a Song/My Sunday Gal
11057 Mobile Bay/Linger Awhile
11258 Some Saturday/Subtle Slough

With Cootie Williams (1-5):

Variety

527 Downtown Uproar/Blue Reverie
555 Diga Diga Do/I Can't Believe That You're in Love with Me

Vocalion

3814 Downtown Uproar/Blue Reverie
3818 Diga Diga Do/I Can't Believe That You're in Love with Me
3890 I Can't Give You Anything But Love, Baby/Watching
3922 Jubilesta/Pigeon and Peppers
3960 Echoes of Harlem/Lost in Meditation
4061 Swingtime in Honolulu/Carnival in Caroline
4086 Ol' Man River/Lesson in "C"
4324 Blues in the Evening/Sharpie
4425 Swing Pan Alley/Chasin' Chippies
4574 Delta Mood/Boys from Harlem
4636 Mobile Blues/Gal-Avantin'
4726 Ain't the Gravy Good/Boudoir Benny
4958 Black Beauty/Night Song
5411 She's Gone/Beautiful Romance
5618 Blues A Poppin'/Black Butterfly
5690 Dry Long So/Give It Up
6336 Top and Bottom/Toasted Pickle

With Warren Mills Serenaders (20):

Victor

35962 St. Louis Blues/Blackbirds Medley

With Joe Turner and Memphis Men (5):

Columbia

1813 Mississippi Moan (36157)/Freeze and Melt

With Sonny Greer and Memphis Men (5):

Columbia

1868 Beggars' Blues/Saturday Night Function

With the Gotham Stompers (2-3):

Variety

541 Did Anyone Ever Tell You/Where Are You
629 Alabamy Home/My Honey's Lovin' Arms

With Harlem Hot Chocolates (3):

Hit of the Week

1045 Sing You Sinners
1046 St. James Infirmary

With Harlem Hot Shots (3):

Perfect

15841 Black and Tan Fantasy/Sugar Blues

With the Lumberjacks (3):

Cameo

  8352 Black Beauty

With Mills' Ten Blackberries

Velvetone

  7082 Black and Tan Fantasy/Hot
         and Bothered

Cameo

  5331 Black and Tan Fantasy/Hot
         and Bothered

Diva

  6056 Black and Tan Fantasy/Hot
         and Bothered

With the Memphis Hot Shots (3):

Harmony

  1377 I'm So in Love/I Can't Real-
         ize You Love Me

Velvetone

  2455 I'm So in Love/I Can't Real-
         ize You Love Me

With the Dixie Jazz Band (3):

Oriole

  1730 Doin' the Voom Voom/Sat-
         urday Night Function

With the Six Jolly Jesters (15):

Vocalion

  1449 Oklahoma Stomp

With the Ten Blackberries (5):

Velvetone

  7082 Hot and Bothered/Black and
         Tan Fantasy

Cameo

  5331 Hot and Bothered/Black and
         Tan Fantasy

Perfect

  15272 St. James Infirmary/When
          You're Smiling

Clarion

  5331 Hot and Bothered/Black and
         Tan Fantasy

Banner

  0594 Rent Party Blues
  0598 Jungle Blues

Jewel

  5854 Jungle Blues

Oriole

  1854 Jungle Blues

Romeo

  1215 Jungle Blues
  1218 When You're Smiling

With Johnny Hodges (retail-3):

Variety

  576 Foolin' Myself/You'll Never
        Go to Heaven
  586 A Sailboat in the Moonlight

Vocalion

  3948 My Day/Silvery Moon &
         Golden Sands

With Johnny Hodges (retail-3)—
continued

4046 I Let Song Go Out of My
Heart/If You Were in My
Place
4115 Jeep's Blues/Rendezvous
with Rhythm
4213 Empty Ballroom Blues/You
Walked Out of Picture
4242 Pyramid/Lost in Meditation
4309 A Blues Serenade/Jitterbug's
Lullaby
4335 Swingin' in the Dell/Love in
Swingtime
4351 Krum Elbow Blues/Some-
thing About an Old Love
4386 Prelude to a Kiss/Jeep Is
Jumpin'
4573 Hodge Podge/Wanderlust
4622 Dancing on the Stars/I'm in
Another World
4710 Swingin' on the Campus/
Like Ship in Night
4849 Dooji Wooji/Mississippi
Dreamboat

With Johnny Hodges (retail-3)—
continued

4917 You Can Count on Me/
Kitchen Mechanic's Day
4941 Dance of the Goon/Home
Town Blues
5100 Rent Party Blues/The Rabbit's Jump
5170 Savoy Strut/Good Gal Blues
5330 Truly Wonderful/My Heart
Jumped Over Moon
5353 Dream Blues/I Know What
You Do
5533 Skunk Hollow Blues/Tired
Socks
5940 Moon Romance/Your Love
Has Faded

Bluebird

11021 Junior Hop/Day Dream
11117 That's the Blues Old Man/
Good Queen Bess
11447 Squaty Roo/Things Ain't
What They Used to Be

FAZOLA, Irving (real name Prestopnick). *Clarinet, alto saxo-*
phone. Born Dec. 10, 1912, New Orleans, La., where he attended
high school. He took a few piano lessons, but in 1925 studied both the
clarinet and music generally under private teachers—Jeon Poquay
and Santo Guiffre. Launched his professional career with Louis Prima
and Candy Candido (1927) and after a few years of local jobbing
performed with Sharkey Bonano (1930-34—but not consecutively).
Joined Roy Teal (1934-35), Ben Pollack (1935-36), Gus Arnheim
(1936), Glenn Miller (1937), Bob Crosby (1938-40), Claude Thornhill (1941), Muggsy Spanier (1942), Teddy Powell (1942-43),
Horace Heidt (1943). Illness forced him to return to native city for
a rest, but during the past year (1944) he has been playing local jobs
at radio station WWL with Pinky Vidacovich and with Leon Prima

at the Plaza Club. Recorded with Pollack, Crosby, Seger Ellis, Jess Stacy, Thornhill. Solos: *Deep Elm, In a Sentimental Mood* (Pollack); *Clarinet Blues* (Stacy); *Milk Cow Blues, March of the Bobcats, Jazz Me Blues, Louise, High Society, Mournin' Blues* (Crosby).

FIELDS, Herbert (Herbie). *Tenor, alto, clarinet, vocal, leader.* Received 4 New Star points as alto: *Cavanaugh, Feather, Jax, Thiele;* 1 New Star point as tenor: *Stacy;* 1 New Star point as leader: *Burley.* Born May 24, 1919, Elizabeth, N. J., where he attended high school, during which time he conducted an orchestra at junior high, played solo clarinet in Union County Symphony orchestra. Studied flute, oboe, bassoon, in addition to piano at age 6, C Melody saxophone at 9, clarinet at 13, alto at 14, tenor at 16. Played in local dance bands from 1931. Attended Juilliard (1936-38). Began professional career with Reggie Childs (1937); fronted own unit (1939-40); then joined Leonard Ware (1940), Slam Stewart (1940), Raymond Scott (1940); led Army band at Fort Dix, N. J. (Apr. 1941-Sept. 1942), then to leadership of Army Air Corps Band in Atlantic City (Sept. 1942-Sept. 1943), at which time he received a medical discharge. Again organized own band (1943-44). Recorded with Woody Herman. Solo: *Perdido* (Herman).

FILHE, George. *Trombone, baritone horn.* Born Nov. 13, 1872, New Orleans, La., where he attended high school. He studied music with special teachers, picked up his own knowledge of the jazz trombone. At 20 he was playing with Cousto & Desdunes (1892-1906) and with the Onward Brass Band (1892-1912). There followed engagements with Bab Frank and Charlie McCurtis' Peerless Band (1907-08), The Imperial Band (1909-12), after which he migrated to Chicago to take up his trade of cigar-making (1913-15 and again 1930-39), with his music-making as a sideline. In Chicago he headed his own band for two years (1915-16) at Tommy Thomas' cabaret, then at the De Luxe Café (1917-19), where cornetist Manuel Perez, clarinetist Tio, Bechet and the great master of the jazz piccolo, Bab Frank, played with him. In 1920 Filhe worked with Carroll Dickerson; from 1921-25 with King Oliver during most of his Chicago engagements; then he joined Dave Peyton at the Big Grand Theatre

(1926-29), after which he retired only to play occasionally for local gig dates.

FOSTER, George (Pop). *String Bass*. Received 9 points: *Avakian, Smith, Williams*. Born May 19, 1892, McCall, La., where he attended grammar school. Foster comes from a musical family, having studied his instrument under his father and receiving much assistance from his sister, Mrs. Elizabeth Foster Mitchell, also a bassist. Began study of music on the cello at age 9, took up string bass at 13. Had first job with Roseals Orchestra in 1906. In New Orleans he played in countless parades for Mardi Gras, funerals, advertising wagons, etc., and with many early bands, including the Eagle Band, Magnolia Band (1907), Freddie Keppard and Kid Ory. He next attracted the attention of Fate Marable who hired him to play with the Steamer *Capitol* Orchestra on Mississippi excursions in the company of Armstrong, Baby Dodds, Sam Dutrey and St. Cyr (1918-20); joined Charlie Creath in St. Louis (1921); and in 1923 went to California to play in a taxi-dance hall with Kid Ory, Liberty Syncopators, and other small groups. He then went to New York to join Luis Russell (1929-34), who is credited with having taught him to read music. In 1935 he joined Louis Armstrong for several years. Recorded with T. Dorsey, J. Dorsey, Jack Teagarden, Armstrong, Russell.

GARLAND, Ed. *String bass, brass bass*. Born Jan. 9, 1895, Irish Channel district New Orleans, La. Participated in Mardi Gras parades, playing tuba or bass drum and played with Frankie Duson and the Excelsior Band under Billy Marrero. Left New Orleans in 1914, going to Chicago, worked at the De Luxe Café, later playing with Manuel Perez and Charlie McCurtis at the famous Pekin and under King Oliver at Dreamland Café. In 1921 he went to California with Oliver and has remained there. In 1922 he worked at the Leeks Lake resort, then going to a taxi-dance hall in Los Angeles, where he worked for about 10 years. He was a member of the first New Orleans Negro band to record when Kid Ory's band made six sides in 1921 for the Sunshine label. He has recently been a member of Ory's Creole band on its West Coast broadcasts.

GILLESPIE, John (Dizzy). *Trumpet, arranger*. Received 5 New Star points as trumpet: *Braveman, Dexter, Jax, Stacy, Ulanov;* 1 New Star point as arranger: *Braveman*. Born Oct. 21, 1917, Chehaw, S. C., where he attended school. Was graduated from Laurinburg Institute, Laurinburg, N. C. First played with Frankie Fairfax (1935); also worked with Teddy Hill, Edgar Hayes, Cab Calloway, Ella Fitzgerald, Benny Carter and Les Hite; has had a band of his own, and has played with Fletcher Henderson, Earl Hines, Duke Ellington. Is now appearing with Billy Eckstine, for whom he arranges.

GOODMAN, Benjamin (Benny). *Carinet*. Received 48 points: *Burley, Braveman, Cavanaugh, Dexter, Feather, Goffin, Hammond, Jovien, Levin, Lim, Miller, Mize, Simon, Stacy, Thiele, Ulanov;* 1 point as New Star vocal: *Simon*. Born May 30, 1909, Chicago, Illinois, where he attended school. Studied at Chicago's Hull House. Encouraged by his parents, he began learning his instrument at the age of 10. While still in short pants (1923) he played with local bands, which activity led to his getting a job with Ben Pollack (1927-29). He subsequently played with Arnold Johnson, Red Nichols and numerous gig bands in the New York area. Free-lanced in New York radio stations. Organized his own band in 1933, which gained its initial success on the Let's Dance radio show (1933-34). By 1936 the band had attained sensational bigtime status. In 1944, due to difficulties and differences with his booking office business agents, he disbanded in mid-year, has appeared since only as guest artist. Currently, however, he is appearing with a quintet in *Seven Lively Arts*. Recorded with the Five Pennies, Charleston Chasers, Joe Venuti, Red Norvo, Rube Bloom, Reginald Foresythe, Gene Krupa, own band, trio, quartet and sextet. Solos: *Blues in My Flat, Caprice Paganini XXIV, Clarinet à la King, Sing, Sing, Sing* (own band); *The Sheik* (Five Pennies); *Tiger Rag* (own trio); *The Man I Love* (own quartet). His band has made appearances in Carnegie Hall, New York City; Symphony Hall, Boston; and Ravinia Park, near Chicago. Has appeared as clarinet soloist with Budapest String Quartet, NBC Symphony, Lewisohn Stadium Orchestra, New York. In the symphonic field has recorded with the Budapest String Quartet and with Joseph Szigeti and Béla Bartók in a trio; and has become an instructor at the Juilliard School. For a complete Goodman Discography, refer to pages 168-78 of the 1944 ESQUIRE JAZZ BOOK.

GREEN, Frederick William (Freddie). *Guitar.* Received 8 points: *Braveman, Hammond, Thiele.* Born March 31, 1911, Charleston, S. C., where he began his education, finishing grammar and high school study in New York City. Mostly self-taught, he began the study of guitar at the age of 21. In 1936 he launched his professional career as guitarist for Count Basie's band, where he has played ever since. Recorded with Basie, Teddy Wilson, Billie Holiday, Benny Goodman.

HALL, Edmond (Ed). *Clarinet.* Received 27 points: *Braveman, Feather, Goffin, Hammond, Hoefer, Jax, Levin, Lim, Miller, Mize, Smith, Stacy, Ulanov.* Born May 15, 1901, New Orleans, La. Attended high school in Reserve, La. Self-taught, with the help of his father, Hall's first instrument was the guitar (1917-18). It was then he switched to clarinet, coming under the influence of New Orleans clarinetists such as Picou, Tio, Dodds and cornetist Buddy Petit, in whose band he worked (1920-22), having previously launched his professional career with Thomas Valentine in Reserve, La. (1917), and with Bud Roussell, with cornetist Lee Collins (1919), following which he played short engagements with Jack Carey and Chris Kelley (1920) before moving over to Petit. In 1923 Hall joined Mack Thomas, a trumpeter, in whose band Al Morgan played bass and George Morris trombone. This band played in and around Pensacola, Fla., where Hall joined pianist Eagle Eye Shields (1924-26) in the Jacksonville-Miami area. Next he worked with Alonzo Ross (1927-28) in tours of the South and a short stay at New York's Savoy Ballroom; Cootie Williams was a member of this band too, and Hall and Williams joined forces in a small band at Happyland Ballroom in New York (1928), after which Hall played with pianist Happy Ford in Atlantic City. Back in New York, Hall transferred his activities to Charlie Skeets (1929), then to Claude Hopkins (1929-35), Lucky Millinder (1936-37), Billy Hicks (1938), Zutty Singleton (1939), Joe Sullivan (1939), Red Allen (1940), Teddy Wilson (1941-44), until finally in the summer of 1944 he headed his own group at Café Society Downtown & Uptown. Recorded with Ross, Hopkins, Sullivan, Allen, Wilson, W. C. Handy, Lionel Hampton, Singleton, Hicks, Art Tatum, Frankie Newton, Billie Holiday, Ida Cox, Eddy Howard, Leonard Feather's All-Stars and many recording groups under his own name. Solos: *Washington Squabble, How'm I Doin', Mystic Moan* (Hopkins); *Please Don't Talk About Me When I'm Gone, Who's Sorry Now, Brittwood Stomp* (Newton); *My Buddy* (Hampton); *Rompin' in '44, Seein' Red, Night Shift Blues, Profoundly Blue, Royal Garden Blues* (own band).

HALL, Fred (Tubby). *Drums.* Born Oct. 12, 1895, Sellers, La. Attended high school in New Orleans. Studied instrument at school, his interest in music having appeared at the age of 10. Began playing professionally around 1915, with the Crescent Band in New Orleans, with whom he stayed for one year; with Silverleaf band (1916-17); came to Chicago with a New Orleans band and worked there for 6 months (1917); served in World War I; toured with Clarence Miller band (1920); Jimmie Noone (1921), Carroll Dickerson (1922), Dr. Watson (1922-23), returned to Dickerson (1924-25), Louis Armstrong (1926-27), Clarence Black (1927-28), Boyd Atkins (1929), rejoined Louis Armstrong (1931-32), Half-Pint Jackson (1933), rejoined Noone (1934-35). Stopped playing for three years and is now leading a small band of his own. Recorded with Noone, Armstrong.

HAMPTON, Lionel. *Vibraharp, drums, leader.* Received 16 points as vibraharp: *Burley, Braveman, Lim, Mize, Simon, Stacy, Ulanov;* 12 points as leader and 6 points as New Star leader: *Burley, Goffin, Feather, Mize, Simon, Ulanov.* Born 1913, Louisville, Kentucky. He attended high school in Chicago. Evinced first interest in music at St. Elizabeth's school in Chicago and continued under private teachers and on his own. Migrated to Los Angeles about 1930 and was soon playing with Les Hite (1932-36). Joined Benny Goodman (1936-40), organized his own band (fall of 1940-44). Recorded with pick-up bands under his own name for the Victor label with Goodman, and most recently with his own band. Vibra solos: *Blues in My Flat, Moonglow, Liza* (Goodman Quartet); *Buzzin' Around with the Bee, Shoeshiner's Drag* (own band). Drum solo: *Drum Stomp* (own band). Piano solo: *Piano Stomp* (own band). Vocalisms: *Blues in Your Flat, Vibraphone Blues* (Goodman Quartet). For a comprehensive Hampton Discography refer to pages 180-82 of the 1944 ESQUIRE JAZZ BOOK.

HARDY, Emmett Louis. *Cornet*. Born June 12, 1903, Gretna, La.; died June 16, 1925, New Orleans, La. Evinced an early interest in the cornet and by age 15 was already playing with local New Orleans bands. From 1916 to 1924 he worked with numerous bands, mostly in New Orleans, but also doing time on the Orpheum Circuit with Tony Catalano's riverboat band, with the New Orleans Rhythm Kings in Chicago and with Carlisle Evans in Davenport, Ia. Hardy was ill and unable to play during the two years before his death. No recordings, but in the opinion of many musicians who heard him, his style preceded and was identical with—even better than—Bix Beiderbeck's.

HARRIS, Willard (Bill). *Trombone*. Received 4 New Star points: *Feather, Jax, Lim, Stacy*. Born Oct. 28, 1916, Philadelphia, Pa., where he attended high school. Studied music on his own, taking up the trombone at the age of 22. Began playing professionally in November, 1942, with Buddy Williams; then joined Bob Chester (Feb. 1943-Sept. 1943), Benny Goodman (Sept. 1943-May 1944), own band (June 1944-Aug. 1944), Woody Herman (since Aug. 1944). Recorded with Joe Bushkin. Solo: *Pickin' at the Pic, Slow Joe* (Bushkin).

HAWKINS, Coleman. *Tenor saxophone*. Received 45 points: *Braveman, Cavanaugh, Dexter, Feather, Hoefer, Jax, Jovien, Levin, Lim, Miller, Mize, Simon, Smith, Stacy, Thiele, Ulanov*. Born Nov. 21, 1907, St. Joseph Missouri. He began study of piano and cello at age 5, under his mother's encouragement. Switched to tenor at 9. Continued his studies during his three years at Washburn College, Topeka. In addition to tenor, he also studied harmony and composition. During his attendance at Washburn he played with local bands. Then joined Mamie Smith's Jazz Hounds in Kansas City (1923). Upon his arrival in New York with this group, he moved to Fletcher Henderson (1924-34), toured England and the Continent as soloist, leader and sideman (1934-39). On returning to the U. S. in the Fall of 1939 he organized his own band, first a large one which was not too successful and then a small one which has been playing nightspots in New York and the Middle West. Recorded with his own bands, the Chocolate Dandies, Spike Hughes, Mound City Blue Blowers, McKinney's Cotton Pickers, Henderson and many pick-up bands during his European sojourn. Solos: *Queer Notions, It's the Talk of the Town, PDQ Blues, Tozo, Sugar Foot Stomp, Stockholm Stomp* (Henderson); *Heartbreak Blues* (own band); *Firebird* (Hughes); *I'd Love It* (McKinney). For an extensive Hawkins Discography refer to pages 183-87 of the 1944 ESQUIRE JAZZ BOOK.

HAZEL, Arthur (Monk). *Cornet, drums, Melophone E Flat, valve trombone*. Born Aug. 15, 1903, Harvey, La. Went to school in Gretna and New Orleans, La. Became interested in music at an early age, studying on his own, and at the age of 8 was paid to play in New Orleans Mardi Gras parades. First real job was with Emmett Hardy in 1920. Also played with Bill Cruger, Happy Schilling, Abbie Brunies, Jules Bauduc (New Orleans); Rhythm Kings, Tony Parenti, Johnny Hyman, own band, Jack Pettis (New York); own band, Gene Austin, Lloyd Dantin. Appeared on radio show, Hollywood on the Air, in 1934, with Gene Austin. Recorded with Tony Parenti, Jimmy Hyman, own band, Jack Pettis, Gene Austin and made numerous records between 1929 and 1931 for Irving Mills with various house bands, white and colored. Cornet solos on recordings with Gene Austin; Melophone solos on recordings with Jack Pettis, Mat Brusiloff, trio, own band. Has retired from music business for the duration of the war and is now working in an industrial alcohol manufacturing plant.

HEWWOOD, Eddie, Jr. *Piano. Received 4 New Star points as* pianist: *Braveman, Jax, Stacy, Thiele;* 2 New Star points as leader: *Cavanaugh, Hammond*. Born Dec. 4, 1915, Atlanta, Ga., where he received his primary education and attended Moorhouse College. Became interested in music at the age of 8, studying in school and under his father. At 14 he had his first paying job in a theatre pit orchestra. Played under Clarence Love (1935), joined Benny Carter (1940-41), formed his own band (1944). Recorded with Carter, Edmond Hall, own band.

HIGGINBOTHAM, Jay C. (Higgie). *Trombone*. Received 23 points: *Burley, Braveman, Feather, Hammond, Hoefer, Jovien, Lim, Miller, Mize, Smith.* Born May 11, 1906 Atlanta, Georgia. Attended school in Cincinnati, Ohio; continued his education at Morris Brown University. Music mostly self-taught. He originally intended to become a tailor, but joined a local Cincinnati band, Wes Helvey (1924-25). Went to Buffalo, N. Y., played with Eugene Primos, later taken over by Jimmy Harrison (1926-27), went to New York, also playing with local bands there during this period (1926-27), joined Luis Russell (1928-30), Fletcher Henderson (1930-31), Chick Webb (1932-33), Blue Rhythm Band (1934-36), Louis Armstrong (1936-40), Red Allen (1940-44)—a period intermittently taken up with free-lancing in New York area. Recorded with Russell, Armstrong, Webb, Henderson, his own recording combinations, Allen, M. Mesirow, The Port of Harlem Seven, Blue Rhythm Band, King Oliver. Solos: *Ease on Down, Muggin' Lightly* (Russell); *Mighty Blues, Rockin' the Blues* (Port of Harlem Seven); *Weary Land Blues* (own Quintet); *West End Blues* (Oliver); *Feeling Drowsy, Patrol Wagon Blues, Swing Out* (Allen).

J. C. HIGGINBOTHAM DISCOGRAPHY

With Louis Armstrong (retail-5):

Okeh

8669 I Can't Give You Anything But Love
8680 Mahogany Hall Stomp

Decca

1347 Red Cap/Public Melody No. One
1353 Cuban Pete/She's Daughter of Planter
1369 Sun Showers/Yours & Mine
1408 Alexander's Ragtime Band/ I've Got Heartful of Rhythm
1635 Jubilee/True Confession
1636 Satchel Mouth Swing/I Double Dare You

With Louis Armstrong (retail-5)—continued

1653 Trumpet Player's Lament/ Sweet as Song
1660 On the Sunny Side of/Once in a While
1661 Struttin' with Some Barbecue/Let That Be a Lesson to You

Okeh

8756 I Ain't Got Nobody/Rockin' Chair
8774 Dallas Blues/Bessie Couldn't Help It
41350 St. Louis Blues
41375 Song of the Islands/Blue Turning Grey

With Fletcher Henderson (4-6):

Columbia

2559 Sugar/Blues in My Heart
2565 Singin' the Blues/It's the Darnest Thing
2615 Business in F
2732 Honeysuckle Rose/Underneath the Harlem Moon

With Connie's Inn Orchestra (20-30):

Crown

3191 Sugar Foot Stomp/Low Down Bayou
3212 Milenberg Joys/Twelfth Street Rag

With Fletcher Henderson (3):

Vocalion

3485 Slummin' on Park Avenue/What Will I Tell My Heart
3487 It's Wearin' Me Down/Rhythm of the Tambourine
3511 Rose Room/Back in Your Own Back Yard
3534 Stampede/Great Caesar's Ghost

With the Blue Rhythm Band (3-6):

Columbia

2963 Out of a Dream/Let's Have a Jubilee
2994 Solitude/Keep Rhythm Going
3020 Back Beats/Spitfire
3038 African Lullaby/Swingin' in E Flat
3044 Brown Sugar Mine/Dancing Dogs

With the Blue Rhythm Band (3-6) —continued

3071 Harlem Heat/There's Rhythm in Harlem
3078 Cotton/Truckin'
3083 Dinah Lou/Waiting in the Garden
3087 Ride, Red, Ride/Congo Caravan
3111 Yes, Yes/Broken Dreams of You
3134 Jes Naturally Lazy/Everything Is Still Okay
3135 St. Louis Wiggle Rhythm/Red Rhythm
3147 Merry Go Round/Until the Real Thing Comes Along
3148 In a Sentimental Mood/Carry Me Back to Green Pastures
3156 Balloonacy/Barrelhouse
3157 Moon Is Grinning at Me/Showboat Shuffle
3158 Mister Ghost Goes to Town/Algiers Stomp
3162 Calling Your Bluff/Big John Special

With Mezz Mezzrow (1):

Victor

25612 Hot Club Stomp/Swing Session's Called to Order
25636 Blues in Disguise/That's How I Feel Today

With Jelly Roll Morton (5-10):

Victor

23402 Jersey Joe/Sweet Peter
23424 Mississippi Mildred

With The Chocolate Dandies (15):

Okeh

8728 That's How I Feel/Six or Seven Times

With Benny Carter (4-6):

Columbia

2898 Devil's Holiday/Symphony in Riffs

Okeh

41567 Lonesome Nights/Blue Lou

With Coleman Hawkins (30):

Okeh

41566 Jamaica Shout/Heartbreak Blues

With Buster Bailey (20):

Vocalion

2887 Shanghai Shuffle/Call of the Delta

With King Oliver (5-10):

Victor

38034 West End Blues
38039 Call of the Freaks/Trumpet's Prayer
38521 Freakish Light Blues/I've Got That Thing

With Jack Purvis (10-15):

Okeh

8782 Poor Richard/Down Georgia Way
8808 Dismal Dan/Be Bo Bo

With Henry Allen (4-8):

Victor

38073 Biffly Blues/It Should Be You
38080 Feeling Drowsy/Swing Out
38088 Funny Feather Blues/How Do They Do It That Way
38107 Pleasin' Paul/Make a Country Bird Fly Wild
38121 Everybody Shout/Dancing Dave
38140 Sugar Hill Function/You You Might Get Better

With Lou & Gingersnaps (20):

Banner

6536 Broadway Rhythm
6540 The Way He Loves Is Just Too Bad

With Luis Russell (5-30):

Okeh

8734 New Call of the Freaks/Jersey Lightning
8766 Doctor Blues/Feelin' the Spirit
8772 Give Me Your Telephone Number/Higginbotham Blues
8780 Saratoga Shout/Song of the Swanee
8811 Louisiana Swing/On Revival Day
8830 Poor Li'l Me/Muggin' Lightly
8849 Panama/High Tension

Vocalion

1579 Case on Down/Saratoga Drag

With Red Allen (1-3):

Vocalion

2997 I Wished on the Moon/Roll Along Prairie Moon
2998 Truckin'/Dinah Lou
3097 Red Sails in the Sunset/I Found a Dream
3098 On Treasure Island/Take Me Back to My Boots and Saddle
3214 I'll Bet You Tell That to All the Girls/Lost
3215 Touch of Your Lips/Every Minute on the Hour
3244 You/Would You
3245 Tormented/Nothing's Blue but the Sky
3261 Take My Heart/On the Beach at Bali Bali
3262 You're Not the Kind/Chloe

With Port of Harlem Seven (retail):

Blue Note

3 Mighty Blues/Rockin' the Blues
6 Pounding Heart Blues
7 Blues for Tommy/Basin St. Blues
14 Port of Harlem Blues

With Own Quintet (retail):

Blue Note

501 Weary Land Blues/Daybreak Blues

Session

10013 JC Jumps/Shorty Joe
12016 Dear Old Southland/Confessin'

HINES, Earl (Father). *Piano.* Received 16 points: *Bravenian, Hoefer, Jax, Jovien, Mize, Thiele.* Born Dec. 28, 1903, Duquesne, Pa. Gained piano fundamentals under his mother's guidance, further studies under private teachers. Launched professional career as accompanist for Louis Deppe in Pittsburgh (1918), after which he played with local bands. Migrated to Chicago, played solo at the Elite and Entertainers cafés (1923-24), then joined Erskine Tate (1925-26), Carroll Dickerson (1926-27), Jimmie Noone (1927-28), organized his own band, playing at the Grand Terrace from 1928 to 1938, and has since been touring the country. Recorded solos for QRS, Brunswick, Okeh. As band pianist recorded with Louis Armstrong, Jimmie Noone, Cozy Cole, Charlie Shavers, his own band. Solos: *West End Blues, Weather Bird* (Armstrong); *Monday Date, I Know That You Know* (Noone); *Deep Forest, Blue Drag, Rock and Rye, Fat Babes* (own band); *Stardust* (Shavers).

HINTON, Milton John. *String bass.* Received 10 points: *Braveman, Hoefer, Lim, Miller.* Born June 23, 1910, Vicksburg, Miss. Educated in Chicago. Began study of violin in 1923, later learning brass and string bass in high school and through his own efforts, as well as subsequently studying under private teachers. Began his career with Eddie South, then played with Erskine Tate (1932), Eddie South, for the second time (1933-36), Cab Calloway (1937-44). Recorded with Teddy Wilson, Chu Berry, Calloway. Solos: *Ebony Silhouette, Plucking the Bass* (Calloway).

HODGES, John Cornelius (Johnny). *Alto and soprano saxophone.* Received 42 points: *Burley, Braveman, Cavanaugh, Dexter, Goffin, Hammond, Hoefer, Jax, Jovien, Levin, Lim, Mize, Simon, Smith, Stacy, Thiele, Ulanov.* Born July 25 1906, Cambridge, Massachusetts, where he attended high school. Initiated his musical studies at school and studied under private teachers. Entered upon his career with Bobby Sawyer (1925), Lloyd Scott (1926), Chick Webb (1927), Duke Ellington (1928-44). Recorded with Ellington, Lionel Hampton, Teddy Wilson, Johnny Dunn and his own studio combinations for the Variety, Vocalion and Okeh labels. Alto solos: *Warm Valley, I Let a Song Go Out of My Heart, The Gal from Joe's, Saratoga Swing* (Ellington); *Buzzin' Around with the Bee, Ring Dem Bells* (Hampton). Soprano solos: *Dear Old Southland, The Sheik* (Ellington).

JOHNNY HODGES DISCOGRAPHY

With Own Band (retail-2):

Variety

576 Foolin' Myself/You'll Never Go to Heaven
586 A Sailboat in the Moonlight

Vocalion

3948 My Day/Silvery Moon & Golden Sands
4046 I Let Song Go Out of My Heart/If You Were in My Place

With Own Band (retail-2)—continued

4115 Jeep's Blues/Rendezvous with Rhythm
4213 Empty Ballroom Blues/You Walked Out of Picture
4242 Pyramid/Lost in Meditation
4309 A Blues Serenade/Jitterbug's Lullaby
4335 Swingin' in the Dell/Love in Swingtime
4351 Krum Elbow Blues/Something About an Old Love

With Own Band (retail-2)—continued

4386 Prelude to a Kiss/Jeep Is Jumpin'
4573 Hodge Podge/Wanderlust
4622 Dancing on the Stars/I'm in Another World
4710 Swingin' on the Campus/ Like Ship in Night
4849 Dooji Wooji/Mississippi Dreamboat
4917 You Can Count on Me/ Kitchen Mechanic's Day
4941 Dance of the Goon/Home Town Blues
5100 Rent Party Blues/The Rabbit's Jump
5170 Savoy Strut/Good Gal Blues
5330 Truly Wonderful/My Heart Jumped Over Moon
5353 Dream Blues/I Know What You Do
5533 Skunk Hollow Blues/Tired Socks
5940 Moon Romance/Your Love Has Faded

Bluebird

11021 Junior Hop/Day Dream
11117 That's the Blues Old Man/ Good Queen Bess
11447 Squaty Roo/Things Ain't What They Used to Be

With Duke Ellington:

With the Jungle Band:

With the Harlem Footwarmers:

See Duke Ellington Discography

With Lionel Hampton (retail-3):

Victor

25575 Buzzin' Around with the Bee /Who Babe
25586 China Stomp/Rhythm Rhythm
25592 On Sunny Side of Street/I Know That You Know
25601 Stompology
25771 You're My Ideal/The Sun Will Shine Tonight

With the Gotham Stompers:

With Rex Stewart:

With Cootie Williams:

See Duke Ellington Discography

With Johnny Dunn (15):

Columbia

14306 Sergeant Dunn's Bugle Call Blues

With Mildred Bailey (retail):

Decca

18108 Honeysuckle Rose/Willow Tree
18109 Downhearted Blues/Squeeze Me

With Teddy Wilson (2-3):

Brunswick

7867 Carelessly/How Could You
7877 Moanin' Low/Fine & Dandy
7884 There's a Lull in My Life/ It's Sweet of You
7893 I'm Coming Virginia/How Am I to Know
7903 I'll Get By/Mean to Me
7917 Sun Showers/Yours & Mine

HOLIDAY, Billie. *Vocal.* Received 32 points: *Braveman, Cavanaugh, Feather, Goffin, Hoefer, Levin, Lim, Mize, Smith, Stacy, Thiele, Ulanov.* Born Apr. 7, 1915, Baltimore, Md. Moved to New York at 14. Obtained her first singing job at 15 at Jerry Preston's Log Cabin Club. She rapidly rose to national prominence. Sang with the orchestras of Count Basie and Artie Shaw. Since 1940, however, she has been singing solo in nightspots throughout the country. Recorded with Benny Goodman, Shaw, Basie and her own studio combination. For a complete Holiday Discography refer to pages 193-94 of the 1944 ESQUIRE JAZZ BOOK.

JACKSON, Greig Stewart (Chubby). *String Bass.* Received 7 points and 6 New Star points: *Feather, Hoefer, Miller, Simon, Thiele, Ulanov.* Born Oct. 25, 1918, New York City; attended high school in Freeport, N. Y., and went one year to Ohio State University. Both parents and other members of his family were actively interested in music; he studied music at school and with special teachers, playing clarinet in the high school band in 1935. Took up bass at the age of 16 and began playing professionally two years later with Mike Riley (1937-38), then joined Johnny Messner (1938-39), Raymond Scott (1939-40), Jan Savitt (1940), Henry Busse (1940-41), Charlie Barnet (1941-43), Woody Herman (1943-44). Recorded with Messner, Scott, Busse, Barnet, Herman.

JACKSON, Preston, *Trombone.* Born 1903, New Orleans, La. Migrated to Chicago in 1917 and played with Bernie Young (1918-22); Dave Peyton, Erskine Tate, Carroll Dickerson, Louis Armstrong, Half-Pint Frankie Jaxon, Zilner Randolph. Recorded with his own studio combination, Richard M. Jones, Punch Miller, Jimmie Noone. Solo: *The Blues Jumped a Rabbit* (Noone).

JACKSON, Tony. *Piano, vocal.* Born about 1868, New Orleans, La.; died about 1922, Chicago, Ill., while working at the Elite No. 2. Remembered as a fascinating character, a unique pianist and entertainer, a good reader and yet a jive man like Fats Waller who played everything, Jackson first started playing in a New Orleans saloon at Amelia and Tchoupitoulas, in the very neighborhood where he was raised and educated. At the turn of the century and for at least a decade following, he was in terrific demand as a pianist-entertainer by the madames of the best bagnios in the Crescent City. He was a special favorite of Gypsy Schaeffer's, but he also worked for Lulu White, Mae Evans, Helma Berth, Josie Arlington, Jessie Brown, Cora De Witt and at the old "25" and Bonnie Moore's. About 1910 or 1911 he migrated to Chicago, played at the Elite No. 1 at 31st and State Streets and the Elite No. 2 at 35th and State Streets—his two major jobs in the Windy City. In 1918 he headed a band which included Sidney Bechet at the Pekin Cabaret. A prolific melodist whose original tunes would no doubt bear investigation for the wealth of material they might offer, he is remembered mainly for his *Pretty Baby*, which he wrote sometime during his first few years in Chicago. No recordings.

JOHNSON, Willie G. (Bunk). *Cornet, trumpet.* Received 9 points: *Avakian, Russell, Williams.* Born Dec. 27, 1879, New Orleans, La., where he attended school and spent much of his time as an active musician, moving rapidly from one band to another, for various lengths of time, as was common in the early days of jazz in his native city. At age 7 he began taking cornet lessons from Professor Wallace Cutchey of New Orleans University; at 15 he was playing with Tony Jackson in Adam Olivier's Band, after which he joined Buddy Bolden as second cornet (1895-97). Then followed a series of engagements with many of the principal bands and dance groups of New Orleans: John Robichaux, Bab Frank, Bob Russell, The Eagle Band, The Superior Band, The Royal Band, The Independence Orchestra, The Columbia Brass Band, The Excelsior Band, The Algiers and Pacific Band, Allen's Band, The Diamond Stone Band. Throughout Johnson's long career his activities in New Orleans were interrupted by numerous tours, one of which took him to California as early as 1905. At the turn of the century he played and traveled for two years with P. G. Loral's Circus Band; with Clarence Williams, Zue Robertson and others he toured the state of Louisiana and worked for a long time in many Texas towns such as Beaumont and particularly along the Gulf Coast from Port Arthur to Tampico, Mexico. After 1914, when he went across the Lake to teach in Mandeville, La., for a year, he left New Orleans almost entirely as the base of his operations. A year of playing at the Colonial Hotel in Bogalusa, La., brought him to an engagement with The Royal Band at Lake Charles, another with Walter Brundy in Baton Rouge (1917), after which he toured almost constantly with various shows. Among them were *The Georgia Smart Set*, and those of the Vernon Brothers and Davis, traveling through the Southwest and as far north as Kansas City. If a show became stranded he took odd jobs—playing county fairs or in honky-tonks (The Yellow Front in K. C., for example). For several years he was a member of The Banner Band in New Iberia, La., and in the early thirties he joined The Black Eagles Band of Crowley, La. His horn was destroyed one night at a dance in Rayne, La., when the Eagle's leader, Evan Thomas, was killed; and since Johnson was losing his teeth, besides, he decided to give up music. For ten years he worked in the Louisiana rice fields, hauling sugar cane in the New Iberia vicinity. A set of false teeth and a new trumpet eventually enabled him to make a comeback. He rapidly regained his old form and in 1942 waxed his first records in New Orleans for the Jazz Information label distributed by Commodore. In April 1943 he returned to California for a 14-month stretch when he appeared in a series of concerts at the Museum of Art in San Francisco and at many jam sessions. He recently cut a large group of records in New Orleans; they will probably appear on the market during 1945. Concerning Johnson's importance, Bill Russell remarks: "Bunk's influence on New Orleans jazz and on trumpeters in particular, can hardly be overestimated. Some of his earlier pupils were Buddy Petit, Wooden Joe Nicholas, King Oliver, Chris Kelley; among those of the later period were Tommy Ladnier and Louis Armstrong."

JOHNSON, William Manuel (Bill). *String bass, guitar*. Born Aug. 10, 1872, New Orleans, La., where he attended school. Mostly self-taught, he took up the harmonica at age 11, the guitar at 15, started playing in bands as a guitarist at 18. About 1900 he switched to string bass, played in a trio at Tom Anderson's Annex (1903-09), while simultaneously working with various parade bands such as The Peerless, The Excelsior, The Uptown, The Eagle. He then migrated to California where he organized his Original Creole Band which, with cornetist Freddie Keppard and clarinetist George Baquet, toured vaudeville throughout the country (1912-18). In Chicago, Johnson joined King Oliver (1918-24), from which point forward he headed his own group part of the time, worked with Darnell Howard, Clifford King, Art Sims, Freddie Keppard and John Wycliffe other times. He spent three years with the Simms band at the Wisconsin Roof Garden in Milwaukee. Recorded with Oliver, Sidney Bechet, Ike Robinson.

JONES, Jonathan (Jo). *Drums.* Received 14 points: *Burley, Braveman, Dexter, Hammond, Lim.* Born Oct. 7, 1911, Chicago, Ill. Attended school in Alabama, going on to A. & M. Institute. Played with college dance bands. Joined Count Basie (1936-44).

JONES, Richard M. (My Knee). *Piano, composer, arranger.* Born June 13, 1889, New Orleans, La., where he attended high school. Music was part of his family's heritage; he thus showed an early and avid interest in the instruments he found in his home. He started studying and playing—"always playing," as he remarks—the pedal organ, piano, alto horn and he would even "steal" blows on his uncle's cornet. This was between the ages of 8 and 12. He attended rehearsals of the parade bands, carried water for them on parades and was himself playing alto horn in the Eureka Brass Band at 13. There followed several years of developing interest and knowledge. In 1908, at 19, he started playing solo piano in the Storyville district, working in the best "houses" in town. Coincidentally with his solo work, he fronted his own band at H. Aberdeen's, George Fewclothes and the Poodle Dog, joined the Tuxedo Band at Jack Sheen's roadhouse (1908-19), after which he migrated to Chicago, where he jobbed with local bands, simultaneously serving as manager of the professional department and Chicago retail stores of the Clarence Williams Publishing Company (1919-21). He then operated his own music store (1923-28), but in conjunction with his professional activities: fronting his own band (1923-25); acting as Chicago recording director for Okeh Records (1925-28). In 1931-32 he headed his own band in New Orleans; in 1934 in Chicago. From 1935-39 he was recording consultant and arranger for Decca Records in Chicago. Through the years he has written and arranged, to which tasks he now devotes himself exclusively. Recorded solo for Gennett; with his own band for Okeh, Victor, Session. Composer: *Jazzin' Babies' Blues* (from which *Tin Roof Blues* was stolen), *Red Wagon, Hollywood Shuffle,*

Trouble in Mind, St. Peter Blues, Riverside Blues, Late Hours Blues and many others.

RICHARD M. JONES DISCOGRAPHY

With Own Band (retail-5):

Bluebird

6569 Black Rider/Trouble in Mind
6963 Trouble in Mind

Paramount

12705 Hot & Ready/It's a Low-down Thing

Okeh

8260 Spanish Shawl/29th and Dearborn
8290 Wonderful Dreams/New Orleans Shag
8349 Mushmouth Blues/Kin To Kant Blues
8390 Baby O' Mine
8431 Dusty Bottom/Scagamore Green
8437 Streetwalker's Blues

Victor

20812 Dark Alley/Hollywood Shuffle

With Own Band (retail-5)—continued

20859 Smoked Meat Blues/Good Stuff
21203 Jazzin' Babies' Blues/Boar Hog Blues
21345 African Hunch
38040 Tickle Britches Blues (Blu 6627)/Novelty Blues (Blu 6627)

Session

12-006 N. O. Hop Scop Blues/29th & Dearborn
12-007 Canal St. Blues/Jazzin' Babies Blues

Piano Solo (8):

Gennett

5174 Jazzin' Babies Blues/12th St. Rag

JORDAN, Louis Thomas. *Vocal, leader, tenor and alto saxophone, clarinet.* Received 8 points as vocal: *Burley, Jovien, Levin;* 2 points as leader: *Miller.* Born July 8, 1908, Brinkley, Arkansas, where he attended high school, and continued his education at the Arkansas Baptist College at Little Rock. Began musical studies at age 7, under his father's tutelage; continued during school and on his own. After playing with Ruby Williams in Hot Springs, Ark., migrated to Philadelphia, joining Charlie Gaines (1930), to New York, and work with Kaiser Marshall, Leroy Smith, then Chick Webb (1932-39), organized own band (1939-44). Recorded with Webb, own band. Solos: *Clap Hands, Here Comes Charlie* (baritone and vocal), *Rusty Hinge* (alto and vocal)—both Webb; *Gee, But You're Swell* (alto and vocal)—own band.

KAMINSKY, Max. *Trumpet, leader.* Received 7 points as trumpet: *Hoefer, Levin, Smith;* 4 points as leader and 3 points as New Star leader: *Avakian, Goffin, Smith.* Born Sept. 7, 1908, Brockton, Massachusetts. Attended high school in Dorchester. Took up the cornet while in school, playing in the school band. Studied under private teachers. By 1921 he was playing with local orchestras in Boston and continued his gigging until 1928 when he came to Chicago and played with Frank Teschemacher and George Wettling at the Cinderella Ballroom. There followed engagements with Red Nichols (1929), Jacques Renard, Leo Reisman and other radio bands (1930-34), Tommy Dorsey (1935), Artie Shaw (1937 and again, 1941-42), Bud Freeman and Pee Wee Russell (1938), Tony Pastor (1940), Artie Shaw's Navy Band (1942-43); organized own band (1943-44). Recorded with Shaw, Dorsey, Russell, Eddie Condon, Chocolate Dandies, Bud Freeman, Joe Bushkin, Willie (The Lion) Smith, Pastor, Art Hodes, own band. Solos: *Maple Leaf Rag* (Dorsey); *There'll Be Some Changes Made* (Russell); *Tennessee Twilight, Madame Dynamite, Basin St. Blues* (Condon).

KEPPARD, Fred (Freddie). *Trumpet.* Born 1883, New Orleans, La.; died 1932 in Chicago. Almost a legendary figure by the time he died, Keppard's activities dip far back into jazz history. Took violin lessons at age 8, changed to cornet at 16, when he had already formed his own small Chitterling band which featured chitterling struts and house-rent stomps. By 1903 he was playing in New Orleans hot spots and a few years later was playing with the best bands in town, attracting citywide attention with his uncommonly loud, boisterous and low-down trumpeting. In 1912, he left New Orleans with the Original Creole Band, touring the entire country for the next six years and landing in Chicago in 1918, where he played with Doc Cooke, Jimmie Noone, Erskine Tate, John Wycliffe, and fronting his own band (1918-30). His health began to fail rapidly and he succumbed to tuberculosis and a complication of stomach troubles.

Solos: *Salty Dog, Stockyard Strut* (own band); *Spanish Mama, Steady Roll* (Cooke); *High Fever, Messin' Around* (Cookie's Ginger-snaps).

FREDDIE KEPPARD DISCOGRAPHY

With Own Band (25):

Gennett

12399 Stockyards Strut/Salty Dog

With Doc Cook (10-15):

Gennett

5360 The One I Love/So This is Venice

5373 Moanful Man/Lonely Little Wallflower

5374 Memphis Man/Scissor Grinder Joe

With Doc Cook (10-15)—continued

Columbia

727 Spanish Mama/Hot Tamale Man

813 High Fever/Brown Sugar

With Cookie's Gingersnaps (20-30):

Okeh

8369 High Fever/Hot Tamale Man

8390 Messin' Around

KERSEY, Kenneth. *Piano.* Received 10 points: *Burley, Feather, Lim, Ulanov.* Born Harrow, Ontario, Canada, 1916. Studied at the Detroit Institute of Music and launched his professional career in 1938 with Lucky Millinder. He then played with Billy Hicks, Frankie Newton, Roy Eldridge, Red Allen (1941); Cootie Williams (1942); Andy Kirk (1942). Entered the Armed Services (1943-44). Recorded with Allen.

KRUPA, Gene. *Drums, leader.* Received 12 points as drummer: *Burley, Cavanaugh, Goffin, Jovien, Simon, Stacy.* Born Jan. 15, 1909, Chicago, Ill., where he attended high school. First evinced interest in drums in 1927 and since then has studied his instrument extensively. Professionally, he started with Joe Kayser, a Wisconsin band, about 1927-28. Subsequently played with Red Nichols (1929-30); Irving Aaronson (1931); Russ Columbo (1932); Mal Hallet, Buddy Rogers (1933-34); Benny Goodman (1935-38). Organized his own band in April, 1938, and quickly attained big-name status. Disbanded his group in mid-1943, then again returned to Benny Goodman (1943), Tommy Dorsey (1943-44), after which he again fronted his own orchestra in the summer of 1944. Recorded with Goodman, his own band, Nichols. Solos: His drum work is particularly effective in the Goodman trio and quartet records.

LADA, Anton. *Drums, songwriter*. Born about 1895, New Orleans, La. Began playing with small local bands; then migrated to Chicago in December, 1914, in the company of Nick LaRocca, Yellow Nunez, Harry Ragas and Eddie Edwards. This group played for exactly two weeks at the Casino Gardens, Clark and Kinzie Streets, when the band broke up because of personal quarrels. LaRocca obtained Johnny Stein, drummer, and Larry Shields, clarinetist, from New Orleans and set up his own band, which later became known as the Original Dixieland Band. Lada, on the other hand, obtained Charlie Pannelli, trombonist; Joe Calway, pianist; and Karl Kalberger, banjoist, and set up his own band which later became known as The Louisiana Five. Although the LaRocca Original Dixieland group is generally believed to be the first white New Orleans jazz band to reach New York City, the actual facts do not verify this. Lada's Louisiana Five was playing at Bus Stanabies Restaurant at 39th and Broadway in New York as early as July, 1915. The LaRocca contingent did not arrive in the big city until December, 1916. When the rivalry between the two groups finally came to a head in December, 1917, they were both playing at Reisenweber's Restaurant in competition with each other. Lada wrote many songs, including *Church Street Sobbin' Blues, Arkansas Blues, Yelpin' Hound Blues*, on which he still collects royalties. After the band broke up in 1924, Lada went to Hollywood, became musical director of KFWB and KFI (1924-28). The Louisiana Five recorded for the Victor, Edison, Okeh, Gennett, Emerson and Columbia labels. It earned as much as $5,000 a night.

LADNIER, Thomas (Tommy). *Cornet*. Born May 28, 1900; died June 4, 1939. Brought up in Mandeville, across Lake Pontchartrain from New Orleans. He learned to play cornet in 1914 when Bunk Johnson went across the lake to teach and organize a band. Migrated to Chicago about 1920, and by January of 1922 the Lincoln Gardens was advertising the Vassar Orchestra "with the sensational cornetist 'Tommy.' " In 1923 he made his first records with Ollie Powers

and Jimmie Noone, for Paramount, and began a long series of recordings with Lovie Austin's Blues Serenaders for Paramount. Played
with King Oliver (1924); Fletcher Henderson (1926-27). Went to
Europe several times, and played in France, Germany and Russia,
returned to U. S. during the Depression, dropping into obscurity
until November, 1938, when he came to New York to record with
Bechet, Mezzrow, Jelly Roll Morton.

LAMARE, Nappy. *Guitar*. Born June 14, 1910. New Orleans,
La., where he attended school and began to play with local bands,
the first professional job being with the Midnight Serenaders (1925).
He became associated with Wingy Manone, migrated to New York
where he worked with numerous local bands until he joined Ben
Pollack (1934). A year later the band was headed by Bob Crosby
and Lamare stayed (1935-43), since which time he has been free-
lancing on the West Coast, most recently playing with the newly
organized Eddie Miller orchestra. Recorded with Crosby, Miller,
Manone.

LaROCCA, Dominic James (Nick). *Cornet*. Born April 11, 1889,
New Orleans, La., where he attended high school. Self-taught, he
first evinced an interest in the cornet at age 11, later dabbled in the
guitar and piano also. About 1910 or 1911 he was playing under Jack
(Papa) Laine; in 1914 he migrated to Chicago with a group of white
New Orleans jazzman and when a dispute caused friction among
the band members, it split, with LaRocca calling up several musician-
friends from his native city and it was this group which became
the Original Dixieland Jazz Band, which recorded the historically
important discs for the Victor, Okeh and Aeolian-Vocalian label.
The LaRocca Dixieland played in Chicago (1914-16); New York
(late 1916-18); London (1918-29); back in New York (1920-26)
after which the group disbanded, to return for a vaudeville tour
(1936-38). Retired from music now, LaRocca engages himself in
work as a carpenter and builder. Recorded with Original Dixieland
Band.

LEWIS, George. *Clarinet*. Received 9 points: *Avakian, Russell,
Williams*. Born July 13, 1900, New Orleans, La. At age 7 he already

was intensely interested in parade bands and when, a little later, his family moved to a house directly in back of Hope Hall, where many of the great bands played for dances, his interest developed to even greater heights. His mother wanted him to play the violin, but his heart was set on the clarinet. When, at 9, his mother gave him 25 cents to buy a toy fiddle, he bought instead a tin flute, which he played as he followed the parades as a spectator. At 16 he was able to buy a real clarinet at a pawn shop for $4. He fixed it up as best he could, began to practice daily. This resulted in his joining the Black Eagle Band at Mandeville, La. (1917), after which followed engagements with Buddy Petit (1920), Earl Humphrey, Lee Collins, Kid Punch Miller; Chris Kelley (1926-28); Kid Rena, Evan Thomas in Crowley, La., in which band Bunk Johnson was playing (1929). More recently Lewis has been a member of the Tulane Brass Band and the Tuxedo Brass Band. Recorded with Bunk Johnson, his own band.

LINDSEY, John. *String bass, trombone.* Born Aug. 23, 1894, Algiers, La., where he attended school. At 16 he was playing bass in a family group consisting of his father on guitar, his brother on violin, himself on bass. Just before the United States' entry into World War I he played that instrument with local band. Served in the Armed Forces (1917-18). Upon his return he again jobbed locally with different bands, switched to trombone and performed on that instrument with John Robichaux (1920-23), Armand Piron (1924) in New Orleans and New York; King Oliver (1924), Willie Hightower (1925-28), Carroll Dickerson, Jimmy Bell and other local bands (1929-30) in Chicago. He returned to the string bass, joined Louis Armstrong (1931) since which he again has been working with local Chicago bands, including Jimmie Noone. Recorded with Jelly Roll Morton (1926) and with Armstrong, Piron, Richard M. Jones, the Harlem Hamfats, Lonnie Johnson, Georgia White.

MADISON, Louis (Kid Shots). *Cornet.* Received 2 points: *Russell.* Born Feb. 19, 1899, New Orleans, La. First learned to play drums in the band in Jones' Home, where Armstrong was a member of the band. Was a member of Armstrong's vocal quartet which roamed the streets of New Orleans, sang at amateur nights, etc., and as a boy he followed the street parades. Studied cornet with Dave Jones, Louis Dumaine and Joe Howard. His first important job was with the Tuxedo orchestra under Celestin at the Suburban Gardens. At various times he worked with Frankie Duson, Big Eye Louis Nelson, Alphonse Picou, Manuel Manetta and other New Orleans musicians, playing at the Pelican, Pete Herman's, the Black and Tan Cabaret, etc. Now works at the P. & L. Club on Lake Ponchartrain and plays regularly in the Eureka Brass Band.

MANONE, Joseph (Wingy). *Trumpet, vocal.* Born 1904, New Orleans, La. Early in life, an accident robbed him of one of his arms, but this handicap did not stop him from his interest in the trumpet. Played with numerous bands in the South, came to Chicago about 1924, then went to New York; in both places he jobbed and recorded with many different outfits. For more than 10 years he has intermittently led his own band. Recorded with his own band, Gene Gifford, Red Nichols, Adrian's Tap Room Gang, Joe Mannone's Harmony Kings, New Orleans Rhythm Kings, Benny Goodman, The Cellar Boys, Barbecue Joe & His Hot Dogs, Harlem Hot Shots, The Red Heads. Solos: *Corrine Corrina* (Nichols); *Panama* (Rhythm Kings); *Isle of Capri, Walkin' the Streets* (own band).

WINGY MANONE DISCOGRAPHY

With Own Band (1-5):

Champion
16153 Tar Paper Stomp/Tin Roof Blues

Okeh
41569 She's Cryin' for Me/Just One Girl
41570 Royal Garden Blues/Zero
41573 Nickel in the Slot/Swing Brother

Brunswick
6911 No Calling Card/Strange Blues
6940 Send Me/Walkin' the Streets

With Own Band (1-5)—continued

Vocalion
3070 You Are My Lucky Star/ Got Feelin' You're Foolin'
3071 I've Got a Note/Every Now & Then

Bluebird
10266 Corrine Corrina/I'm a Real Kinda Poppa
10289 Jumpy Nerves/Casey Jones
10296 Downright Disgusted/ Boogie Woogie
10331 Royal Garden Blues/In the Barrel

With Own Band (1-5)—continued

10401 Farewell Blues/Beale St.
Blues

10432 Limehouse Blues/Fare Thee
Well

10560 Sudan/When the Saints Go
Marching In

10749 How Long Blues/Blue Lou

With Joe Mannone (10-15):

Vocalion

15728 Downright Disgusted/Fare
Thee Well

15797 Trying to Stop My Crying/
Isn't There Little Love

With the Cellar Boys (20):

Vocalion

1503 Barrel House Stomp/Wail-
ing Blues

*With New Orleans Rhythm Kings
(1):*

Decca

161 Tin Roof Blues/San Antonio
Shout

162 Panama/Jazz Me Blues

229 Dixieland One Step/Ostrich
Walk

464 Sensation/Bluin' the Blues

*With Barbecue Joe & Hot Dogs
(3-5):*

Champion

16127 Weary Blues/Up the Country Blues

16192 Butter & Egg Man/Shake
That Thing

MARES, Paul. *Trumpet.* Born 1900, New Orleans, La. Began
career on the SS *Capitol,* a Mississippi excursion boat (1919). The
following year he came to Chicago, worked with a resort band, then
joined the New Orleans Rhythm Kings (1921-24); after which he
retired from music. He now operates a barbecue restaurant in Chicago. Solos: *Maple Leaf Rag, Nagasaki* (his own recording group).

MARRERO, Lawrence. *Guitar.* Received 9 points: *Avakian,
Russell, Williams.* Born Oct. 24, 1900, New Orleans, La. Under the
tutelage of his father and brothers, he first took up string bass, then
guitar and tenor banjo. Not long after World War I he began playing with numerous New Orleans bands, including those of Paul
Barnes, Bush Hall, Chris Kelley, Buddy Petit, Sam Morgan, Manuel
Manetta, John Robichaux, Manuel Perez, Lee Collins; he headed his
own group, the Young Tuxedo Band, for a time. Recorded with
Bunk Johnson and George Lewis.

MATTHEWS, Dave. *Tenor and alto saxophone, arranger.* Received 7 points as tenor: *Hoefer, Miller, Mize,* 4 points as arranger: *Jax, Jovien.* Born June 6, 1911, McAllister, Okla. Educated at University of Oklahoma and the Chicago Musical College. Joined Ben Pollack (1935); Jimmy Dorsey (1936-37); Benny Goodman (1937-39); Harry James, as altoman and arranger (1939-41); Hal McIntyre, alto and arranger (1941-42); Woody Herman, as arranger, (1942-43). Recorded with Pollack, Goodman, James, McIntyre, The Capitol Jazzmen. Alto solo: *Lullaby in Rhythm* (James); tenor solos: *Solitude, Clambake in B Flat* (Jazzmen).

MILLER, Eddie. *Tenor saxophone, clarinet.* Received 4 points on tenor: *Dexter, Smith;* 2 points as Armed Forces Favorite: *Simon.* Born June 23, 1911, New Orleans, La., where he attended school. He began his musical studies in school, added to his knowledge with self-study. He entered music professionally with Ben Pollack (1930-34), after which he joined Bob Crosby (1935-43). Upon the breakup of the Crosby band, he took over its leadership for a time before he entered the Armed Services; upon his discharge in the late summer of 1944, he organized a new big band in California. Recorded with Crosby, The Capitol Jazzmen, his own band. Clarinet solo: *Dogtown Blues* (Crosby). Tenor solos: *Clambake in B Flat* (Jazzmen); *Stomp Mr. Henry Lee, Yesterdays* (own band); *Panama, Little Rock Getaway, Muskrat Ramble* (Crosby).

MILLER, Ernest (Punch). *Trumpet.* Born Dec. 24, 1897, Raceland, La., where he attended school. Studied instrument on his own, with some direction from local musicians, beginning at age 14. Launching his professional career in 1918, he successively played with Frank Davis in Houston, Tex.; Erskine Tate in Chicago and in that city also with Al Wynn, François' Louisianians (1928-31), since which time he has fronted his own groups and jobbed with local Chicago bands. Recorded with Wynn, François, Jimmy Bertrand, and with his own Trio on the S-D label (to be released in 1945) and his own band on the Session label (to be released in 1945).

MOORE, Oscar Fred. *Guitar.* Received 19 points: *Burley, Cavanaugh, Feather, Lim, Simon, Stacy, Ulanov.* Born Dec. 25, 1916,

Austin, Texas. Attended school in Phoenix, Ariz., studying music under private teachers and beginning study of the guitar at the age of 6. First professional date was played with his brothers in 1934. Joined forces with Nat Cole to form the King Cole Trio in September 1937 and has been with him ever since. Has worked mostly on the West Coast, doing recording work in film studios, also in Hollywood and Los Angeles night clubs. During 1941-42 played at Nick's and Kelly's Stable in New York. Recorded with King Cole Trio, Lionel Hampton (*Jack the Bellboy*), Art Tatum (*Lonesome Graveyard*).

MORGAN, Al (Sharp). *String bass.* Received 2 points: *Goffin.* Born Aug. 19, 1908, New Orleans, La., where he attended high school. Studied music at school, on his own and with special teachers. Interest in music began with clarinet and drums at age 9, string bass at 10. First job was with Fate Marable on river boats and in St. Louis, Mo. (1927-30); he then went to New York to join Cab Calloway (1931-36); then to California to form his own band (1936); played with Les Hite (1938-40); Zutty Singleton (1940-41); Sabby Lewis, in Boston (1941-44); Louis Jordan (1944). Recorded with Calloway, Red McKenzie.

MORTON, Henry Sterling (Benny). *Trombone.* Received 11 points: *Cavanaugh, Levin, Lim, Miller.* Born 1907, New York City, where he attended school and began his musical studies. Worked with local bands, including that of Billy Fowler (1924-30), then joined Fletcher Henderson (1931-32), Don Redman (1932-39), Count Basie (1939-40), Joe Sullivan (1941), Teddy Wilson (1940-44); Edmond Hall (1944); fronted his own combination (1944). Recorded with his own studio combination, Redman, Henderson, Eddie Condon, Benny Carter. Solos: *I Got Rhythm, Nagasaki* (Redman); *Sugar Foot Stomp, Just Blues* (Henderson); *Basin St. Blues* (Condon).

MORTON, Ferdinand Joseph (Jelly Roll). *Composer, piano, leader.* Born Sept. 20, 1885, New Orleans, La.; died July 10, 1941, Los Angeles, Calif. Started studying and playing the guitar at age 7, almost simultaneously taking to the piano as well, since there was one in his home. "It was then considered a female instrument," said Morton of the piano. He explained that he was "always called a freak of a pianist, or considered I could not play on account of this peculiar style that's called jazz; but I always managed to pull the crowd any place I played.... All fast pieces I would play them slow with a precise tempo and I noticed the world fell for that tempo, but I arranged a mixture of Spanish with Negro ragtime and it sounded great it seemed to the world, because when I played I was almost mobbed, people trying to get a peek at me."

Considering his propensity to exaggerate actual occurrences, it is important to point out these facts: that he spent his childhood and early youth in Gulfport, Miss., where he played and gained a small reputation before returning to New Orleans about 1909. That upon his return he was taken under the wing of pianist Richard M. Jones and cornetist Sullivan Spraul, who not only contributed to his musical education, but who found a job and an abode for him and came to his aid in numerous little ways. Soon Morton was soloing at Tom Anderson's Annex and there followed a period (1909-15) in which he was a Storyville favorite, but in which he also made frequent excursions to distant points such as Mobile, Atlanta, Seattle, Chicago. In 1915 he migrated to California, where he stayed for a number of years, always, however, moving around the country to some extent. Chicago became his next base of activities (1923-28), after which he went to New York (1928-35); to Washington, D. C., where he owned and ran his own night club (1936-38); and then to the West Coast. Recorded for many different labels, both with band and as soloist: as pianist with Wilton Crawley, Johnny Dunn; made piano rolls for QRS, American, Wurlitzer and others; toured in vaudeville; held a recording contract with Victor (1927-30).

JELLY ROLL MORTON DISCOGRAPHY

Acc. Lizzie Miles (5):

Victor

38571 Don't Tell Me Nothin' Bout My Man/I Hate a Man Like You

Piano Solos (values after name of label):

Gennett (20-30):

3043 Tia Juana/Mamamita
5218 Grandpa's Spells/Kansas City Stomp

Piano Solos—continued

5289 King Porter Stomp/Wolverine Blues

5323 The Pearls

5486 Perfect Rag/New Orleans Joys

5515 Tom Cat/Bucktown Blues

5552 Jelly Roll Blues/Big Fat Ham

5590 Shreveport Stomp/Stratford Hunch

Paramount (20):

12216 Mamamita/35th Street Blues

Vocalion (20):

1019 Fat Meat and Greens/Sweetheart of Mine

1020 King Porter Stomp/The Pearls

Victor (6-8):

38527 Seattle Hunch/Freakish

38627 Fat Frances/Pep

General (retail):

4001 Original Rags/Mamie's Blues

4002 Michigan Water Blues/Naked Dance

4003 The Crave/Buddy Bolden's Blues

4004 Mister Joe/Winnin' Boy Blues

4005 King Porter Stomp/Don't You Leave Me

With Own Band (values after name of label):

Paramount (10):

12050 Big Fat Ham

20251 Muddy Water Blues

20332 Steady Roll/Mr. Jelly Roll

Autograph (15-20):

606 Fish Tail Blues/High Society

607 Weary Blues/Tiger Rag

617 King Porter Stomp/Tom Cat

623 My Gal/Wolverine Blues

Gennett (15):

3259 Mr. Jelly Lord

Okeh (15):

8105 London Blues/Someday Sweetheart

Victor (4-8):

20221 Black Bottom Stomp/Chant

20252 Sidewalk Blues/Dead Man Blues

20296 Smokehouse Blues/Steamboat Stomp

20405 Someday Sweetheart/Jelly Roll Blues

20415 Doctor Jazz Stomp

20431 Cannon Ball Blues/Grandpa's Spells

20772 Billy Goat Stomp/Hyena Stomp

20948 The Pearls/Beale St. Blues

21064 Wolverine Blues/Mr. Jelly Lord

21345 Jungle Blues

With Own Band—continued

21658 Shoe Shiner's Drag/Shreve-
   port
22681 Blue Blood Blues
23004 I'm Looking for a Little Blue-
   bird/Mushmouth Shuffle
23019 That'll Never Do/Fickle Fay
23307 Crazy Chords/Gambling
   Jack
23321 If Someone Would Only
   Love Me/Oil Well
23334 Mint Julep/Low Gravy
23351 Strokin' Away/Each Day
23402 Sweet Peter/Jersey Joe
23424 Load of Coal/Mississippi
   Mildred
23429 Load of Coal I and II
27565 Seattle Hunch/Freakish
   (38627)
38010 Bugaboo/Kansas City Stomp
38024 Mournful Serenade/Georgia
   Swing
38055 Red Hot Pepper/Deep Creek
   Blues
38075 Burnin' the Iceberg/Tank
   Town
38078 Pretty Lil/New Orleans
   Bump
38093 Courthouse Bump/Sweet
   Anita Mine
38108 Turtle Twist/Smilin' the
   Blues Away
38113 Try Me Out/Down My
   Way
38125 Fussy Mabel/Ponchatrain
38135 Little Lawrence/Harmony
   Blues
38601 My Little Dixie Home/
   That's Like It Ought To Be

With Own Band—continued

Bluebird (retail-1):
10254 Cannon Ball Blues/Grandpa's
   Spells
10255 Doctor Jazz/Original Jelly
   Roll Blues
10256 Wild Man Blues/Jungle
   Blues
10429 Oh Didn't He Ramble/
   Winin' Boy Blues
10434 High Society/I Thought I
   Heard Buddy Bolden Say
10442 Climax Rag/West End Blues
10450 Don't You Leave Me Here/
   Ballin' the Jack

General (retail):
1703 Sweet Substitute/Panama
1704 Good Old New York/Big
   Lip Blues
1706 Why/Get the Bucket
1707 If You Know/Shake It
1710 Mama's Got a Baby/My
   Home Is in a Southern Town
1711 Dirty, Dirty, Dirty

With New Orleans Rhythm Kings
   (10-20):

Gennett
5217 Milenberg Joys
5219 Sobbin' Blues
5220 Mr. Jelly Lord

With Wilton Crawley (3-10):

Victor
23292 Big Time/Sweetest Smile
38116 You've Got What I Need/
   Keep Your Busines to Yourself
38136 Futuristic/Got to See My
   Gal

NANCE, Raymond (Ray). *Trumpet, violin.* Received 6 points as New Star violin: *Feather, Lim, Simon, Stacy, Thiele, Ulanov.* Born Dec. 10, 1913, Chicago, Ill., where he attended school and began his study of music under private teachers and on his own. Formed his own band in 1932, but gained most of his professional experience as a night club entertainer. Later played with Earl Hines (1938), Horace Henderson (1940), Duke Ellington (1940-44). Trumpet solos: *Kitty on Toast* (Henderson); *Perdido, Take the A Train* (Ellington). Violin solos: *Moon Mist* (Ellington). Vocalisms: *Bli-Blip* (Ellington).

NELSON, Louis Delile (Big Eye Louis). *Clarinetist.* Born Jan. 28, 1885, New Orleans, La. Took to music early in life; learned the accordion, led a small combination at age 13. Played violin, guitar, eventually clarinet—which he learned under the tutorship of the Tio brothers (about 1906). Joined the Imperial Band (1907); subsequently played with many of the famous New Orleans bands of that day (1908-24); many of the groups were pick-up organizations and sometimes he was the leader. During this period he joined the Original Creole Band on part of its vaudeville tour of the U. S. (1916-17), but all his other activities centered in New Orleans and vicinity. Recorded in 1940 for the Delta label.

BAND DISCOGRAPHY

NEW ORLEANS BOOTBLACKS

Columbia (10)
14337 Mad Dog/Flat Foot
14465 I Can't Say/Mixed Salad

NEW ORLEANS FOOTWARMERS

See Sidney Bechet Discography.

NEW ORLEANS OWLS

Columbia (1-3)
459 Stomp Off, Let's Go/Oh Me, Oh My

NEW ORLEANS OWLS—*continued*

605 Owl's Hoot
688 Tampeekoe/West End Romp
823 Blowin' Off Steam/Brotherly Love
862 White Ghost Shivers
943 Eccentric/Nightmare
1045 Pretty Baby/Dynamite
1158 Meat on the Table/Piccadilly
1261 Goose Pimples/Throwin' the Horns
1547 That's a Plenty/New Twister

NEW ORLEANS RHYTHM KINGS

Gennett (10-21)

5102 Wolverine Blues/Weary Blues
5105 Tin Roof Blues/That's a Plenty
5106 Shimme-Sha-Wabble/Da Da Strain
5217 Milenberg Joys/Marguerite
5219 Sobbin' Blues/Angry
5220 Mr. Jelly Lord/Clarinet Marmalade
5221 London Blues/Mad

On Okeh (5-10):

40327 She's Cryin' for Me/Golden Leaf Rag
40422 Baby/I Never Knew

On Victor (3):

19645 She's Cryin' for Me/Everybody Loves My Baby

NEW ORLEANS WANDERERS

Columbia (15)

698 Gate Mouth/Perdido St. Blues
735 Too Tight/Papa Dip

NICHOLAS, Albert (Al). *Clarinet, tenor saxophone.* Born May 27, 1900, New Orleans, La. Evinced an early interest in music, and at age 14 studied with Lorenzo Tio, after which by 1916, he was playing gig dates with greats such as Buddy Petit and King Oliver. He signed up with the Navy (1916-19), playing in a band on the U.S.S. *Olympia.* Upon his return to his native city he worked with the Maple Leaf Band (1920-21), Arnold De Pas (1921-22), Manuel Perez (1922-23), fronted his own band at Tom Anderson's Cabaret (1923-24). He then was called to Chicago to join King Oliver (1924-26), subsequent to which he joined Jack Carter to play the Plaza Hotel, Shanghai, China (1926-27), Grudo Curti in Cairo, Egypt (1927-28), Benedetti's Six Crackerjacks in Alexandria, Egypt (1928). Back in New York, he joined Luis Russell (1929-33), with whom he had played in his own band at Tom Anderson's. Then came engagements with Chick Webb (1934), Sam Wooding (1934), The Blue Chips (1934), Bernard Addison (1935), again fronted his own small group (1935), Louis Armstrong (1936-39), Zutty Singleton (1940). The following year he gave up music and took a job as a subway guard in New York. Recorded with Oliver, Red Allen, Russell, Bernard Addison, Little Ramblers, Fats Waller, Freddie Jenkins, Armstrong, Richard M. Jones, Jelly Roll Morton. Clarinet Solos: *Sugar Foot Stomp, Too Bad, Deep Henderson, Jackass Blues* (Oliver); *29th and Dearborn, Spanish Shawl* (Jones); *Song of the Swa-*

nee, Feelin' the Spirit (Russell); *Blue Blood Blues, Mushmouth Shuffle, West End Blues, Climax Rag* (Morton).

NICHOLAS, Joe (Wooden Joe). *Cornet.* Born 1883, New Orleans, La. Learned to play cornet under the influence of Bunk Johnson and Buddy Bolden. Received the nickname "Wooden Joe" because of his reputation for power and stamina in the New Orleans parades, and according to Sidney Bechet, his tone is "still so strong he can balance an entire brass band." For the past thirty years he has led his own small group in neighborhood New Orleans night clubs. Although his reputation is for the most part a local one, "he is," claims William Russell, "known as being able to play one of the hottest horns in New Orleans."

NOONE, Jimmie. *Clarinet, leader.* Born Apr. 23, 1895, on a farm near New Orleans; died April 19, 1944, Los Angeles, Calif. Began the study of his instrument at age 15, on his own and with Sidney Bechet and the Tio Brothers. Soon was playing with Kid Ory and Armand Piron (1917-18). Migrated to Chicago and worked with King Oliver (1918-19), Freddie Keppard (1919-21), Doc Cook's Dreamland Orchestra (1922-27). Organized his own small combination and went into the Apex Club (1927-29), since which he played nightspots—mainly in Chicago. In 1943 he moved to California and up to the time of his death he fronted his own small group playing a long engagement at the Streets of Paris. He took part in the Orson Welles jazz broadcasts over a limited West Coast CBS network (1944). Solos: *My Daddy Rocks Me* (both Cook and own band); *Monday Date, I Know That You Know, The Blues Jumped a Rabbit, Sweet Lorraine* (own band).

JIMMIE NOONE DISCOGRAPHY

With Ollie Powers (10):

Claxtonola

40263 Play That Thing

Paramount

12059 Play That Thing (Pa 20263)
/Jazzbo Jenkins

With Cookie's Gingersnaps (20-30):

Okeh

8369 Here Comes the Old Tamale
Man/High Fever

8392 Messin' Around

40675 Love Found You for Me

With Cook's Dreamland Orchestra
(*10-15*):

Gennett

5360 The One I Love/So This Is
Venice

5373 Moanful Man/Lonely Little
Wall Flower

5374 Memphis Maybe Man/Scissor Grinder Joe

Acc. Lillie Delk Christian (*2-4*):

Okeh

8596 Too Busy/Was It Dream

8607 You're a Real Sweetheart/
Last Night I Dreamed You
Kissed Me

8650 Sweethearts on Parade/I
Can't Give You Anything
But Love, Baby

8660 Must Have That Man/Baby

With Own Band

Vocalion (20-35):

1184 I Know That You Know/
Sweet Sue

1185 Four or Five Times/Every
Evening

1188 Ready for the River/Forevermore

1207 Sweet Lorraine/Apex Blues

1215 Blues My Naughty Sweetie
Gives to Me

1229 King Joe/Monday Date

Vocalion (3-10):

1238 Let's Sow a Wild Oat/It's
Tight Like That

With Own Band—continued

1240 Some Rainy Day/She's
Funny That Way

1267 Chicago Rhythm/I Got a
Misery

1272 Wake Up Chillun'/Love Me
or Leave Me

1296 Birmingham Bertha/Am I
Blue

1415 True Blue Lou/'Sposin'

1416 Satisfied/Through

1436 I'm Doin' What You're Doin'
/He's a Good Man to Have
Around

1439 Love Me/Love

1466 Have a Little Faith in Me/
Cryin' for the Carolines

1471 Should I/I'm Following You

1490 El Rado Shuffle/Deep Trouble

1497 When You're Smilin'/I Lost
My Gal from Memphis

1506 I'm Driftin' Back to Dreamland/On Revival Day

1518 So Sweet/Virginia Lee

1531 Moonlight on the Colorado/
Little White Lies

1554 Three Little Words/Something to Remember You By

1580 He's Not Worth Your Tears
/Travelin' All Alone

1584 Bring It on Home to
Grandma/You Rascal You

2619 Inka Dinka Doo/Like Me a
Little Bit Less

2620 Dixie Lee/Delta Bound

2779 Apex Blues (Br 7096)/My
Daddy Rocks Me (Br 7096)

2862 Anything for You/Liza

2888 Porter's Love Song/Shine
2907 It's Easy to Remember/Soon
2908 Lullaby of Broadway/Here
Comes Cookie

Vocalion (4-5):

15819 Off-Time/Ain't Misbehavin'
15823 Anything You Want/That
Rhythm Man

Brunswick (2-4):

6174 I Need Lovin'/When It's
Sleepy Time Down South
6192 River Stay Way from My
Door/It's You
7124 My Melancholy Baby/After
You've Gone

Decca (retail):

1584 I Know That You Know/
Bump It

1621 Japansy/Four or Five Times
1730 I'm Walking This Town/
Call Me Darling, Call Me
Sweetheart, Call Me Dear
18095 New Orleans Hop Scop
Blues/Keystone Blues

English Parlophone (5):

R2281 Way Down Yonder in New
Orleans/Sweet Georgia
Brown
R2303 Blues Jumped a Rabbit/He's
a Different Type of Guy

With the Capitol Jazzmen (retail):

Capitol

10009 Clambake in B Flat/I'm
Sorry I Made You Cry
10010 Casanova's Lament/Solitude

NORVO, Kenneth (Red). *Vibraharp, xylophone, marimba.* Received 44 points on vibes: *Burley Braveman, Cavanangh, Dexter, Feather, Goffin, Hammond, Hoefer, Jax, Jovien, Levin, Mize, Simon, Smith, Stacy, Thiele, Ulanov;* 4 points as leader: *Cavanaugh, Levin.* Born March 31, 1908, Beardstown, Ill., where he attended school. First musical interest was the piano, but he switched to xylophone during high school. At 17 he entered music professionally with a chautauqua troupe, after which he toured vaudeville with a band called The Collegians. At the Oriental Theatre in Chicago he played with Paul Ash (1926) and then became a single solo act (1926-27). At the Eagles Ballroom in Milwaukee he fronted his first band (1928), then went to radio station KSTP, Minneapolis, again as a single (1928). Back in Chicago he played briefly with Victor Young, Ben Bernie—and more than a year as an NBC staff musician (1928-30). Joined Paul Whiteman (1930-34), after which he organized his own band (1935-44). Joined Benny Goodman & Teddy Wilson in a

Quintet for *Seven Lively Arts* (1944). Switched to vibes in 1943. Recorded with own band, Hoagy Carmichael, Edmond Hall, Teddy Wilson, Mildred Bailey. Xylophone solos: *Smoke Dreams, Knockin' on Wood, Blues in E Flat, Hole in the Wall* (own band); *Just a Mood* (Wilson Quartet). Marimba solos: *Dance of the Octopus, In a Mist* (solos). Vibe solos: *Seein' Red, Blue Interval* (Edmond Hall). For comprehensive Norvo discography refer to pages 203-04 of the 1944 ESQUIRE JAZZ BOOK.

O'DAY, Anita. *Vocal.* Received 6 points and 4 as New Star: *Feather, Mize, Simon, Stacy.* Born Dec. 18, 1919, Chicago, Ill., where she attended high school. She began the study of music without any particular instruction, taking up voice at the age of 17. First sang professionally with the Max Miller combination which played at Chicago's Three Deuces in 1939. Joined Gene Krupa (1941-43); retired from music for a short period and joined Stan Kenton orchestra in 1944. Recorded with Krupa and Kenton. Solos: *Let Me Off Uptown, Side by Side.*

OLIVER, Joseph (King). *Trumpet, leader.* Born 1885, New Orleans; died April 10, 1938, Savannah, Ga. Began studying and playing trumpet at an early age and soon was part and parcel of the hectic jazz activity in the New Orleans of 1910-18. Was a member of the Onward Brass Band, became leader of the famous Olympia Band (1916-18). Migrated to Chicago, where he opened at Dreamland Café with celebrated King Oliver Creole Jazz Band (1918-19); moved to the Royal Garden Café (1919-20). Took his band to California for about a year and on his return to Chicago again played at the Royal Garden (1922-24) and it was here that Armstrong joined the group. Oliver continued in Chicago at various night spots in addition to tours until 1928, when he went to New York where, under his recording contract with Victor, he waxed many recordings with pickup bands, all under his name. Played in southeastern U. S. 1931-37. Solos: *Sugar Foot Stomp, Snag It, Jackass Blues, Deep Henderson* and many others, all with his own band.

It was the collaboration of Oliver and his band and Richard M. Jones that resulted in the now famous and highly prized recordings by Oliver on the Paramount and Gennett and Okeh labels. Having himself made some discs for Paramount and Gennett, and having been asked by those companies to form a band of his own for recording purposes, Richard Jones declined to organize a band, saying that already there was a fine one in existence—one which he could highly recommend: that of King Oliver. Then it was that Oliver and his men began this series of great recordings.

KING OLIVER DISCOGRAPHY

With Own Band (30-50):

Paramount

12088 Southern Stomps
20292 Riverside Blues/Mabel's Dream

Columbia

13003 New Orleans Stomp/Chattanooga Blues
14003 Camp Meeting Blues/London Café Blues

Gennett

5132 Dipper Mouth Blues (HRS 4)/Weather Bird Rag (UHCA 75-76)
5133 Canal St. Blues/Just Gone
5134 Mandy Lee/I'm Goin' Away
5135 Chimes Blues/Froggie Moore
5184 Snake Rag (UHCA 75-76)
5274 Alligator Hop/Krooked Blues
5275 Zulu's Ball/Workingman Blues
5276 If You Want My Heart/That Sweet Something Dear

Okeh

4906 Sobbin' Blues/Sweet Lovin' Man

With Own Band (30-50)—continued

4918 Dipper Mouth Blues/Where Did You Stay Last Night
4933 Snake Rag/High Society Rag (HRS 12)
4975 Jazzin' Babies Blues
8148 Room Rent Blues/Ain't Gonna Tell Nobody
8235 Mabel's Dream/Sweet Baby Doll
40000 Tears (HRS 12)/Buddy's Habits
40034 Riverside Blues/Working Man Blues

With Own Band (5-25):

Vocalion

1007 Too Bad/Snag It (Br 80039)
1014 Deep Henderson/Jackass Blues
1033 Sugar Foot Stomp/Wa Wa Wa
1049 Tack Annie/Wang Wang Blues
1059 Someday Sweetheart/Dead Man Blues
1112 Black Snake Blues/Willie the Weeper
1114 Every Tub/Showboat Shuffle

With Own Band (5-25)—continued

1152 Sobbin' Blues/Farewell Blues
1189 West End Blues/Tin Roof Blues
1190 Lazy Mama/Sweet Emmaline
1225 Speakeasy Blues/Aunt Hagar's Blues
..... Unissued:
The Hobo's Prayer
Messin' Around
Doctor Jazz
Aunt Jemima
Crab House Blues
Janitor Sam
Where That Ol' Man River Flows

With Own Band (2-25):

Brunswick

4028 Got Everything/Four or Five Times
4469 Watching the Clock/Slow & Steady
6053 Stop Crying/Papa De Da Da
6065 I'm Crazy About My Baby/ Sugar Blues

Victor

22298 St. James Infirmary/When You're Smiling (Blu 5466)
22681 Olga
23001 Struggle Buggy/Don't You Think I Love You
23009 Shake It & Break It/Stingaree Blues (Blu 10707)
23011 Passing Time with Me/ What's Use of Living Without Me

With Own Band (2-25)—continued

23029 I'm Lonesome/Can't Stop
23388 New Orleans Shout/Nelson Stomp
38034 West End Blues
38039 Call of the Freaks/Trumpet's Prayer (Blu 7705)
38049 My Good Man Sam/Can I Tell You
38090 What You Want Me To Do/Too Late
38101 Sweet Like This/I Want You Just Myself
38109 Frankie & Johnny/Everybody Does It in Hawaii
38124 You're Just My Type/I Must Have It
38134 Mule Face Blues/Boogie Woogie (Blu 6778)
38137 Rhythm Club Stomp/Edna

With The Savannah Syncopators (4):

Brunswick

6046 Who's Blue

With The Chocolate Dandies (10):

Vocalion

1610 Loveless Love/One More Time
1617 When I Take My Sugar to Tea

Duet With Jelly Roll Morton (20):

Autograph

617 King Porter Stomp/Tom Cat (Session)

ORY, Edward (Kid). *Trombone, leader.* Received 7 points as trombone: *Avakian, Russell, Williams:* 2 points as leader: *Avakian.* Born Dec. 25, 1889, La Place, La. At age 11, Ory and four other kids organized a "string" band—their instruments were homemade. This group played for local dances, saved money to buy real instruments. On one of his occasional trips to New Orleans Ory purchased a trombone, became acquainted with trumpeter Buddy Bolden; on future trips (1905-10), he "sat in" with the Bolden outfit. During this period and later, Ory studied his instrument under private teachers. He brought his own band to New Orleans (1911-18), played at numerous New Orleans spots; migrated to Los Angeles, sent for his band, which worked regularly in that area (1919-24). He then joined Louis Armstrong in Chicago (1924), for a few months; moved to King Oliver (1924-27), Dave Peyton (1928), Clarence Black (1928-29), the Chicago Vagabonds (1929). Returned to Los Angeles (1929), played with local bands until 1931, then retired from music. He took up chicken ranching with his brother and when, in 1938, his brother died, he felt the new interest in swing would warrant his return to the music field. Encouraged by the publication of his *Muskrat Ramble,* he started writing again and soon after was again playing with some of his old New Orleans friends in Los Angeles. He became a member of Barney Bigard's group in 1942, simultaneously taking up string bass so he would have a double opportunity of obtaining jobs. Appeared with Bunk Johnson at the Geary Theatre concerts in San Francisco (1943), played the Orson Welles broadcasts (1944) and the Standard Oil West Coast Educational broadcasts (1944). For several years now he has been fronting his own small combination in Frisco. Recorded with Armstrong, Oliver, Jelly Roll Morton, Tiny Parham, his own band, Lil's Hot Shots, New Orleans Wanderers. Solos: *Savoy Blues, Hotter Than That* (Armstrong); *Drop That Sack* (Hot Shots); *Sugar Foot Stomp, Jackass Blues, West End Blues, Tack Annie, Snag It* (Oliver).

PALMIERI, Remo. *Guitar.* Received 10 points and 9 points as New Star: *Cavanaugh, Feather, Goffin, Jovien, Levin, Lim, Miller, Simon, Ulanov.* Born March 29, 1923, Manhattan, New York, N. Y., where he attended high school. Began the study of music on his own and started the study of his instrument at the age of 11. Between

12 and 16 he also studied bass. Launched his professional career with his own 4-piece band. Also played with Nat Jaffe (Jan. 1943-Apr. 1943), Coleman Hawkins (Apr. 1943-Dec. 1943), with Red Norvo (since Feb. 1944). Recorded with Red Norvo, Phil Moore, Teddy Wilson.

PARENTI, Anthony (Tony). *Clarinet, alto saxophone.* Born Aug. 6, 1900, New Orleans, La., where he attended high school. Studied under special teachers, first the violin at age 13, then the clarinet at 14. Launched his professional career fronting his own band in New Orleans, playing the La Vida Club (1922-24) and at the Liberty Theatre. During this time his band recorded 12 sides for the Victor label, 12 sides for Brunswick, 6 sides for Columbia and 2 sides for Okeh, all of which were waxed in his native city. In 1927 he migrated to New York to work with Paul Ash (1928), Arnold Johnson (1929), B. A. Rolfe's Lucky Strike Orchestra (1930-32), the Kate Smith show orchestra (1932-34), CBS staff (1934-38), Ted Lewis (1938-44). Recorded with his own band.

TONY PARENTI DISCOGRAPHY

With Own Band (1-3):

Brunswick

4184 Gumbo/You Made Me Like It

Cameo

0180 Old Man Rhythm

Columbia

545 Midnight Papa/Cabaret Echoes
836 New Crazy Blues/Up Jumped the Devil
1264 African Echoes/Weary Blues

With Own Band (1-3)—continued

1548 In the Dungeon/When You and I Were Pals

Okeh

40308 That's a Plenty/Cabaret Echoes

Victor

19647 Twelfth Street Blues/Creole Blues
19697 Dizzy Lizzy/French Market Blues
19698 Be Yourself/La Vida

PAUL, Les. *Guitar*. Received 8 points: *Hoefer, Jovien, Miller*. Born 1916, Waukesha, Wisconsin, where he attended high school. Began self-study of guitar at an early age and hasn't quit yet. Became staff artist at KMOX, St. Louis (1931), then to WLS, WBBM, WJJD, WIND—all Chicago, on all of which he worked as staff guitarist (1932-37). Joined Fred Waring (1938-41), after which he again returned to WBBM as staff artist (1941-42), then radio work in California (1943-44).

PAVAGEAU, Alcide (Slow Drag). *String bass*. Received 3 points: *Russell*. Born Mar. 7, 1888, New Orleans, La. Is self-taught, both on guitar, which he started playing at the age of 17, and on string bass which he did not take up until 1933, when he built up an instrument of his own. Has become prominent as bass player only in recent years. First professional job was with a washboard band called the Undertaker Band, in which he played guitar. Has played in many New Orleans clubs on Bourbon St. and in the French Quarter and is currently with George Lewis and Herb Morand's orchestra at a New Orleans nightspot.

PEREZ, Manuel. *Cornet*. Born about 1879, New Orleans, La., where he atteneded school and engaged in most of his early musical activities. He began playing professionally in the 1890's and was best known as the leader of the Imperial Band, beginning in 1898. Later he led the Onward Brass Band. He migrated to Chicago where he played the Arsonia Café and other spots (1915-18). Both in his native city and in Chicago he engaged also in his daytime trade as a cigarmaker. Now retired from music, he helps run a furniture store on Orleans Street in his native city.

PETTIFORD, Oscar, *String bass*. Received 20 points: *Burley, Braveman, Feather, Levin, Simon, Thiele, Ulanov*. Born Sept. 30, 1922, Okmulgee, Okla. His father gave up practicing medicine to form a band consisting of members of the family—11 children, all of whom were taught to be musicians or entertainers. When Oscar was three, the family moved to Minneapolis and the boy's first appearance musically was as singer with this band. At the age of 10 he began piano lessons; he is self-taught on the bass, and in 1936 appeared as bassist with the family band, remaining until 1941. During this time they toured Georgia, the Carolinas, and Alabama. Returning to Minneapolis, he started working with local bands, continually experimenting with complex bass rhythms. Here he was heard by Charlie Barnet, who hired him, even though it meant having two men on this instrument. As a result, Pettiford perfected a *Concerto for Two Basses*. Worked with Roy Eldridge (1943); Billy Eckstine (1944), Boyd Raeburn (1944). Recorded with Feather's All-Stars, Sid Catlett, Edmond Hall, Coleman Hawkins, Earl Hines.

PHILLIPS, Joseph Edward (Flip). *Tenor saxophone*. Received 6 points as New Star: *Burley, Cavanaugh, Jax, Jovien, Miller, Thiele*. Born 1915, Brooklyn, N. Y., where he attended school. During those school days he launched his musical efforts with the alto sax, which he played in local bands. With his own trio he worked an engagement at Schneider's Lobster House, Brooklyn (1934-39), then joined Frankie Newton (1940-41), Larry Bennett (1941-43), Woody Herman (1944).

PICOU, Alphonse. *Clarinet*. Born Oct. 19, 1878, New Orleans, La., where he attended high school. He was given a good musical education: at 14 he was studying the guitar, at 15 he took up the clarinet. By 1894 he was playing in the Accordiana Band, after which he worked with various important New Orleans groups, among others his own Independent Band and the Superior Band with Bunk Johnson about 1908. He migrated to Chicago in 1917, played with Manuel Perez and with Dave Peyton's Grand Theatre Orchestra. He is still playing with local groups in his native city. Recorded for the first time in 1940 with Kid Rena's Jazz Band. During the thirties he devoted much of his time to tinsmithing, playing only occasionally in the parades at Carnival time. Solo: *High Society* (Rena), in which he performs the part which he himself made famous.

PRION'S NEW ORLEANS ORCHESTRA

Columbia (1):

99 Bright Star Blues/Ghost of the Blues
14007 West Indies/Sud Bustin'

Okeh

40021 Bouncing Around/Kiss Me Sweet
40189 Louisiana Swing/Sittin' On Curb

Prion Orchestra Discography—continued

Victor

19223 New Orleans Wiggle/
       Mama's Gone

19255 Do Doddle Oom/West In-
       dies Blues
19646 Red Man Blues/Do Just As
       I Say

POWELL, Gordon (Specs). *Drums*. Received 10 points and 6 points as New Star: *Cavanaugh, Hammond, Jax, Levin, Stacy, Ulanov*. Born June 5, 1922, New York, N. Y., where he attended high school. Studied the piano until he was about 15 years old, under private teachers and then began study of drums. First professional job was with Edgar Hayes in 1939; played with Eddie South (1939-40); John Kirby (1940-41); Benny Carter (1941-42); Red Norvo (1942); Raymond Scott (1943, with whom he plays now as staff drummer for CBS). Recorded with South, Kirby.

POWELL, Mel. *Piano*. Received 9 points as Armed Forces Favorite and 6 points as New Star: *Burley, Braveman, Feather, Goffin, Jax, Stacy*. Born Feb. 12, 1923, New York City, where he attended high school, graduating at age 14. Began playing piano during pre-grammar school days, studied in school and under a private teacher. Organized his own band at 12—The Dixieland Six—which held down a job at the Palais Royale, Nyack, N. Y., for six months. After graduation played with local bands (Singleton, Brunis, McPartland, Hackett); became acquainted with pianist Willie (The Lion) Smith, who gave him further informal instruction. Powell joined Muggsy Spanier (1940), then moved to Benny Goodman (1940-42), Raymond Scott's CBS band (1942-43), entered Armed Services (1943-44). Solos: *The Earl, Tuesday at Ten, Caprice Paganini XXIV, Pound Ridge* (Goodman).

RAPPOLO, Leon Joseph. *Clarinet*. Born March 16, 1902, Lutheran, La.; died Oct. 5, 1943, New Orleans, La. He started studying music at an early age under private teachers. Ran away from home, joined Bee Palmer's troupe (1916); after playing with other southern bands (Emmett Hardy included), he joined the New Orleans Rhythm Kings (1921-23). Lost his health and was forced to retire from active participation in music. Solos: *Eccentric, Tin Roof Blues, Clarinet Marmalade* (New Orleans Rhythm Kings).

ROBERTSON, C. Alvin (Zue). *Trombone*. Born March 7, 1891, New Orleans, La. Interest in music began on piano at age 5; turned to trombone at 13, studied under private teacher. Played locally (1909), then joined Kit Carson's Wild West Show (1910); headed own band (1911-13) at a nightspot in New Orleans' Storyville district; joined road show, subsequently played with many of the famous New Orleans bands of the day (1913-17); with a Chicago group which numbered among its members trumpeter Freddie Keppard and Bab Frank, a hot piccolo player (1918-19); with Jelly Roll Morton, also in Chicago (1921-24), followed by short stints with King Oliver, W. C. Handy, Dave Peyton (1924-25); joined road show, landed in New York, started playing piano again and became pianist and organist at New York's Lincoln and Lafayette Theatres (1926-29), a period interspersed with vaudeville tours and work with local groups. Retired from music about 1930.

ROBINSON, James (Jim). *Trombone*. Received 8 points: *Avakian, Russell, Williams*. Born Dec. 25, 1892, Deeringe, La. First studied the guitar and did not take up the trombone until he was 24 years of age, when he studied by himself, later having some instruction from Charles Henry. Played trombone for twelve years in Sam Morgan's Jazz Band, touring with them from Florida to Texas and once as far north as Chicago. Recorded with Sam Morgan, Kid Rena, Bunk Johnson, George Lewis.

SACHS, Aaron. *Clarinet, alto saxophone*. Received 6 points as New Star clarinet: *Braveman, Cavanaugh, Feather, Goffin, Jax, Lim*. Born July 4, 1923, New York, N. Y., where he attended high school. Studied music with private teachers, beginning at the age of 12. First job was with Babe Russin (1941); played with Red Norvo (1941-42); Van Alexander (1942-43); rejoined Red Norvo (1943-44). Recorded with Norvo, Teddy Wilson, Eddie Heywood. Solos: *Man I Love/ Blues* (Teddy Wilson); *Rosetta/Flying Home* (Norvo).

SAUTER, Eddie. *Arranger, trumpeter*. Received 9 points as arranger: *Cavanaugh, Levin, Lim, Simon*. Born Dec. 2, 1914, Brooklyn, N. Y. Attended high school in Nyack, N. Y. Became interested in music during high school days and played with local bands. First big-time job with Archie Bleyer; then joined Charlie Barnet; Red Norvo (1936-39); Benny Goodman, as arranger (1939-42), since which time he has free lanced.

SCOTT, Arthur Budd (Bud). *Guitar, banjo*. Received 6 points: *Avakian, Russell, Williams*. Born Jan. 11, 1890, New Orleans, La. Played with Buddy Bolden just after the turn of the century; then with John Robichaux, The Olympia Band, Freddie Keppard, Big Eye Louie Nelson, many others. He began traveling when very young as a musician-entertainer with road shows, playing not only his instruments but frequently working as a vocalist. He migrated to New York not long after the end of World War I, then to Los Angeles where he became a member of Kid Ory's band (1922), then to Chicago where he played and recorded with King Oliver, Jelly Roll Morton, Jimmie Noone. For the past 15 years he has lived in Los Angeles, where he has recently again played with his old New Orleans friends, Kid Ory, Mutt Carey, Noone and others; and where, for several years, he has led his own string trio.

SIMEON, Omer Victor, Jr. (Simmie). *Alto saxophone, clarinet*. Born July 21, 1902, New Orleans, La. Raised in Chicago where he attended high school. Began his musical studies in 1920 under special teachers, among them, Lorenzo Tio, Jr. Joined Charlie Elgar (1923-27), King Oliver (1927), rejoined Elgar (1927-28), Luis Russell (1928), Erskine Tate (1928-30), Jerome Carrington at the Regal Theatre, Chicago (1931), Earl Hines (1931-37), Horace Henderson (1938-39), Coleman Hawkins (1940), Walter Fuller (1940-41), Jimmie Lunceford (1942-44). Recorded with Jelly Roll Morton, Hines, Oliver, Dixie Rhythm Kings, Jabbo Smith, Harry Dial, Paul Mares, his own combination on the Brunswick label—*Beau Koo Jack/ Smoke House Blues* (7109). Clarinet solos: *Shreveport Stomp, Someday Sweetheart, Smoke House Blues, The Chant, Black Bottom Stomp* (Morton); *Rosetta* (Hines); *Reincarnation, Maple Leaf Rag. Nagasaki* (Mares).

SINGLETON, Arthur James (Zutty). *Drums*. Received 6 points: *Avakian, Dexter, Smith*. Born May 14, 1898, Bunkie, La., but attended school in New Orleans. Initial interest in drums at age 7; mostly self-taught. Began professional playing with Big Eye Louie Nelson and Steve Lewis in New Orleans (1920), then went on to the Tuxedo Band (1921), John Robichaux (1922), the Maple Leaf Band (1922), Fate Marable (1923), Charlie Creath (1924). In Chicago he joined Doc Cook (1925), Dave Peyton (1925), Jimmie Noone (1926), Clarence Jones (1926), Carroll Dickerson (1927-28), Louis Armstrong (1929-30); then East to Alonzo Ross (1930-31), Fats Waller (1931), Vernone Andrade (1932-34), Roy Eldridge (1935-36—this was again in Chicago at the Three Deuces); Bobby Hackett (1937), after which came free-lancing, including a period with Bud Freeman (1940). Oftentimes he headed some small group. During the past several years he has spent much time in California, free-lancing and playing with many different small outfits. In the fall of 1944 he was a member of an act headed by Shelton Brooks, Jr. Zutty has recorded with his own band, Pee Wee Russell, The Rhythmakers, Louis Armstrong, The Capitol Jazzmen.

SMITH, Willie. *Alto saxophone.* Received 17 points as Armed Forces Favorite: *Goffin, Jovien, Levin, Lim, Miller, Stacy, Ulanov.* Born 1908, Charleston, S. C., where he attended high school. He continued his education at Fisk University, Nashville, Tennessee, majoring in chemistry. Began clarinet studies at age 10 under private teachers. Started alto studies in college, but mostly self-taught. Played in school band. Entered professional career with Jimmie Lunceford (1930-41); then joined Charlie Spivak (1942); entered Armed Services (1942-44) from which he received his discharge in the fall of 1944. Alto solos: *I'll See You in My Dreams, Avalon, Uptown Blues, Swingin' Uptown.* Clarinet solos: *Sophisticated Lady, Put on Your Old Grey Bonnet* (Lunceford).

SPANIER, Francis (Muggsy). *Trumpet.* Received 7 points: *Dexter, Goffin, Jax.* Born Nov. 9, 1906, Chicago, Ill., there attending school. Studied instrument under private teachers and at school. Began career with Sig Meyers (1922-24), played with other local bands including Floyd Towne (1925-26), later joined Joe Kayser (1926), Ray Miller (1927-28), Ted Lewis (1928-35), Ben Pollack (1936-38), after which he retired from music because of illness, until April,

1939, when he reappeared as leader of his own small group which later expanded to a full-size orchestra (1940-42). Rejoined Ted Lewis (1943-44), after which he once more organized his own group in New York (1944). Recorded with Miller, Pollack, Lewis, Charlie Pierce, Chicago Rhythm Kings, the Bucktown Five, Bechet-Spanier Quartet, Mound City Blue Blowers, Dorsey Brothers and more recently, with his own small combination on the Bluebird label. Solos: *Relaxin' at the Touro, Dipper Mouth, Sister Kate, Riverboat Shuffle, Big Butter and Egg Man* (own band); *Lazy River* (Bechet-Spanier).

SPENCER, O'Neill. *Drums*. Born Nov. 25, 1909, Cedarville, O.; died July 24, 1944, New York City. Attended high school in Springfield, O. Studied at school and on his own. Began playing locally in Buffalo, N. Y. (1926-30). Joined the Blue Rhythm Band (1931-36), John Kirby (1937-43). Recorded with his own band on the Decca label and with Blue Rhythm, Milt Herth Trio and Kirby.

O'NEILL SPENCER DISCOGRAPHY

With Benny Carter (5):

Columbia

2439 Blues in My Heart/Minnie the Moocher
2504 Moanin'/Blue Rhythm
2638 I Can't Get Along Without My Baby/Low Down on the Bayou

With Blue Rhythm Band (2-5):

Perfect

15605 Cabin in the Cotton/Scat Song
15606 Heat Waves/Minnie the Moocher's Wedding Day
15621 Growl/Mighty River
15629 White Lightning/Rhythm Spasm
15634 Doin' the Shake/Wild Waves

With Blue Rhythm Band (2-5)—continued

15652 Sentimental Gentleman from Georgia/You Gave Me Everything but Love
15676 Old Yazoo/Reefer Man
15696 Jazz Cocktail/Smoke Rings
15822 Feelin' Gay/Jazz Martini

English Vocalion

6 Harlem After Midnight

Bluebird

5688 The Growl/Stuff Is Here

Victor

24442 Harlem After Midnight/Love's Serenade
24482 Kokey Joe/Break It Down

With Blue Rhythm Band (2-5)—
continued

English Columbia

  734 Buddy's Wednesday Outing/
     Ridin' in Rhythm

Brunswick

  7534 Tallahassee/Once to Every
      Heart

Columbia

  2963 Out of a Dream/Let's Have
      a Jubilee
  2994 Solitude/Keep Rhythm
      Going
  3020 Back Beats/Spitfire
  3038 African Lullaby/Swingin' in
      E Flat
  3044 Brown Sugar Mine/Dancing
      Dogs
  3071 Harlem Heat/There's
      Rhythm in Harlem
  3078 Cotton/Truckin'
  3083 Dinah Lou/Waiting in the
      Garden

Vocalion

  3808 Blue Rhythm Fantasy/Har-
      lem Madness
  3817 Prelude to a Stomp/Rhythm
      Jam

Variety

  604 Image of You/Lucky Swing
  624 Camp Meeting Jamboree/
     When Irish Eyes Are Smiling

With Henry Allen (1):

Vocalion

  3261 On the Beach at Bali/Take
      My Heart
  3262 You're Not the Kind/Chloe

With Buster Bailey (3-5):

Vocalion

  3846 Dizzy Debutante/Afternoon
      in Africa
  4089 Sloe Jam Fizz/Planter's
      Punch

With New Orleans Feetwarmers
(1):

Decca

  7429 Sweet Patootie/Viper Mad

With Johnny Dodds (1):

Decca

  1676 Stack O'Lee Blues/Melan-
      choly
  7413 Blues Galore/Shake Your
      Can

With Billy Kyle (3):

Variety

  531 Margie/Big Boy Blues (Voc.
     3815)
  574 Havin' a Ball/Sundays Are
     Reserved

With Frank Newton (3-5):

Variety

  616 Easy Living/Where or
     When (Voc. 3777)
  647 Onyx Hop (Voc. 3839)

With Jimmie Noone (1):

Decca

  1584 Bump It/I Know That You
      Know
  1621 Four or Five Times/Japansy

With Willie Smith (retail-1):

Decca

1366 Peace, Brother, Peace/Knock Wood

1380 Old Stomping Grounds/Get Acquainted with Yourself

1553 Dipsy Doodle/That's a Plenty

1612 Bei Mir Bist Du Schon/Big Dipper

With Own Trio (1):

Decca

1873 Afternoon in Africa/John Henry

1941 Baby Won't You Please Come Home/Lorna Doone Short Bread

With John Kirby (retail-1):

Vocalion

4624 Effervescent Blues/It Feels So Good

4653 Dawn on the Desert/The Turf

With John Kirby (retail-1)—continued

4890 Anitra's Dance/Drink to Me Only

5048 I May Be Wrong/Opus 5

5187 Royal Garden Blues/Blue Skies

5520 Front and Center/Nocturne

5542 Minute Waltz/You Go Your Way

5570 Little Brown Jug/ Impromptu

Decca

2216 A Flat to C/Undecided

2367 Pastel Blue/Rehearsin' Nervous Breakdown

Victor

27568 Bugler's Dilemma/Close Shave

27598 Fifi's Rhapsody/Only a Paper Moon

27667 Tweed Me/Night Whispers

27890 Comin' Back/Keep Smilin' Keep Laughin'

27926 St. Louis Blues/No Blues at All

STEWART, Leroy (Slam). *String bass.* Received 14 points: *Cavanaugh, Feather, Goffin, Lim, Stacy.* Born Sept. 21, 1914, Englewood, N. J. First musical instrument was violin—at age six—which he studied for two years. It was not until 1934 that he became interested in the bass; first played that instrument in a local Newark, N. J., band. Attended Boston Conservatory of Music for a year, worked with local Boston bands two more years. Joined Peanuts Holland in Buffalo (1938), formed team of Slim & Slam with Slim Gaillard (intermittently, 1938-42), joined Art Tatum Trio (1943), free-lanced in Hollywood (1942)—included recordings and movies. Recorded with Slim & Slam; co-composer of *Flat Foot Floogie.*

STRAYHORN, William (Billy). *Arranger.* Received 16 points: *Feather, Goffin, Jax, Jovien, Stacy Simon.* Born 1915, Dayton, O. Attended high school in Pittsburgh, Pa. Began study of piano at age 15 under private teacher. Soon became interested in composing and arranging and took further lessons on these subjects. Entered big-time field with Duke Ellington (Dec., 1938-44).

TATUM, Art. *Piano.* Received 21 points: *Braveman, Cavanaugh, Feather, Goffin, Jax, Jovien, Stacy, Simon.* Born 1915, Dayton, O. Started playing violin at 13, later giving it up in favor of the piano. Studied for about five years in Toledo before going to work. Appeared in local amateur radio show and his first professional job was with this station (WSPD), where he remained three years, doubling in Toledo nightspots. As accompanist for Adelaide Hall he went to New York (1932), returning to Toledo, thence to Chicago (Three Deuces, 1937). Toured Europe (1938) and since his return has been featured as soloist and with his Trio in nightspots in Hollywood, Chicago, New York. Solos: for Brunswick and Decca. For comprehensive Tatum Discography refer to pages 215-16 of the 1944 ESQUIRE JAZZ BOOK.

TEAGARDEN, Welden John (Jack). *Trombone, Vocal.* Received 13 points as trombonist: *Dexter, Hoefer, Jovien, Mize, Thiele;* 8 points as vocalist: *Dexter, Hoefer, Jovien.* Born Aug. 20, 1905, Vernon, Tex. Evinced interest in the piano at age 5, but by 7 found his real love in the trombone, which he picked up mostly on his own. Attended high school in Chapel, Neb., but quit at the end of his second year to work with his father in the cotton gin business. After working as a garage mechanic in Oklahoma City, he went to San Angelo, Tex., to take a job running a motion picture projection machine. It was here that he began to "sit in" with local bands, soon accepted an offer to play at San Antonio's Horn Palace (1920-21), then joined Peck's Bad Boys (pianist Peck Kelley's group), in Houston (1921-22)—both Pee Wee Russell and Leon Rappolo played clarinet in the band, each during part of the period. In Kansas City he played with Willard Robison (1922-23), then went to Wichita Falls, Kans., where he took over a local band and played in that vicinity (1923-25). Joined Doc Ross (1925-26), became acquainted with Wingy Manone, who also played in the band. Jack migrated to New York (1927) and was soon recording with Red Nichols, Willard Robison, Roger Wolfe Kahn, Sam Lanin. Accepted an offer from Ben Pollack (1928-32), did a stint at Chicago World's Fair with a pick-up band (1933), returned to New York for more free-lancing, including a date with Mal Hallett. Joined Paul Whiteman (1935-39), after which he formed his own band (1940-44). Recorded with his own band, Whiteman, Nichols, Pollack, Robison, Lanin, Kahn, The Charleston Chasers, Venuti-Lang All Stars, Frankie Trum-bauer, Benny Goodman, Mound City Blue Blowers, Adrian Rollini and numerous pick-up bands comprised of contingents of the Pollack band. Solos: *The Blues* (own band on the Varsity label); *The Sheik, After You've Gone, China Boy* (Nichols' Five Pennies); *Tailspin Blues* (Blue Blowers); *Beale St. Blues, Someday Sweetheart* (All Stars); *Riverboat Shuffle* (Rollini). For comprehensive Teagarden Discography refer to pages 217-24 of the 1944 ESQUIRE JAZZ BOOK.

THOMPSON, John (Johnny). *Arranger.* Received 7 points and 4 points as New Star: *Levin, Lim, Simon, Hammond.* Born June 11, 1918, Dallas, Tex. First professional job was at radio station KRLD, Dallas (1933). Between 1937 and 1940 he attended Juilliard Institute and studied with Joseph Schillinger. Arranged for Red Norvo (1941-42), Benny Goodman (1942-43), Harry James (1943-44).

TOUGH, Dave. *Drums.* Received 19 points: *Feather, Hoefer, Jax, Jovien, Miller, Simon, Thiele.* Born April 26, 1908, Oak Park, Illinois, where he attended high school, later going on to Lewis Institute, intermittently over a period of three years. At Lewis he met the Austin High gang, joined them under their engagements with Husk O'Hare (1925-26). Worked at the Commercial Theatre, South Chicago, with Eddie Condon (1927). Went to Europe with Danny Polo, played with many different jazz bands there (1928-31). Inactive in musical circles from 1932-35, after which he joined Tommy Dorsey (1936-37 and again 1939), Bunny Berigan (1938), Benny Good-man (1938), Jack Teagarden (1939), Joe Marsala (1939 and again 1940), Goodman again (1940), Artie Shaw (1940-1941), Charlie Spivak (1942), Woody Herman (1942), U.S.N.R. Band No. 501—The Artie Shaw Rangers (1942-44). After a medical discharge from the Navy he again returned to Woody Herman (1944). Recorded with bands with which he has played since 1935.

TURNER, Joe. *Vocal.* Received 17 points: *Burley, Dexter, Feather, Hammond, Jax, Lim, Ulanov.* Born in Kansas City, Mo. Music mostly self-taught. Attained local recognition in Kansas City where he worked as a bartender at the Hawaiian Gardens. Through association with Pete Johnson he got started as a singer, in 1938 and came to the attention of recording companies. Has also sung with Joe Sullivan, the Boogie-Woogie Trio, Duke Ellington and performed in Carnegie Hall. Records for Decca. Solo: *Doggin' the Dog.*

VINSON, Eddie. *Vocal.* Received 6 points and 5 points as New Star: *Hoefer, Jax, Jovien, Lim, Stacy.* Born December 18, 1917, Houston, Texas. Having a musical heritage on the paternal side, he first taught himself to play piano. During high school he obtained his first saxophone (he is an altoman as well as vocalist); later he studied this instrument more carefully, was hired by Milt Larkin. While with that band he vocalized as a "stunt"—which became a regular part of his musical equipment. Joined Floyd Ray (1940-41), Cootie Williams (1942-44).

VIDACOVICH, Irvine (Pinky). *Clarinet, alto saxophone.* Born Sept. 14, 1904, New Orleans, La., where he attended high school. Began his musical activities by studying flute, oboe, then mandolin, but not the clarinet until 1922. Almost immediately he was playing in local bands, among them Norman Brownlee, the New Orleans Owls (for a four-year stretch), Max Fink, Josef Chiarniavsky and his own band. He now leads the staff orchestra at radio station WWL, New Orleans. Recorded all the Columbia discs cut by the New Orleans Owls.

WALLER, Thomas (Fats). *Piano.* Born May 21, 1904, New York City. Died December 15, 1943, Kansas City. Studied intensively both piano and organ. His family wanted him to become a minister, but his musical inclinations were so strong that he was soon playing both as soloist and with his own band in various New York nightspots (1921-24). His recording activities began as early as 1922 when he played accompaniments for Sara Martin, joined Erskine Tate in Chicago (1925-26), returned to New York for more solo work (1927-30). Became staff artist at WLW, Cincinnati (1931-32). Organized his own band (1933-43), solo work, wrote music for new musical show (1943). Recorded with his own band, Louisiana Sugar Babes, Thomas Morris, McKinney's Cotton Pickers, Fletcher Henderson, The Rhythmakers. Piano and organ solos for the Victor label. Compositions: *Ain't Misbehavin', Honeysuckle Rose, Alligator Crawl, Variety Stomp, Whiteman Stomp, Lennox Avenue Blues, Stealin' Apples,* etc.

FATS WALLER DISCOGRAPHY

With Fletcher Henderson (15-30):

Columbia

654 Stampede/Jackass Blues
817 Henderson Stomp/The Chant
970 Rocky Mountain Blues/Tozo
1059 Whiteman Stomp/I'm Coming Virginia

Victor

20944 St. Louis Shuffle/Variety Stomp

With McKinney's Cotton Pickers (5-8):

Victor

38097 Plain Dirt/Gee Ain't I Good
38102 Miss Hannah/Way I Feel Today
38133 Peggy/I'd Love It

With The Rhythmakers (25-30):

Banner

32502 Mean Old Bedbug Blues/ Yellow Dog Blues
32530 Yes Suh/Anything for You

With The Rhythmakers (25-30)— continued

Melotone

12457 Mean Old Bedbug Blues/I'd Do Anything
12481 Yellow Dog Blues/Yes Suh

With Jack Teagarden (3):

Columbia

2558 You Rascal You

With Morris Hot Babies (2-3):

Victor

20776 Savannah Blues/Won't You Take Me Home
20890 Fats Waller Stomp
21127 Red Hot Dan
21202 He's Gone Away/Please Take Me Out
21358 Geechee

With Louisiana Sugar Babes (2):

Victor

21346 Thou Swell/Persian Rug
21348 Willow Tree/'Sippi

With Chocolate Dandies (10):

Okeh

8728 That's How I Feel Today/
Six or Seven Times

Victor Jam Session (retail):

Victor

25569 Honeysuckle Rose/ Blues

With Ted Lewis (2-10):

Columbia

2428 Egyptian Ella/I'm Crazy
'Bout My Baby
2467 Dip Your Brush in the Sunshine
2527 Dallas Blues/Royal Garden
Blues
2786 Lazy Bones

With Own Band (1-2):

Victor

24641 Wish I Were Twins/Armful
of Sweetness
24648 Do Me a Favor/Porter's Love
Song
24708 Have a Little Dream/I'll Be
Tired of You
24714 Don't Let It Bother You/
Georgia May
24737 Sweetie Pie/How Can You
Face Me
24738 Mandy/You're Not the Only
Oyster in the Stew
24742 Serenade for a Wealthy
Widow/Let's Pretend

With Own Band (1-2)—continued

24801 Dream Man/I'm Getting
Fonder of You
24808 If It Isn't Love/Believe It Beloved
24826 Honeysuckle Rose/Breakin'
the Ice
24846 Baby Brown/Once Upon a
Time
24853 Night Wind/I Believe in
Miracles
24863 You Fit into the Picture/100
Per Cent for You
24867 Baby Brown/100 Per Cent
for You (without vocal)
24888 I Ain't Got Nobody/Oh
Suzanna
24889 What's the Reason/Pardon
My Love
24892 Rosetta/Whose Honey Are
You
24898 Louisiana Fairy Tale/Cinders
25026 Rosetta/I Ain't Got Nobody
25027 Whose Honey Are You/
What's the Reason
25039 You're Cutest One/Hate to
Talk About Myself
25044 Taking Lessons in Love/I'm
Gonna Sit Right Down
25063 Sweet & Slow/Lulu's Back in
Town
25075 My Very Good Friend the
Milkman/You're the Picture,
I'm the Frame
25078 Take It Easy/There's Gonna
Be the Devil to Pay
25087 Sweet Sue/Twelfth Street
Rag
25116 Truckin'/The Girl I Left Behind Me

25120 I'm On a See Saw/You're So Darn Charming

25123 Thief in the Night/Got a Bran' New Suit

25131 Rhythm and Romance/A Sweet Beginning Like This

25140 Woe Is Me/Loafin'

25175 Georgia Rockin' Chair/ Brother Seek and Ye Shall Find

25192 Sweet Thing/A Little Bit Independent

25194 Sugar Blues/Somebody Stole My Gal

25211 I've Got My Fingers Crossed /Spreading Rhythm Around

25222 You Stayed Away Too Long /When Somebody Thinks You're Wonderful

25253 West Wind/Sing an Old Fashioned Love Song

25255 Oooh! Looka There/That Never-to-be-Forgotten Night

25266 Sugar Rose/Panic Is On

25281 Moon Rose/Garbo Green

25295 Christopher Columbus/Us on a Bus

25296 All My Life/It's No Fun

25315 Cabin in the Sky/Cross Patch

25342 Big Chief DeSota/It's a Sin to Tell a Lie

25345 Let's Sing Again/The More I Know You

25359 Paswonky/Black Raspberry Jam

25363 You're Not the Kind/Why Do I Lie to Myself

25374 Crazy 'Bout My Baby/Until the Real Thing Comes Along

25388 Bye Bye Baby/There Goes My Attraction

25394 Curse of Aching Heart/I Just Made Up

25398 Nero/Please Keep Me in Your Dreams

25409 At Mercy of Love/Copper Colored Gal

25415 Posin'/Floatin' Down to Cotton Town

25430 La-de-da/Lounging at the Waldorf

25471 Dinah/Latch On

25478 'Tain't Good/Things Are Rosy Now

25483 Thousand Dreams of You/ Swingin' Them Jingle Bells

25488 'Tain't Good/Things Are Rosy Now

25490 Thousand Dreams of You/ Swingin' Them Jingle Bells

25491 Rhyme for Love/I Adore You

25499 One in a Million/Who's Afraid of Love

25505 Havin' a Ball/Sorry I Made You Cry

25514 Spring Cleaning/You've Been Reading My Mail

25530 You're Laughing at Me/I Can't Break the Habit

25536 Meanest Thing You Ever Did

25537 Did Anyone Ever Tell You/ When Love Is Young

25550 Old Plantation/Where Is the Sun

With Own Band (1-2)—continued

25551 Cryin' Mood/To a Sweet & Pretty Thing
25554 Spring Cleaning/You've Been Reading My Mail
25563 Love Bug Will Bite You/Boo Hoo
25565 San Anton/You Showed Me the Way (without vocal)
25571 Sweet Heartache/New Lease on Love (without vocal)
25579 San Anton/You Showed Me the Way
25580 Sweet Heartache/New Lease on Love
25604 Don't You Know/Lost Love
25608 Smarty/I'm Gonna Put You in Your Place
25652 Fractious Fingering
25656 Fractious Fingering
25671 She's Tan, She's Tall, She's Terrific/I'm Always in the Mood
25672 Beat It Out/Got Me under Your Thumb
25679 More Power to You/You're My Dish
25681 Rather Call You Baby/Our Love Was Meant to Be
25689 Joint Is Jumpin'/Hopeless Love Affair
25712 How Ya Baby/That Will Do in the Morning
25749 Every Day's a Holiday/Neglected
25753 My First Impression/I'm in Another World
25762 My Window Faces South/Why Do Hawaiians Sing

With Own Band (1-2)—continued

25779 Honeysuckle Rose/Blue Turning Grey
25806 Florida Flo/I Love to Whistle
25812 Lost & Found/You Went to My Head
25817 Don't Try to Cry/Something Tells Me
25847 The Shiek/In the Gloaming
25891 Honey on the Moon/Fair & Square
26045 Hold My Hand/Inside
36206 Honeysuckle Rose/Blue Turning Grey (12")

With Own Band (5-10):

Victor

38050 Minor Drag/Harlem Fuss
38086 Lookin' Good But Feelin' Bad/I Need Someone Like You
38110 Lookin' for Another Sweetie /When I'm Alone
38119 Ridin' But Walkin'/Won't You Get Off It Please

With Own Band (retail-1):

Bluebird (including many reissues from Victor label)

7885 Tell Me With Your Kisses/ Shame! Shame!
10000 Two Sleepy People/I'll Never Forgive Myself
10016 Swingin' Them Jingle Bells/ A Porter's Love Song to a Chambermaid

With Own Band (retail-1)—continued

10035 Yacht Club Swing/Muskrat Ramble

10078 I Wish I Had You/Georgia May

10100 Havin' a Ball/Don't Try Your Jive on Me

10109 San Anton/Baby Brown

10116 Hold Tight/You Outsmarted Yourself

10129 You're the Cutest One/Good for Nothin' But Love

10136 Kiss Me with Your Eyes/Last Night a Miracle Happened

10143 Good Man Is Hard to Find/How Can You Face Me

10149 Patty Cake, Patty Cake/Armful o' Sweetness

10156 S'posin'/Rosetta

10184 Undecided/Step Up and Shake My Hand

10185 The Minor Drag/Harlem Fuss

10192 'Tain't What You Do/Some Rainy Day

10205 Spider and the Fly/Remember Who You're Promised To

10261 Dream Man/You're Not the Only Oyster in the Stew

10262 Sweetie Pie/Serenade for a Wealthy Widow

10288 Ain't Misbehavin'/Georgia Rockin' Chair

10322 There'll Be Some Changes Made/Blue Because of You

With Own Band (retail-1)—continued

10346 Honey Hush/You Meet the Nicest People in Your Dreams

10369 Anita/I Used to Love You

10393 Bless You/It's the Tune That Counts

10405 Squeeze Me/Wait and See

10419 Who'll Take My Place/Abdullah

10437 Bond Street/What a Pretty Miss

10500 Your Feet's Too Big/Suitcase Susie

10527 It's You Who Taught It to Me/You're Letting the Grass Grow Under Your Feet

10573 Darktown Strutter's Ball/I Can't Give You Anything But Love, Baby

10624 Moon Is Low/Black Maria

10658 Oh Frenchy/Cheatin' on Me

10698 Old Grandad/Little Curly Hair in a Highchair

10730 Send Me Jackson/Square from Delaware

10744 Mighty Fine/Eeep, Ipe, Wanna Piece of Pie

10779 Too Tired/You Run Your Mouth, I'll Run My Business

10803 Fat and Greasy/At Twilight

10829 Hey, Stop Kissing My Sister/Stop Pretending

10841 I'll Never Smile Again/Stayin' at Home

10858 Fats Waller's Original E Flat Blues/Swing a Dallas Street (organ)

With Own Band (retail-1)—continued

10892 Dry Bones/My Mommy Sent Me to the Store

10943 Blue Eyes/I'm Gonna Salt Away Some Sugar

10967 'Tain't Nobody's Business If I Do/Abercrombie Had a Zombie

10989 Scram/Everybody Loves My Baby

11010 Liver Lip Jones/Come Down to Earth

11078 Shortnin' Bread/Mamacita

11102 All That Meat & No Potatoes/Buckin' the Dice

11115 Wanna Hear Swing Songs/Let's Get Away

11175 Pantin' in Panther Room/I Understand

11188 Headlines in the News/I Repent

11222 Twenty-Four Robbers/Do You Have to Go

11262 Chant of the Groove/Come & Get It

11296 Sad Sap Sucker/Rump Steak Serenade

11324 Bells of San Raquel/Buck Jumpin'

11518 Jitterbug Waltz/We Need a Little Love

11539 Don't Give Me That Jive/You Must Be Losing Your Mind

11569 Swing Out to Victory/By the Light of the Silvery Moon

Piano Duet with Bennie Paine (3):

Victor

22371 St. Louis Blues/After You've Gone

Piano and Organ Solos (2-10):

Columbia

14593 Draggin' My Heart Around/I'm Crazy 'Bout My Baby (Voc. 3016)

Victor

20357 St. Louis Blues/Lenox Avenue Blues

20470 Loveless Love/Soothin' Syrup

20492 Sloppy Water/The Rusty Pail

20655 Stompin' the Bug/Messin' Around with the Blues

20890 Beale St. Blues

21127 I Ain't Got Nobody

21358 The Digah's Stomp

21525 Hog Maw Stomp/Sugar

22092 I've Got a Feeling/Love Me or Leave Me

22108 Ain't Misbehavin'/Sweet Savannah Sue

23260 Loveless Love/That's All

24030 African Ripples/Alligator Crawl

25015 Clothes Line Ballet/Viper's Drag

25338 Numb Fumblin'/Smashing Thirds

38508 Handful of Keys/Numb Fumblin'

38554 Gladyse/Valentine Stomp

Piano and Organ Solos (2-10)—continued

38568 My Fate Is in Your Hands/ Turn on the Heat
38613 My Feelin's Are Hurt/ Smashing Thirds

Bluebird Reissues (retail):

5093 Sugar/I Ain't Got Nobody
10098 Alligator Crawl/Clothes Line Ballet
10099 Star Dust/Keepin' Out of Michief Now
10115 African Ripples/Basin Street Blues

Piano and Organ Solos (2-10)—continued

10133 I Ain't Got Nobody/Viper's Drag
10263 Valentine Stomp/Love Me or Leave Me
10264 Waitin' At the End of the Road/Sweet Savannah Sue

Okeh

4757 Muscle Shoal Blues/Birmingham
8043 'Tain't Nobody's Business/ You Got
8045 Last Go Round Blues/ Mama's Got the Blues

WEBSTER, Ben. *Tenor saxophone.* Received 7 points: *Burley, Levin, Stacy.* Born Mar. 27, 1909, Kansas City, Mo. where he attended high school, later going to Wilberforce. Studied violin and piano at an early age, but turned to tenor, on which he is mostly self-taught. Began professional career with an Enid, Oklahoma, band with which he played piano. Subsequently played with Dutch Campbell (piano), Gene Coy (first alto and then switching to tenor in that band in 1929). In rapid succession he then played with Blanche Calloway, Bennie Moten, Andy Kirk, Fletcher Hendersen (1934 and again 1937-38), Benny Carter, Willie Bryant, Cab Calloway (1935-37), Stuff Smith, Roy Eldridge, Duke Ellington (Jan. 1940-42), own small combination (1943-44). Recently he has been appearing as a soloist. Recorded with both Calloways, Moten, Carter Bryant, Henderson, Ellington, Teddy Wilson, Billie Holiday. Solos: *Limehouse Blues, Memphis Blues* (Henderson); *Sweet Lorraine, Seventy-one* (Wilson); *Some Saturday, Linger Awhile* (Rex Stewart); *Conga Brava, Cotton Tail, Blue Serge, Giddybug Gallop* (Ellington).

WHALEY, Wade. *Clarinet.* Received 2 points: *Williams.* Born 1895, New Orleans, La. Studied with and was influenced by Lorenzo and Louis Tio, although he first studied guitar and string bass, on which instruments he played at house parties. As a clarinetist his first job was with Armand Piron at the Temple Theatre, subsequently to which he worked with numerous New Orleans bands, including John Robichaux, Manuel Perez, Chris Kelley, Manuel Manetta, Kid Ory, The Crescent Band. In 1916 he fronted his own band. The following year he migrated to California in the company of Buddy Petit and Frankie Duson—to join Jelly Roll Morton in Los Angeles. After several years with Morton, Whaley again worked with Kid Ory, who by that time also was in California. There followed several years as leader of his own group in the San Francisco-Oakland area and work in the pit band for the Capitol Burlesque until the Depression hit. In 1934 he grabbed a job in San José, stayed there to work in a shipyard. But he came out of "retirement" to play in the All-Star New Orleans Band at the Geary Theatre, San Francisco, in May 1943. A year later (Apr. 1944) he journeyed to Los Angeles to broadcast with Kid Ory and Mutt Carey. Recorded with Bunk Johnson in L.A. (July 1944).

WILLIAMS, Charles Melvin (Cootie). *Trumpet.* Received 32 points: *Braveman, Dexter, Feather, Hammond, Hoefer, Jovien, Levin, Miller, Simon, Stacy, Thiele, Ulanov.* Born July 24, 1908, Mobile, Ala., where he attended high school. Interest in music originated on drums at age 14, but he soon changed to trumpet. Studied in school and played in the school band. Professional career began in Florida with Eagle Eye Shields' band (1925-26), then joined Alonzo Ross (1926-28), Chick Webb (three weeks only, 1928), Fletcher Henderson (1928-29), Duke Ellington (early 1929-Nov., 1940), Benny Goodman (1940-41), organized his own band (1942-44). Recorded with Ellington, Goodman, Teddy Wilson, Lionel Hampton and his own studio combinations. Composition: *Echoes of Harlem.* Solos: *East St. Louis Toodle-oo* (on Master label), *Black and Tan Fantasy* (Victor); *Echoes of Harlem, Concerto for Cootie*—all Ellington; *Buzzin' Around with the Bee, Ring Dem Bells* (Hampton).

COOTIE WILLIAMS DISCOGRAPHY

With Own Band (1-5):

Variety

527 Blue Reverie/Downtown
  Uproar
555 Diga Diga/Can't Believe
  You're in Love

Vocalion

3890 Watching/Can't Give You
  Anything Love
3922 Pigeons & Peppers/Jubilesta
3960 Echoes of Harlem/Lost in
  Meditation
4061 Swingtime in Honolulu/Car-
  nival Caroline
4086 A Lesson in C/Ol' Man River
4324 Blues in the Evening/Sharpie
4425 Swing Pan Alley/Chasin'
  Chippies
4636 Mobile Blues/Gal-Avantin'
4726 Boudoir Benny/Ain't the
  Gray Good
4754 Delta Mood/Boys from Harlem
4958 Black Beauty/Night Song
5411 She's Gone/Beautiful
  Romance
5618 Black Butterfly/Blues-a-
  Poppin'
5690 Give It Up/Dry So Long
6336 Toasted Pickle/Top & Bottom

With Duke Ellington:

With The Gotham Stompers:

With Johnny Hodges:

With Barney Bigard:

See Duke Ellington Discography.
Most Ellington Victors, all Brunswicks and Masters there listed include Cootie Williams as one of the
featured instrumentalists.

With Teddy Wilson (2-3):

Brunswick

7867 Carelessly/How Could You
7877 Moanin' Low/Fine & Dandy

With Lionel Hampton (retail-3):

Victor

25575 Buzzin' Around with the Bee
  /Who Babe
25601 Stompology
25771 You're My Ideal/The Sun
  Will Shine Tonight

With Benny Goodman (retail-1):

Columbia

35349 Seven Come Eleven/Shivers
35466 The Shiek/Poor Butterfly
35482 I Surrender Dear/Boy Meets
  Goy
35810 Royal Garden Blues/Wholly
  Cats
35901 Benny's Bugle/As Long As I
  Live
35938 On the Alamo/Gone with
  What Draft
35962 Let Doorknob Hitcha/
  Perfidia

With Benny Goodman (retail-1)—
continued

36039 Breakfast Fued/I've Found New Baby
36099 A Smo-o-oth One/Good Enough to Keep

With Benny Goodman (retail-1)—
continued

55001 Benny Rides Again/The Man I Love
55002 Superman/More Than You Know

CLARENCE WILLIAMS & ORCHESTRA

See Also Sidney Bechet Discography for Clarence Williams listings

Bluebird (retail-1):

4169 Liza
6918 Top of the Town/More Than That
6932 Cryin' Mood/Wanted
11368 Thriller Blues/Uncle Sam

Brunswick (1-2):

3580 Zulu Wail/Slow River
3664 Baltimore
7000 Cushion Foot Stomp/PDQ Blues
7017 Baltimore/Take Your Black Bottom Dance Outside

Columbia (1-2):

1735 Have You Ever Felt That Way/If You Like Me
2806 High Society/Shim Sham Shimmy
2863 Organ Grinder/You Ain't Too Old
14164 Nobody But My Baby
14193 Jazz Lips/Gravier Street
14241 Shootin' Pistol/When I March
14244 You'll Long for Me/Bottomland

14287 Dreaming Hours Away/ Close Fit Blues
14314 Sweet Emmaline/Any Time
14348 Walk That Broad/Keyboard Express
14362 I'm Busy/Jeannine
14422 Mountain City Blues/Breeze
14434 Them Things Get Me/Our Cottage of Love
14447 I'm Not Worrying/Whoop It Up
14460 Freeze Out/Pane in the Glass
14468 Railroad Rhythm/Nervous Breakdown
14488 Zonky/You've Got to be Modernistic
14555 High Society/Lazy Levee Loungers
35957 Mandy Make Up Your Mind /I'm a Little Blackbird

HRS Reissues (retail):

6 Coal Cart Blues
31 Terrible Blues

Melotone (1):

13328 Milk Cow Blues/Black Gal

Odeon (1):

36083 Whip Me With Plenty of Love/Worn Out Blues

Okeh (1-5, except* 25-50):

3055 *Farewell Blues/Gulf Coast Blues

4925 *Wildcat Blues/Kansas City Man Blues

4927 Oh Daddy Blues/I've Got the "Yes We Have No Bananas" Blues

4966 Achin' Hearted Blues/Tain' Nobody's Business If I Do

4975 *New Orleans Hop Scop Blues

4993 Oh Daddy Blues/Old Fashioned Love

8073 Barefoot Blues/Do It a Long Time Papa

8089 Original Charleston Strut/If You Don't

8144 Old Fashioned Love/Open Your Heart

8149 Prove It/I Want To Go Back

8151 Agitate Me Blues/Never Knew What Blues

8159 Stranger Blues/Mama Place

8160 Mississippi Blues

8171 *House Rent Blues/Texas Moaner Blues

8181 *Everybody Loves My Baby /Of All the Wrongs You've Done

8193 *Who'll Chop Your Suey

8215 *Papa De Da Da

8245 *Santa Claus Blues/Coal Cart Blues

8267 Shake That Thing/Get It Fixed

8269 Walk That Broad/Have You Ever Felt That Way

8272 *Just Wait Till You See My Baby/Livin' High

With Own Band—continued

8286 Pile of Logs and Stone/I've Found a New Baby

8342 You Can't Shush My Katie

8440 Candy Lips/Nobody But

8462 Take Your Black Bottom Outside/Cushion Foot Stomp

8465 Old Folks Shuffle/Black Snake Blues

8510 Close Fit Blues/Baby Won't You Please Come Home

8525 Yama Yama Blues/Church St. Sobbin' Blues

8572 Sweet Emmaline/Log Cabin Blues

8584 Red River/Shake It Down

8592 Lazy Mama/Mountain City Blues

8604 Wildflower Rag/Organ Grinder Blues

8615 My Handy Man/Organ Grinder Blues

8617 I'm Busy and You Can't Come In/Organ Grinder Blues

8629 Walk That Broad/Have You Ever Felt That Way

8645 In the Bottle Blues/What Ya Want Me To Do

8663 Freeze Out/Watchin' the Clock

8672 Steamboat Days/Mississippi Blues

8706 High Society/Whoop It Up

8738 I've Got What It Takes/You Gotta Give Me Some

8752 What Makes Me Love You/ You Don't Understand

8763 I Found a New Baby/Left All Alone

With Own Band—continued

8790 Whip Me/Worn Out Blues
8798 Look Like a Monkey/He Wouldn't Stop
8806 Michigan Water Blues/You Rascal You
8821 Shout Sister Shout/Where That Old Man River Flows By
8842 Loving/Papa De Da Da
40006 *Shreveport Blues/Mean Blues
40172 My Own Blues/Gravier St. Blues
40206 *I'm a Little Blackbird/ Mandy Make Up Your Mind
40321 *Cake Walking Babies from Home
40330 *Castaway
40598 What's the Matter Now/ Jackass Blues
81865 Church St. Sobbin' Blues/ Yama Yama Blues

Paramount (1-2):

12587 Shake 'Em Up/Jingles
12870 Saturday Night Jag

Perfect (1):

15387 Papa De Da Da/Baby Won't You Please Come Home
15403 Hot Lovin'/Shout Sister

QRS (1-2):

7004 Long Deep and Wide/Speakeasy
7009 Shake It Black Bottom/I Don't Care

With Own Band—continued

7033 Midnight Stomp/Wildflower Rag
7034 Bozo/Bimbo
7035 Hole in the Wall/Don't Turn Your Back
7040 I'm Through/Longshoremen's Blues

Victor (1-2):

19094 Sugar Blues/Gulf Coast Blues
24039 Charlie Two-Step/Sleep Come and Take Me
24083 Red Blues
38063 Lazy Mama/In Our Cottage of Love
38630 I'm Not Worrying/Touchdown

Vocalion (1-3):

1088 PDQ Blues/Cushion Foot Stomp
1130 Baltimore
2541 Beer Garden Blues/Breeze
2563 Right Key but Wrong Keyhole/Little Bit Left
2584 Dispossessin' Me/Chocolate Av.
2602 Harlem Rhythm Dance/For Sale
2616 Swaller Tail Coat/Looka There Ain't She Cute
2630 How Can I Get It/Sunny Side of the Street
2654 New Orleans Hop Scop Blues/I've Got Horses on My Mind

With Own Band—continued

2674 Ill Wind/As Long As I Live
2676 St. Louis Blues/Mr. Will You Serenade
2689 I Can't Dance/Christmas Night in Harlem
2718 Won't You Come Over/ Pretty Baby
2736 Old Street Sweeper/After Tonight
2759 Gonna Wash My Sins Away /Let's Have a Showdown
2778 Bimbo/Way Down Home
2788 Trouble/I Can't Beat You
2805 Sugar Blues/Ain't Gonna Git None of My Jelly Roll
2838 Sashay Oh Boy/Big Fat Mama
2854 Chizzlin' Sam/Jerry the Junker
2871 Organ Grinder Blues/Nobody's Business
2889 Tell the Truth/Getting My Bonus in Love
2899 Rhapsody in Love/I Saw Stars
2909 Saving for Baby/Jungle Creep

With Own Band—continued

2927 Milk Cow Blues/Gonna Be the Devil to Pay
2938 Black Gal/A Foolish Little Girl Like You
2958 Can See You All Over the Place/Anything But You
2991 Yama Yama/Lady Luck Blues
03013 Wipe It Off
3195 Sunday Off/Mother's Day
03350 Mississippi Basin/Walk That Broad
4157 Bluer Than Blue/Cozy
4169 Liza
8763 I Found a New Baby/Left All
25009 Black Eyed Susan Brown/ Mama Stayed All Night
25010 Like to Go Back/High Society

Piano solos (1):

Victor

38524 Too Low/Pane in the Glass

Okeh

Mixing the Blues

WILLIAMS, Fred J. (Freddie). *Drums.* Born Dec. 29, 1898, New Orleans, La., where he attended high school. Picked up his own knowledge of drums, beginning at age 13. Not long after he was playing with Fischer's Ragtime Band (1912-13), after which he played with Jack (Papa) Laine (1913-14), Brown's Band (1914-15), Happy Schilling in Chicago at the Arsonia Café (1915-16), Merritt Brunis at the Casino Gardens in Chicago (1916-19), Freddie Newroth at the Burnham Inn, Burnham, Ill. (1919). When this spot closed because of prohibition, he returned to his native city, retired from music to join the New Orleans Police Department, in which he now holds the rank of Captain.

WILSON, Theodore (Teddy). *Piano.* Received 24 points: *Cavanaugh, Dexter, Goffin, Hammond, Levin, Lim, Miller, Simon, Stacy.* Born Nov. 24, 1912, Austin, Texas. He attended high school Tuskagee, Alabama, and went on to Tulladega College in Alabama. Began study of music at an early age under his parents' guidance. Became really interested in the piano during his college days. Went to Detroit, playing with local bands (1929), joined Milton Senior in Toledo (1930-31). With this band he traveled to Chicago, there playing with Erskine Tate, Jimmie Noone, François' Louisianians, Benny Carter (1933), Willie Bryant (1934-35), the Charioteers (1935-36), Benny Goodman (spring, 1936-39). Organized his own band (1939-44). Joined the Benny Goodman Quintet for the music revue, *The Seven Lively Arts* (1944). Recorded with Louis Armstrong, Bryant, the Chocolate Dandies, Goodman, Bob Howard, Red Norvo and his own numerous studio combinations. Solos: on the Brunswick label: *Just a Mood, Blues in C Sharp Minor* (own band); *Blues in E Flat* (Norvo); *The Man I Love, Body and Soul, Tiger Rag* (Goodman).

TEDDY WILSON DISCOGRAPHY

With Own Band (2-4):

Brunswick

7498 Sunbonnet Blue/What a Little Moonlight Can Do (Co 36206)

7501 I Wished on the Moon/Miss Brown to You (Co 36205)

7514 Sweet Lorraine/Painting the Town Red

7520 Too Hot for Words/What a Night What a Moon

7550 Yankee Doodle Never Went to Town/24 Hours a Day

7554 If You Were Mine (Co 36206)/Eeney Meeney Miney Mo

With Own Band (2-4)—continued

7577 These 'n That 'n Those

7581 Spreadin' Rhythm Around/You Let Me Down

7612 Life Begins When You're in Love

7640 Christopher Columbus/All My Life

7663 Mary Had a Little Lamb/Too Good to be True

7684 Warmin' Up/Blues in C Sharp Minor

7699 These Foolish Things/Why Do I Lie About You

With   Own   Band   (2-4)—continued

7702 Guess Who/Like Reaching for the Moon
7729 I Cried for You (Co 35862)
7736 You Turned the Tables on Me/Sing, Baby, Sing
7739 You Came to My Rescue/ Here's Love in Your Eyes
7762 Easy to Love/Just the Way You Look Tonight
7768 Who Loves You/With Thee I Swing
7781 Sailin'/I Can't Give You Anything But Love, Baby
7789 Pennies from Heaven/That's Life I Guess
7797 Right or Wrong/Lazy River Goes By
7816 Tea for Two/I'll See You in My Dreams
7824 This Year's Kisses/He Ain't Got Rhythm
7840 My Last Affair/You Showed Me the Way
7844 Mood I'm In/Sentimental & Melancholy
7859 Why Was I Born (Co 36283) /Must Have That Man (Co 36207)
7867 Carelessly/How Could You
7877 Moanin' Low/Fine & Dandy
7884 It's Sweet of You/There's a Lull in My Life
7893 I'm Coming, Virginia/How Am I to Know
7903 Mean to Me/I'll Get By (Co 35926)
7911 Easy Living (Co 36208)/ Foolin' Myself (Co 36207)

With   Own   Band   (2-4)—continued

7917 Yours & Mine/Sun Showers
7926 Never Be the Same/Found a New Baby
7940 Remember Me/You're My Desire
7943 Hour of Parting/Coquette
7954 Big Apple/You Can't Stop Me From Dreaming
7960 If I Had You/Brought a New Kind of Love
7964 Ain't Misbehavin'/Honeysuckle Rose
7973 Just a Mood (I and II)
8008 My Man/I Can't Help Loving That Man
8015 Nice Work if You Can Get It/Things Are Looking Up

Piano Solos (2-3):

Brunswick

7543 Every Now and Then/It Never Dawned on Me
7563 Liza/Rosetta
7572 I Found a Dream/On Treasure Island
7599 Breaking in a Pair of Shoes/ I Feel Like a Feather in the Breeze
8025 Don't Blame Me/Between the Devil and the Deep Blue Sea

With Louis Armstrong (1-2):

Victor

24232 Mahogany Hall Stomp/High Society

**With Louis Armstrong (1-2)—con-
tinued**

24233 Hustlin' and Bustlin' for
Baby/I Gotta Right to Sing
the Blues
24245 I've Got the World on a
String/Sittin' in the Dark
24257 He's a Son of the South/
Some Sweet Day
24351 Basin St. Blues
24369 Snow Ball/Honey Do

Bluebird

4968 Swing You Cats

With Mezz Mezzrow (4-6):

Brunswick

6778 Swinging with Mezz/Love
You're Not the One For Me
7551 Free Love/Dissonance

With Benny Goodman Trio (2-5):

Victor

25115 Body & Soul/After You've
Gone
25181 Someday Sweetheart/Who
25324 All My Life/Too Good to
Be True
25333 China Boy/Lady Be Good
25345 Nobody's Sweetheart/More
Than You Know
25406 Exactly Like You
25481 Tiger Rag
25711 Silhouetted in the Moonlight
25725 Where or When
25822 Sweet Lorraine
26090 I Must Have That Man

**With Benny Goodman Quartet
(2-5):**

Victor

25398 Moonglow/Dinah
25473 Melancholy Baby/Sweet Sue
25481 Whispering
25521 Vibraphone Blues/Stompin'
at the Savoy
25529 Runnin' Wild/Tea for Two
25531 Ida
25644 Avalon/The Man I Love
25660 Liza/Smiles
25705 Handful of Keys/Vieni
Vieni
25725 I'm a Ding Dong Daddy
25751 Bei Mir Bist du Schoen
25822 Dizzy Spells
26044 Blues in Your Flat/Blues in
My Flat
26090 S'Wonderful
26091 Opus ½/Sweet Georgia
Brown
26240 Opus ¾/Sugar

With Chocolate Dandies (4-6):

Columbia

2875 I Never Knew

Okeh

41568 Once Upon a Time/Krazy
Kapers

With Benny Carter (4-6):

Columbia

2898 Devil's Holiday/Symphony
in Riffs

Okeh

41567 Lonesome Nights/Blue Lou

With Benny Carter (4-6)—continued

Vocalion

2870 Synthetic Love/Everybody Shuffle

2898 Shoot the Works/Dream Lullaby

With Red Allen (1):

Vocalion

3244 You/Would You

3245 Tormented/Nothing's Blue but the Sky

With Mildred Bailey (retail-3):

Vocalion

3056 I'd Love to Take Orders from You/I'd Rather Listen to Your Eyes

3057 Someday Sweetheart/When Day Is Done

3367 For Sentimental Reasons/It's Love I'm After

3378 More Than You Know/ 'Long About Midnight

3449 Trust in Me/My Last Affair

3456 Where Are You/You're Laughing at Me

Decca

2201 Honeysuckle Rose/Willow Tree

2257 Downhearted Blues/Squeeze Me

With Willie Bryant (2-5):

Victor

24847 Throwin' Stones at Sun/ Chimes at Meetin'

With Willie Bryant (2-5)—continued

24858 It's Over Because We're Through/Viper's Moan

25038 Rigamarole/Shiek

25045 'Long About Midnight/ Jerry the Junker

25129 Voice of Old Man River/ Long Gone

25160 Liza/Steak and Potatoes

With Putney Dandridge (1-2):

Vocalion

3006 Isn't This a Lovely Day/ Cheek to Cheek

3007 I'm in the Mood for Love/ That's What You Think

3024 Shine/Nagasaki

3122 No Other One/Little Bit Independent

3123 You Hit the Spot/You Took My Breath Away

3252 All My Life/It's a Sin To Tell a Lie

3269 Why Was I Born/Ol' Man River

3399 In a Dancing Mood/With Plenty of Money and You

3409 That Foolish Feeling/Gee But You're Swell

With Billie Holiday (1-2):

3431 One Never Knows/Got My Love to Keep Me Warm

3440 Keep Me in Your Dreams/If My Heart Could Talk

3520 Let's Call the Whole Thing Off/They Can't Take That

3543 Where Is the Sun/Don't Know if I'm Coming

With Taft Jordan (1):

Perfect

16094 Night Wind/If the Moon Turns Green
16102 Devil in the Moon/Louisiana Fairy Tale

With Red Norvo (5):

Columbia

2977 I Surrender Dear/Tomboy
3026 Night Is Blue/With All My Heart & Soul
3059 Old Fashioned Love/Honey-suckle Rose
3079 Blues in E Flat/Bughouse (Co 36158)

With Edmond Hall (retail):

Blue Note

30 Rompin' in '44/Smooth Sailing
31 Blue Interval/Seein' Red

With Coleman Hawkins (retail):

Keynote

609 I Only Have Eyes for You/S'Wonderful
610 Bean at the Met/I'm in the Mood for Love

With Own Band (retail):

Columbia

35926 Mean to Me/I'll Get By
36208 When You're Smiling

WYNN, Albert (Al). *Trombone.* Born July 29, 1907, New Orleans, La., where he attended grammar school; high school in Chicago. With special teachers he began the study of his instrument at age 11. He launched his professional career with Ma Rainey (1922-23), led his own band (1923-28), subsequently playing with Charlie Creath (1928), Louis Armstrong (1928), Levy-Wine in Hamburg, Germany (1928-29), Sam Wooding in Madrid, Spain (1929-31), Harry Fleming (1931), Louis Douglas' Review (1931-32), Fleming again (1932), after which, in October of that year he returned to his native land. In Chicago again he worked with local bands (1932-33), joined Jimmie Noone (1933-34 and again 1939-40), local jobs (1934-37 and 1940-44), Fletcher Henderson (1937-39). Recorded with his own band, Henderson, Charlie Creath, Ma Rainey, Sam Wooding. His records for the Vocalion label, under his own name, include *She's Cryin' for Me*, *Down by the Levee* (just reissued in Brunswick's Riverboat Jazz album) and *Crying My Blues Away.*

YOUNG, Lester (Les.). *Tenor saxophone.* Received 9 points: *Braveman, Cavanaugh, Lim, Hammond.* Best known for his feature solo work with the Count Basie band (1937-41). During the past several years he has been free-lancing on the West Coast, working with his brother's band, in the studios, etc. Rejoined Basie (Dec., 1943-Sept., 1944), at which time he entered the Armed Forces. Solos: *Every Tub, Out the Window* (Basie).

Chapter VIII

Backstage with the Experts

1 Dan Burley	12 Harry Lim
2 Mal Braveman	13 Paul Eduard Miller
3 Inez Cavanaugh	14 J. T. H. Mize
4 Dave Dexter, Jr.	15 William Russell
5 Leonard G. Feather	16 George T. Simon
6 Robert Goffin	17 Charles Edward Smith
7 John Hammond	18 Frank Stacy
8 George Hoefer	19 Robert Thiele
9 Jax (John Lucas)	20 Barry Ulanov
10 Harold Jovien	21 Eugene Williams
11 Mike Levin	22 George Avakian

IN THIS analysis, Esquire's jazz experts will be referred to mostly by the index numbers listed above, to save space. This year's enlarged board of experts comprises every conceivable shade of jazz opinion, from the modernists (2, 5, 20), through the moderates (1, 6, 13, 14, 17) to the reactionaries (15, 21, 22).

Nobody but an embittered musician who didn't win, or a critic whose selections all failed to win, could possibly deny this year that our line-up of voters represents, in fair proportions, every attitude in this branch of musical criticism, and that the list of winners represents fairly the consensus of jazz opinion.

The board last year included several men who were ruled out

254 *Esquire's 1945 Jazz Book*

this time as currently inactive in the field of jazz writing, or not specializing in jazz. The new additions were Nos. 1 (Amsterdam *Star-News*), 2 (*Orchestra World*), 3 (*Band Leaders*), 4 (*The Captiol*), 8, 9, 11 (*Down Beat*), 10 (Associated Negro Press), 14 (*The Musician, School Musician*, etc.), 15 (*The Needle, Jazz Quarterly, Record Changer*), 16 (*Metronome*), 21 (free lance).

The board includes representatives of magazines whose circulations range from barely 1,000 to a national publication with 2,250,000. It includes two Negroes (1, 3).

The over-all picture of these writers gives a varied view of what qualifies a man as a jazz expert. They come from such places as Belgium (6), Laramie, Wyo. (8), Java (12), Lexington, Ky. (1), London (5) and Edgerton, Wis. (13). Only six are native New Yorkers (2, 7, 16, 19, 20, 21). Altogether they are 651 years old and have 199 years' writing experience, making the average expert a man 31 years old who started writing about jazz 9½ years ago.

Their ages range from 21 (Braveman), 22 (Thiele) and 23 (Levin) to 40 (Smith) and 46 (Goffin). Goffin started writing about jazz 25 years ago; Braveman only last spring. Most of them work in other jobs and are jazz experts only as a sideline. Burley is sports and news editor of a New York Negro weekly, Braveman has an M-G-M publicity job; Goffin is a lecturer, lawyer, naturalist and historian. Four men (4, 12, 19, 21) are connected with record companies. Hoefer works in a war plant, Smith is with the OWI, Jovien is an advertising representative for *The Billboard*.

Hammond, Levin, Mize, Avakian and Simon are in the Army, but all were able to conform with the requirement that they vote for musicians they had heard this year, since all of them spent sufficient furlough time in a thorough coverage of the jazz front. (Avakian, who could not be included in this analysis because his information arrived late, has been in the South Pacific area.) Three members of the board—Feather, Miller and Ulanov—are now working as full-time jazz listeners and experts.

Do jazz experts know music? An analysis of the questionnaires sent in provides some enlightening answers. Of the twenty-one, three have had professional experience, are members of the Musicians' Union and creators themselves of the jazz they write about (1, 5, 11). Another (16) is an ex-member. Of the rest, two had training as classical violinists (7, 20), and another plays all the principal band instruments (15), three are amateur reedmen (4, 14, 19) and the others (2, 3, 6, 9, 10, 12, 13, 17, 18, 21) are non-instrumentalists or amateur drummers.

The musical education of the critics varies almost as widely. The men who studied music and harmony extensively are 5, 7, 11, 14, 15, 20. Eight others (2, 6, 8, 9, 10, 13, 17, 21) claimed no musical education (except in a few cases, the usual childhood piano course).

Eight of the men (2, 6, 8, 10, 12, 13, 17, 21) did not claim to be able to read music. Four said they read "slowly" (1, 4, 18, 19) and nine answered "yes." Twelve are non-composers, three write lyrics (3, 4, 16), six compose music (1, 5, 11, 14, 15, 18) and four of these six (5, 11, 14, 15) can also write orchestrations. Their musical careers are as follows:

Burley has had three of his tunes recorded by Lionel Hampton. Feather, writer of music, lyrics and/or orchestrations for over fifty tunes recorded by Ellington, Lunceford, Goodman, Waller, etc., and featured by Count Basie, Benny Carter and Teddy Wilson. He plays piano and is the author of a historical and technical-analytical book, *Duke Ellington Piano Method for Blues* published by Robbins. Levin took courses at Cleveland Conservatory, Harvard, NYU, studied piano, keyboard harmony and musicology, and has often sat in at jam sessions.

Dr. Mize's degrees include B.M. and B.A., Baylor Univ.; M.A., Columbia; M.S., Texas A. & M.; Ph.D., NYU. He was music head at Rye High School, where he conducted a popular music appreciation class and brought in Ellington's band to give the world première of *Black, Brown and Beige*. Russell graduated from Quincy (Ill.) Conservatory, took a conducting course with the National Orchestral Society, had other extensive musical training and is the writer of several compositions published by New Music Edition. Stacy, currently studying piano and arranging, has written a number of compositions, as yet unpublished.

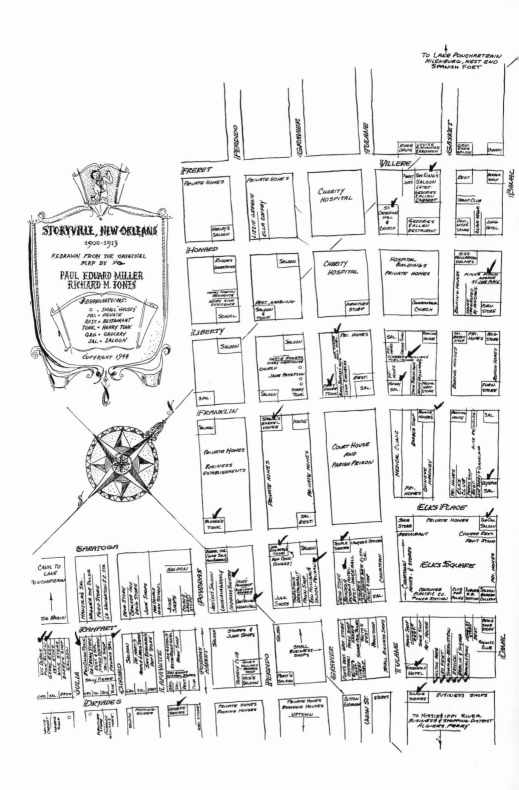

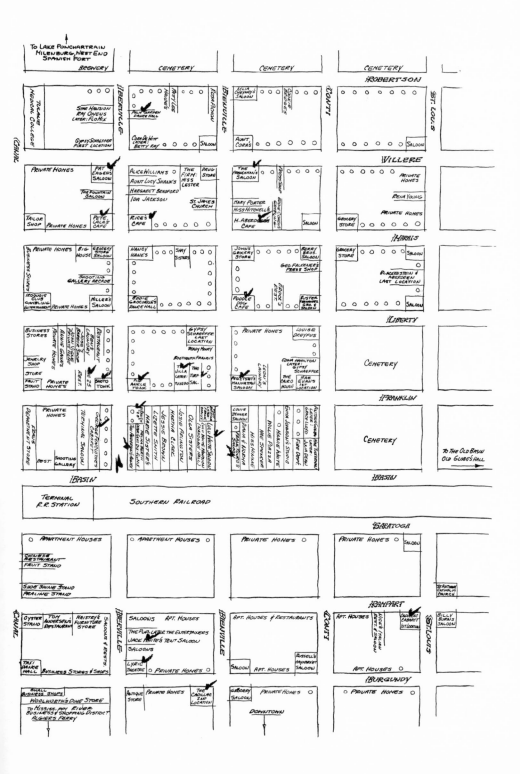